The
Perfect Murder

THE
Perfect Murder

A Study in Detection

David Lehman

THE FREE PRESS
A Division of Macmillan, Inc.
NEW YORK

Collier Macmillan Publishers
LONDON

The Free Press
A Division of Macmillan, Inc.
866 Third Avenue, New York, N.Y. 10022

Collier Macmillan Canada, Inc.

Printed in the United States of America

printing number
1 2 3 4 5 6 7 8 9 10

Library of Congress Cataloging-in-Publication Data

Lehman, David
    The perfect murder : a study in detection / David Lehman.
        p.   cm.
    Bibliography: p.
    Includes indexes.
    ISBN 0-02-919770-8
    1. Detective and mystery stories, American—History and criticism.
    2. Detective and mystery stories, English—History and criticism.
    I. Title.
    PS374.D4L44   1989
    813'.087209-dc20   89-7732
                                                                          CIP

Excerpt from "Crime Club" by Weldon Kees. Reprinted from *The Collected Poems of Weldon Kees*, edited by Donald Justice, by permission of University of Nebraska Press. Copyright © 1962, 1975 University of Nebraska Press.

Excerpts from Raymond Chandler: *The Big Sleep*, copyright © 1939 by Raymond Chandler, copyright © renewed 1967 by Helga Greene; *Farewell, My Lovely*, copyright © 1940 by Raymond Chandler, copyright © renewed 1968 by Helga Greene; *The High Window*, copyright © 1942 by Raymond Chandler, copyright © renewed 1970 by Helga Greene. All reprinted by permission of Random House, Inc. In the British Commonwealth, permission is granted by Hamish Hamilton, Ltd. From *The Long Goodbye*, copyright © 1953 by Raymond Chandler, copyright © renewed 1981 by Helga Greene; *The Simple Art of Murder*, copyright © 1950 by Raymond Chandler, copyright © renewed 1978 by Helga Greene. Reprinted by permission of Houghton Mifflin Company. In the British Commonwealth, permission is granted by Hamish Hamilton, Ltd. From *The Notebooks of Raymond Chandler*, ed. by Frank MacShane, copyright © Helga Greene for the Estate of Raymond Chandler, 1976. First published by The Ecco Press in 1976. Reprinted by permission.

Excerpts from Dashiell Hammett: *Red Harvest*, copyright © 1929 by Alfred A. Knopf, Inc., copyright © renewed 1957 by Dashiell Hammett; *The Big Knockover*, copyright © 1966 by Lillian Hellman; *The Glass Key*, copyright © 1931 by Alfred A. Knopf, Inc., copyright © renewed 1959 by Dashiell Hammett; *The Maltese Falcon*, copyright © 1929, 1930 by Alfred A. Knopf, Inc., copyright © renewed 1957, 1958 by Dashiell Hammett. All reprinted by permission of Random House, Inc. In the British Commonwealth, permission to reprint from *The Big Knockover* is granted by Cassell.

A perfect murder is a nightmare with a happy ending.

Contents

———◆———

Acknowledgments ix
Introduction xi

1. The Corpse on Page One 1
2. The Birth of a New Hero 13
3. Mysteries and Myths 23
4. Murder Considered as a Fine Art 37
5. De Quincey's Irony 45
6. No Police Like Holmes 55
7. The Legacy of Edgar Allan Poe 71
8. No Mask Like Open Truth 83
9. The Double 93
10. Funerals in Eden 101
11. From Paradise to Poisonville 117
12. The Hard-boiled Romance 135
13. Hammett and Chandler 155
14. Ross Macdonald and After 169
15. A Portrait of the Reader as Escapist 181
16. At the Heart of the Maze 197

APPENDIX 1. Further Reading 211
APPENDIX 2. Personal Favorites 217

Index of Concepts 231
Index of Names and Titles 235

Acknowledgments

———◆———

Next in praise to the author of a fine book is the first reader who recommends it to you. Mystery lovers seem to live by this notion—we exchange our enthusiasms freely, frequently, and with the proper spirit of generosity. I couldn't begin to thank everyone who shared tips and leads with me, since the list of my debts—which go back twenty years—was never compiled in a formal or systematic way. To friends who alerted me to particular titles, my thanks are no less sincere for being collectively expressed. Since embarking on this study, I have benefited from consultations with Katrine Ames, Jacques Barzun, Joel Black, Michael Dirda, Tom Disch, Erwin Glikes, Glen Hartley, John Koethe, Alison Lurie, Noreen O'Connor, Robert Polito, Edward Rothstein, Jon Stallworthy, Annalyn Swan, and Frank Tomasulo. Sue Llewellyn, who copy-edited the manuscript, improved it. I am grateful to Tony Clifton and Donna Foote, reporters at *Newsweek*'s London bureau, whose files on P. D. James and Ruth Rendell assisted me beyond the magazine articles for which they were commissioned. I am grateful as well to the magazine editors who have assigned me detective novels and thrillers to review.

Introduction

———◆———

*W*ell, sir, here's to plain speaking and clear understanding.

—THE FAT MAN in *The Maltese Falcon*

The detective story has gone through many transformations in the century and a half since Edgar Allan Poe invented it. The story has grown into the novel and been made into the movie; it has branched out into such related fictional forms as the spy thriller, the crime caper, and the police procedural; it has been adopted by the avant-garde, tampered with, parodied, subverted. What has remained constant is its extraordinary popularity, the potentially addictive spell it casts on writers and readers alike. In the generality of its appeal, the genre seems to transcend—as does perhaps no other form of fiction—the ordinary barriers of class, income level, gender, and education.

From the start the detective story offered a formula or a form that was elastic enough to allow for infinite repetition and variation. The plot centered on life-and-death matters that were stark enough to please a mass readership. On the other hand, the hero was distinguished by properties of mind that ensured the interest of an intellectual class. To this day, no other category of popular fiction so cleverly fuses a visceral impulse with a cerebral one—

the physical action of the crime, the mental action of the detection—or so easily accommodates the best efforts of the Oxford don
and the former steelworker, the prolific spinster and the pseudon-
ymous journalist, the hard-edged experimentalist and the hard-line
feminist, the Anglophile and the Anglophobe, not to mention an
odd assortment of one-of-a-kind authors including the son of one
president (Elliott Roosevelt), the daughter of another (Margaret
Truman), a British poet laureate (C. Day Lewis writing as Nicholas
Blake), and a Welsh poet eager to spoof the whole poet laureate
tradition (Dylan Thomas in *The Death of the King's Canary*, 1940).

For every Edmund Wilson who growls that he doesn't care who
killed Roger Ackroyd, it is easy to name five literary intellectuals
who have fiercely embraced the genre, written odes to it, or otherwise appropriated it for their own purposes. Why has the detective
novel been the darling of successive generations of highbrow critics? In part because the conventions of the genre are intrinsically
interesting, in part because the form has attracted so many estimable talents, and in part because the ardor of its readership demands attention as a phenomenon in its own right. There is one
other reason as well. Virtually all detective novels implicitly and
automatically flatter the literary critic, whose own work so frequently resembles a species of detection.

Critics who may disagree on everything else concur in regarding
Poe as the most significant figure in the detective story's history
and development—though only a handful of Poe's stories can be
called, in his words, "tales of ratiocination." From "The Murders
in the Rue Morgue" alone one might deduce virtually all the primary rules of the genre and many of its secondary rituals. The plot
is triggered by a murder: The fearfully mutilated bodies of Mme.
L'Espanaye and her daughter are discovered in their Paris apartment. It is a locked-room problem, an excursion into the realm of
the seemingly impossible, since all means of entry and egress were
locked at the time of the murders. The formal problem is therefore
not only who dunit but how could *any*one have done it? The identity of the culprit is unknown and brought to light only gradually
by a detective—that is, a private citizen acting without official
sanction: the Chevalier C. Auguste Dupin. Though his deductions
exonerate a wrongly accused citizen, Dupin's interest in solving the
case has less to do with justice than with his determination to out-
wit his rival, the chief of police, and thereby to demonstrate his
mental superiority.

Dupin's companion, the unnamed narrator of "The Murders in

the Rue Morgue," is an avatar of all the Dr. Watsons in the literature; Dupin himself is the prototype of Sherlock Holmes, the aloof genius with the artist's temperament and the scientific mind. The plot is bi-level, as it must be: The story of the murders is framed within the story of the detective's investigation. The two narratives meet at the point where the sleuth reveals his solution to the case. The solution relieves some anxieties and awakens others: Dupin demonstrates that an orangutan belonging to a sailor must have climbed in through a window and committed the murders. You see, Dupin explains in his second story, "The Mystery of Marie Roget," the more "outré" the crime, the easier it is to solve. Nothing to it.

W. H. Auden—a self-confessed detective story addict and one of many poets drawn to it—succinctly defined the detective story's basic formula: "A murder occurs; many are suspected; all but one suspect, who is the murderer, are eliminated; the murderer is arrested or dies." Auden was anxious to distinguish the stories he liked most from spy novels and from crime thrillers told from the murderer's point of view. He summed up the types in his essay "The Guilty Vicarage": "The interest in the thriller is the ethical and eristic conflict between good and evil, between Us and Them. The interest in the study of a murderer is the observation, by the innocent many, of the sufferings of the guilty one. The interest in the detective story is the dialectic of innocence and guilt."[1] Building on Auden's summary, we might extrapolate several worst-case scenarios. The most subversive thing that can happen in a spy thriller is the recognition that Us and Them are not absolutes, that the better man may be on the wrong side, that rival intelligence companies are more alike than different, and that the spy's ultimate end is always to betray and be betrayed. The most subversive thing that can happen in a detective novel is the recognition that the sleuth and the culprit are more alike than different, that chaos is the norm and true detection impossible, and that the detective is therefore doomed to fail or die.

Auden was more confident of his ability to make sharp distinctions—and keep to them—than many readers would be. But even readers less able to discriminate among their impressions know their own biases. And, theoretically at least, you can tell something about a person from knowing what sort of sleuth he or she favors. There are two main categories: The eccentric mastermind (Sherlock Holmes with his cocaine and his fiddle, Lord Peter Wimsey with his patrician monocle, the obese Nero Wolfe with his orchid

collection) is a legacy bequeathed by Poe's Dupin. A rival tradition
sprang up with Dashiell Hammett's hard-boiled novels and came
to full flower in the person of Raymond Chandler's Philip Marlowe:
the gumshoe who gets knocked on the head for his troubles and
wisecracks his way to the truth. The Holmes model ingeniously unravels an apparently insoluble puzzle; the Marlowe model gets to
the bottom of things through a combination of luck, pluck, and
derring-do. The latter goes it alone; the former, for all his aloofness
and pride, usually has a trusty companion, a combination of Boswell and Sancho Panza, who chronicles the Great Detective's exploits and assists with the legwork. The Watson figure tends to be
down-to-earth, a bit obtuse but glad to be of use.

Both traditions have had their heyday. The hard-boiled novel's
last great practitioner was the late Ross Macdonald, whose best
work was done in the 1960s and 1970s. For its part, the classic
whodunit may never have an era to surpass the 1930s, the last days
of the genre's so-called golden age, when Agatha Christie and John
Dickson Carr and Nicholas Blake fashioned their most intricate
puzzles. Yet both traditions remain vital, able to adapt to new conditions. The novel of straight detection cannot admit a greater
amount of psychological implication than the British writer P. D.
James puts into her books. Ruth Rendell's novels of domestic terror
are like detective novels without the detective; they remind us that
there is no better, scarier, likelier place for an uncanny experience
than home. Among the most intellectually ambitious novels of the
past decade, Umberto Eco's *The Name of the Rose* is at its core
an ingenious and elaborate detective story in which, in effect, the
critical talents of Sherlock Holmes and Dr. Watson are pitted
against the artistic genius of Jorge Luis Borges. Meanwhile, the
American private-eye novel has entered a nostalgia phase (where
the wisecracking sleuth takes a time-machine trip back to the
1940s), a regional phase (the Cambridge, Massachusetts, model
sounds like a hip graduate student while the Montana version drives
a pickup truck and snorts a fair amount of cocaine), and a feminist
phase (with attractive heroines who can take care of themselves
perfectly well, thank you, and are as tough, as jaded, and as sex-
ually opportunistic as any of the guys). The police procedurals of
Ed McBain fuse elements from both traditions, demonstrating that
brain-teasing puzzles need not be incompatible with a realistic urban setting.

As far as the publishing industry is concerned, the golden age of crime fiction is now. Hardcover publishers count on thrillers of various stripes to earn them a reliable profit, and then some. Paperback publishers know there's a constant demand for reprints of past classics, perennial favorites. There is the occasional gold mine. Every so often, a steady-selling genre author "breaks out" of the pack into six-figure glory—as when a long-deserving, long-invisible writer is suddenly, as it seems, taken up by all the critics at once. It happened to Elmore Leonard in 1985, and it seems to be happening now with Patricia Highsmith; the process of mass discovery may look orchestrated but is simply the way of the media, which compensates with hyperbole for the belatedness of its recognitions. There are the usual publishing ironies: It could be argued, for example, that Dick Francis was a far better writer of mysteries *before* his leap into bestsellerdom and cover story fame. In recent years publishers and publicists—who formerly favored the word *Kafkaesque*—have switched to *like a detective novel* as an honorific. They count on the term to kindle an interest in the book they're touting, be it a work of science, or a novel, or a scholarly treatise; they know there is no better metaphor for the seeker of knowledge than the detective.

The genre continues to inspire the most extravagant acts of fealty from its devotees. There are Sherlockians who have gone over the entire Sherlock Holmes oeuvre with a magnifying glass—not once but several times—and assemble to discuss it with the passion of contentious Talmudists. In the university seminar room, murder mysteries are getting deconstructed; in the Catskills resort, they are being simulated, on murder mystery weekends, during which the paying guest gets to play sleuth and there are prizes for the most accurate and for the most imaginative solution (the two are seldom the same). There are murder mystery games, kits, quiz books, comic books, TV programs, computer-interactive novels, fine-press editions of classics. In the last two decades, independent bookstores catering to murder aficionados—stores with names like Murder Ink, Scene of the Crime, and Sherlock's Home—began to flourish ahead of the trend toward specialty bookshops. And the traffic will always be heavy at the section of the public library reserved for the books with the bright red skulls on their slip-jacketed spines.

In this book I have concentrated on the detective novel proper, using Auden's definition (broadly constructed). I have not tried to

be comprehensive; my goal isn't a history or a taxonomy but something more immediate. I have therefore felt free to discuss some
writers at length and to ignore others, who are equally worthy, on
grounds that may strike some readers as capricious. I am, for example, an enthusiastic admirer of Ross Thomas, Elmore Leonard,
and Donald E. Westlake, but feel they would be more beneficially
considered in a different context. I came to think of the international thriller, with or without spies, as a separate phenomenon
entirely. Then there is the case of Georges Simenon. The novels
featuring Chief Inspector Jules Maigret are marvelously atmos-
pheric—it is always raining as Maigret nurses his aperitif at the
zinc bar of a Paris cafe—but get scarcely a mention here simply
because in so many ways they are exceptional rather than representative. As Jacques Barzun and Wendell Hertig Taylor write in
their *Catalogue of Crime,* Simenon's psychological thrillers "make
one think of what Proust could have done had he chosen to write
a western. The cowboys' professional skill and purpose in life would
be completely subordinated to their introspection, childhood mem-
ories, and emotional entanglements with particular horses."[2] One
needn't share the Barzun/Taylor animus to agree that Simenon
epitomizes "the art that is farthest from the center of detection."
On the other hand, knowing that any good detective likes making
unpredictable moves and inscrutable decisions, I have not hesitated
to roam much farther afield than Simenon where it suited my purposes. I have called upon thrillers by Eric Ambler and Graham
Greene, short stories by Borges and Nabokov, Greek myth, French
symbolist poetry, Freud, fairy tales, and films, where the work
seemed germane to what Auden called "the dialectic of innocence
and guilt."

The first three chapters of this book treat the consequences of
the detective story's "corpse on page one"—the violent death that
triggers the action. The suggestion is made that the detective story
completes certain Romantic impulses and repudiates others. The
orangutan in "The Murders in the Rue Morgue" would seem to
embody a base view of human nature: the transmogrification of
Rousseau's "noble savage" into Darwin's primal ape. The detective's mission corresponds to that of the ego mediating between
superego and id. Alternatively, the detective may be seen as the
new hero, who arrives to replace the fallen hero (the victim) and
to confront his double (the culprit); it is a mark of the detective's

power that he survives the encounter with his mirror image, which under ordinary gothic circumstances would prove fatal.

Chapters four through six are unified broadly by the shared theme of aesthetics: The detective novel, as a condition of its being, took murder out of the ethical realm and put it into that of aesthetics. By analogy, murder in a murder mystery becomes a kind of poetic conceit, often quite a baroque one; the criminal is an artist, the detective an aesthete and a critic, and the blundering policeman a philistine. The impulse to treat murder as an exotic and perverse art form came to a head in the extravagant whodunits of the 1920s and 1930s, which regarded art as synonymous with artifice. A puzzle like the one devised by Ngaio Marsh in *Overture to Death* (1936) is imperial in the same sense that the Pont du Gare is: It employs ostentatious means to achieve relatively modest ends. In Marsh's book, a pistol hooked up to the pedal of an upright piano is programmed to go off at the right moment of a Rachmaninoff prelude. If all you wanted was to eliminate somebody, there would be easier ways to do it, but clearly the planning of a perfect crime entails more than an itchy trigger finger and a suitable victim. In Thomas De Quincey's words, "Design, gentlemen, grouping, light and shade, poetry, sentiment, are now deemed indispensable to attempts of this nature."

Chapters seven through nine examine specific aspects of Poe's legacy: the locked room, the wrong man, the least likely suspect, the most obvious hiding place (or the open secret), the theme of the double. Chapters ten and eleven are concerned with paradise and "Poisonville" respectively as ideal settings for different sorts of murder stories. Chapters twelve through fourteen focus on the American hard-boiled novel, its chief practitioners, and their governing assumptions. The hard-boiled novel is understood to participate in an American rebellion against the British whodunit. But claims for the hard-boiled novel's greater "realism" must be qualified by the knowledge that the realism in this case was largely a surface victory of style and stylishness. Raymond Chandler's sarcastic hyperboles and side-of-the-mouth similes—"she wore a hat with a crown the size of a whiskey glass and a brim you could have wrapped the week's laundry in"—raise the wisecrack to a stylistic ideal. In a larger sense, the hard-boiled style has obvious affinities with that of *film noir,* including a liking for the shadows, a fierce ambivalence about the female of the species, a certain fatalism, and a tendency to mask the hero's vulnerability as toughness. It is a style that seems admirably suited to the demands of what could be called an existential romance.

Final thoughts are in chapters fifteen and sixteen. The former considers the charge of escapism and proposes three possible portraits of the reader as escapist; the latter considers the examples of Borges and Eco, the limits of detection, and the possibilities of a literature that may long for the old verities but is secretly certain that the detective is dead or obsolete. The book concludes with a bibliography and an annotated list of personal favorites.

My own experience tells me that foreknowledge of a detective novel's secrets needn't diminish the reader's enjoyment of the book. I have therefore felt free to disclose a plot twist or a surprise revelation when it suited my argument to do so. The generic *he* as used in this book—often in imaginary scenarios—is a grammatical convenience and does not necessarily designate the sex of the protagonist.

The detective story is unique among literary forms in that the narrative line flows backward, from effect to cause, causing the reader to become a participant or co-conspirator, since one is continually asked to guess at the meaning of events and to extrapolate an entire scenario from a handful of clues. The action of a detective novel is framed by a fearful symmetry: In the beginning is one expulsion (the victim) and in the end is another (the villain). What does that first corpse stand for? Why does the detective novel begin with death, an ending, and work its way back in time? Why is the classic detective an eccentric while the hard-boiled shamus is a loner? What accounts for the genre's attitude toward the police? Who makes an ideal victim? Why do we read thrillers? In the course of investigating such questions as these, it will become necessary to inquire about corpses in locked rooms and down blind alleys, where no footprints disturb the freshly fallen snow. We will round up the usual suspects and grill them, though a small voice in the back of the head keeps insisting that the least likely of all the suspects may prove to be the guilty party. We will try to crack some airtight alibis and to separate the red herrings from the real clues, and we will search in all the dark places and be prepared to discover that the object of the search was in plain sight all along.

The detective novel and its familiar emblems—the spectral hound on the Devonshire moors or the sculpted falcon whose black enamel is said to conceal priceless jewels—reward multiple approaches. An individual example of the genre is either a gothic nightmare with a happy ending or a parable about justice and guilt (the difficulty of the first, the universality of the second), or it may be the folktale of the modern metropolis, or it's the exposition of a Freudian drama or a (secularized) religious ritual. All are possible and none are final—which makes a further point: This is a genre that prizes puzzles even as it praises the sleuth who solves them. At their most inspired, detective novels yield mysteries that retain their aura of mystery even after the solution is announced. A riddle is answered with an enigma; a false solution like a narrative trapdoor suckers us in the book's penultimate chapter. It turns out that the culprit planned the murder as though it were a work of art, with equal measures of ingenuity and caprice. The result of his efforts is a perfect murder not because it is insoluble but because it has been so artistically conceived.

The detective novel has given its devotees much to be grateful for. How better to celebrate it than by undertaking an investigation into its nature, as though the form itself constituted the most admirable of three-pipe problems, a mystery equal to our capacity for wonderment?

The
Perfect Murder

1

---◆---

The Corpse on Page One

*C*onsider the clues: the potato masher in a vase,
C The torn photograph of a Wesleyan basketball team,
Scattered with checkstubs in the hall;
The unsent fan letter to Shirley Temple,
The Hoover button on the lapel of the deceased,
The note: "To be killed this way is quite all right with me."

—WELDON KEES, "Crime Club"

In the beginning was the corpse.

The genealogy is simple. Guilt comes first, the rank smell of corruption seeping out of locked rooms. Then comes fear, as the body on the carpet is replaced by a police silhouette. Then paranoia, a compound of the two, as reporters arrive at the scene of the crime and some neighbors talk loosely while others clam up, looking terror stricken. Welcome to the art of the murder mystery. Within these boundaries, we are all suspects, witnesses, accomplices, or accessories after the fact, living our lives in the wake of an original crime. It has already been committed and cannot be undone, and there's every likelihood that the trail will lead to more of the same. John Dickson Carr in *The Crooked Hinge* called it "the law of progressive homicide": Every murder threatens to be the first in a series. No one's above suspicion, least of all you, the detective's client, or friend, or lover. It's a rule of the game that you're going

1

to learn early on. "There's one thing you have to realize," says the detective's right-hand man in Lawrence Block's *The Topless Tulip Caper,* a parody of Rex Stout's Nero Wolfe novels. "Everybody's a suspect until proven otherwise." The client objects, reasonably enough, to the implied inversion of our legal system's chief tenet and greatest glory. "I thought everyone's innocent until proved guilty," she says. "Absolutely," comes the not-too-reassuring reply. "And everybody's suspicious until proved innocent. That's how it works." This is perfect, down to the word *suspicious,* a street-smart solecism. In this universe, everyone is not only a suspect but also a suspicious character, an apprehensive observer of everyone else, and what's more we have every right to be on our guard. We are all implicated, whatever our rank or station. The detective's finger may in the end point to any of us, and we read on not only to find out whodunit but to free ourselves—if only until the next title we compulsively pick up—of the suspicion that we need only look in the mirror for the truth.

What we see in the mirror—an ape with a shaving brush—may well terrify us but shouldn't take us by surprise. After all, we've read enough murder mysteries to know that the deed was probably done by the least likely suspect, and what phrase could better describe any of us? "There is still to be written a book in which the murderer is the reader," Umberto Eco notes in his *Postscript to the Name of the Rose.* True: Our killers have come in every form but that. We've read about murders perpetrated by all the suspects combined. We've met more than one culprit who troubles to disguise himself as one of his own putative victims. Now and then we even run across detectives who commit what can at best be called justifiable manslaughter. But the murderer as the reader? Never—which is to say, on some implicit, metaphorical level, always. There was never any reason for the detective novelist to make the identification too plain. Readers of detective novels participate in perfect murders—perfect because they offer us a vicarious and therefore socially acceptable form of releasing our homicidal instincts, and they allow us to do it again and again and again, letting us off the hook each time, without ever having to face the consequences. "Books talk among themselves," writes Umberto Eco, "and any true detection should prove that we are the guilty party."[1]

In the book before you, books will converse among themselves, sometimes quizzically, sometimes in an argumentative mood, for your delectation and in the hope that you will agree to play several roles as you listen. You, who sit in the dock as the accused, are being asked as well to serve as a juror in this trial of ideas. For now, let the dead body in the library prove that the guilty party lurks among us. Let it suggest, too, that the guilt is contagious, leading to other corpses that need to be exhumed, other secrets that call for the services of a sleuth. Let us consider the paradox of our position as mystery readers: These books, the friendliest palliatives in sight, invoke our anxieties for the purpose of assuaging them; they confirm us as murder addicts. Ladies and gentlemen of the jury, these shall be our working premises, and we may hope that true detection will follow from the presentation of evidence. But let us also remind ourselves of another quirk in our behavior as murder addicts: our predilection for mysteries, which we savor rather more than their solutions, though the uncertainties in our lives frighten us and we say we are dying for the truth.

———◆———

The *corpus delicti* awaits us in the locked chamber of the dream. Here is exhibit A: the omnipresent corpse on page one, or near enough as to make little difference. Like Poe's purloined letter, hidden in everyone's full view, this first clue of ours stares us in the face and we must be careful not to overlook it for its very obviousness. Agatha Christie titled one of her murder mysteries *Death Comes as the End* (1944)—a bland and seemingly incontestable fact. Yet exactly the opposite is true in the world of crime fiction, where death comes not only *at* but *as* the beginning. Ed McBain, describing how he writes his 87th Precinct novels, puts it simply: "I usually start with a corpse. I then ask myself how the corpse got to be that way." The corpse: not a person but an indispensable pretext. Though the murder may be made quite exquisitely unthreatening by the murderer's use of some cunningly elaborate stratagem, the twentieth-century detective novel can't do without its corpse; it has to include the fact of violent death as a given. It wasn't always that way, of course. Wilkie Collins's *The Moonstone* (1868), which T. S. Eliot hyperbolically called "the first, the longest and the best of modern English detective novels," centers on a theft rather than a murder; and many a Sherlock Holmes adventure involves a felony of one kind or another, not homicide. But Collins wrote in the 1860s, and Holmes is a product of late-Victorian England, London gaslight, and fog.

We are not too many years into the twentieth century—World War I marks a convenient cutoff date—before the case of the constant corpse supplants all the rest. One reason Dorothy L. Sayers's *Gaudy Night* (1935) is among the least satisfying of her works is the substitution of pranks and threats for homicidal deeds. It's all very well to add depth to the background, as Sayers does with her Oxford dons and their donnish debates in *Gaudy Night,* but not at the expense of a corpse. "If you could order a crime as one orders a dinner, what would you choose?" Hercule Poirot asks his "mascot," Captain Hastings, in Agatha Christie's *The ABC Murders* (1936). "Let's review the menu," Hastings replies. "Robbery? Forgery? No, I think not. Rather too vegetarian. It must be murder—red-blooded murder—with trimmings, of course." Murder, because it is final, irrevocable, and irremediable, is the perfect metaphor, the right objective correlative. Nothing else will do, for nothing else will seem commensurate to the capacity for guilt and the craving for absolution that we bring with us to the reading of mysteries.

Our victim, dead to begin with, can be identified, though not always so easily as at first seems possible. But we can never identify ourselves with him or her. Where a classic catharsis calls for the evocation of both pity and terror in the reader and their exorcism in the reading, the detective novel does away with pity, offering us instead a purgatory of unalloyed terror. The victim is someone else—anyone else but us. And this stands to reason, since not even a victim would want to look at things from the victim's point of view. Thomas De Quincey, whose reflections on murder amount to an anticipatory brief for the detective story, explains why. This is from his celebrated essay "On the Knocking at the Gate in *Macbeth,*" which he published in 1823, some eighteen years before Poe invented the new genre: "Murder, in ordinary cases, where the sympathy is wholly directed to the case of the murdered person, is an incident of coarse and vulgar horror; and for this reason—that it flings the interest exclusively upon the natural but ignoble instinct by which we cleave to life." All victims have this much in common. They exhibit, in De Quincey's words, "human nature in its most abject and humiliating attitude." Death has obliterated any other distinctions among them, and the detective story will make sure that our attention and our sympathy get directed elsewhere.

Nor can we identify ourselves fully with the detective. We may try to outsmart the masterful sleuth or at least keep in step with his implacable tread, but a condition of our admiration is precisely the difference between his abilities and ours. Unlike us, he has little to fear, despite the dangerous nature of his work. Larger than life in his wizardry, he is an exceptional rather than a representative creature, and his resources remind us that our own are pitifully inadequate to the dire tasks at hand. Our powers of deduction pale next to those of Sherlock Holmes or Hercule Poirot; we haven't the toughness of Sam Spade or the fortitude of Philip Marlowe; the saintly Father Brown shames us, and the infinite patience of Inspector Maigret lies infinitely beyond us. No, we are the bystanders, innocent or guilty as the case may be. The jurors in Raymond Postgate's splendid *Verdict of Twelve* (1940) show us in the correct, ambiguous light. A cross-section of London, Postgate's jurors include a woman who once committed murder and got away with it, a woman whose husband was murdered, a foreman with an exaggerated sense of fair play, and a somewhat demented religious fanatic. They and their fellows must decide whether the accused did, as charged, murder her young nephew. But they deliberate not so much on the basis of the evidence as on its effect on themselves— their verdict is a reflection of their own yearning to be free of guilt. Not guilty, they duly declare—to be, as we might have guessed, proved wrong.

Verdict of Twelve is unusual in substituting a highly fallible jury for the detective tag team that we expect in puzzlers of the classic British variety. In such books the character that best represents us is likely to be the narrator, a chap who's deferential, reliable, and slightly obtuse but eager to be of use. We accompany the master sleuth as his trusted sidekick, aware of things as they happen but not aware of what they mean. We can fancy ourselves as Holmes's sensible Dr. Watson on one of our good days or as Poirot's sublimely stupid Captain Hastings on a bad one. But even that is no guarantee that we won't get sucked up into the detective story's eternal dialectic of guilt and innocence. The trick Agatha Christie played on readers of *The Murder of Roger Ackroyd* (1926) proves the point. For here the culprit is none other than the book's sympathetic narrator, Dr. Sheppard, Captain Hastings's stand-in as Poirot's companionable chronicler. If the good Sheppard could have done it, anyone could.

Consider this proposition: Detective stories mesmerize us as they do because our love of mystery is matched only by our longing for certainty—and because we find it hard to tolerate the condition of doubt and guilt in which we are destined to live. The officer in Kafka's "In the Penal Colony," pronouncing his universal verdict, identifies one reason for the mystery genre's enduring popularity. "My guiding principle is this," he declares. "Guilt is never to be doubted." Guilt is what we bring with us to the night table on which a stack of detective novels awaits our perusal. Guilt may be the one thing beyond doubt, the single certainty we have. It's the aching tooth we can't help poking at, needing to reinforce the pain even as we seek a remedy and, finding none, settle for a short-term pain reliever, hoping no one has doctored the pill with cyanide. Guilt is the burden we need to prove and try to shed, and it fascinates us because its cause remains a mystery. Mystified, we keep trying to get at the origins of our condition even when we imagine that we're trying to escape from it, as when we read ourselves to sleep with a detective novel, looking forward to another nightmare with a happy ending.

In this collective dream of ours, all logic resembles a species of retrospective prophecy. Just as scientists go back from effects to likely causes, we must try to intuit the uncertain truths from which an all-too-certain consequence—our guilt—has issued. As we reconstruct what might have happened to produce the corpse on page one, we subject our motives to scrutiny, making few allowances for what we did unknowingly or only in fantasy. Committed as we are to a foreordained verdict of guilty, we can't help uncovering plenty of incriminating evidence, though clever attorneys will interpret it in various, conflicting ways. The defense will argue, correctly, that the only thing some of us may have to feel guilty about is our guilt itself, but that doesn't lessen the burden or obviate our need to do something about it. In fact, we had better keep trying to persuade ourselves that time will separate the innocent from the guilty, that the pollution infecting the city will go away, that rational solutions to our problems do exist. And if that means constructing artificial puzzles just so we can have the satisfaction of seeing them solved, so be it. What we're up against calls for extraordinary measures.

———◆———

The eternal triangle in a detective novel consists of the culprit, the sleuth, and the victim. Of the three, the victim is the least important. The victim exists primarily for one purpose: to get killed, and quickly. True, the reader may cite numerous cases in which the corpse puts in its appearance well after chapter one. Where the murderer impersonates his or her victim, as in Nicholas Blake's *The Widow's Cruise* (1959), it's in the author's devious interests to put us on a nodding acquaintance with the victim—real or pretended—before whisking the body away. In *The Widow's Cruise*, all fingers point to Ianthe Ambrose as the probable murderee; we can tell from the start that she was made for the role. If the wish were father to the deed, many of the passengers aboard the *Menelaos* would have done away with her long before the fatal day the ship was moored off Kalymnos. But there's a reason Ianthe doesn't become a corpse until nearly halfway through the novel: Ambiguities about her identity become, when properly detected and interpreted, revelations about the killer's identity, motive, and *modus operandi*.

Again, in Blake's *Thou Shell of Death* (1936), we get a good long look at the dashing Fergus O'Brien before he is dispatched—but only because *this* victim will turn out to be the posthumous architect of two subsequent murders, one of which proves his ability to live in a nutshell and count himself a king of infinite space. Terminally ill and looking for a dramatic way to go, O'Brien arranges to become a corpse, the victim of a staged and secluded knife fight, but not before he injects an unopened walnut with poison, knowing that one of his targets has a voracious appetite for nuts and tends to crack the shells with his teeth. (The other target will be dispatched in an only slightly less imaginative way.) O'Brien's artistry is exemplary, not least because both his victims were themselves the culprits in crimes that antedate the events in the novel by many years. But so brilliant an exception proves the rule: We customarily meet the victim just long enough to realize that he or she is a thoroughly expendable character. The victim's life ends and the book begins. Its single most important event—the one that will set all the others in motion—has taken place beforehand, offstage, with no one looking over the murderer's shoulder.

"Every fear is a desire," James Fenton writes in his poem "A Staffordshire Murderer." "Every victim is an accomplice." Where Fergus O'Brien actively collaborates in his own demise, most victims play along passively. Even so, their cooperation is essential. When a rare, untraceable poison finds its way into the glass of port on the silver salver served dutifully by the stolid butler, it's clear that the victim no less than the culprit has taken pains to make the murder seem a civilized ritual, an aesthetically pleasing act. A saving grace? Indeed. Providing the corpse is the least that victims can do—and is nine times out of ten the most socially beneficial thing they have ever done. For as a rule these are nasty people and leave no one heartbroken when they exit the scene; guilt is one thing, remorse quite another. When Sigsbee Manderson, plutocrat, has his brains blown out on the first page of E. C. Bentley's *Trent's Last Case* (1912), we're told that the world "lost nothing worth a single tear." On the contrary, "it gained something memorable in a harsh reminder of the vanity of such wealth as this dead man had piled up—without making one loyal friend to mourn him, without doing an act that could help his memory to the least honor." Anyone could have done it because everyone wanted to. "I should say that any one who had anything to do with George was potentially his murderer," says a suspect matter-of-factly in Nicholas Blake's *The Beast Must Die* (1938). Lord Peter Wimsey suavely understates the case in Dorothy Sayers's *Murder Must Advertise* (1933): "I gather that the late Victor Dean was not universally beloved." Wimsey is speaking of victims everywhere. Perfect murders require perfect murderees.

Trent's Last Case, published on the eve of World War I, signaled the arrival of the genteel detective novel, which had its heyday in the 1920s and 1930s. It's commonly thought that such "golden age" crime fiction, of which Christie and Sayers were the reigning royalty, owed a large portion of its popularity to the puzzle element it so prominently displayed. In an interesting essay, George Grella takes issue with this assumption, crediting instead the way that formal detective novels of the period enforced a social code. The whodunit "remains one of the last outposts of the comedy of manners in fiction," Grella contends, going so far as to dub it "the thriller of manners." The analogy is beautifully applicable to the body of the crime, the unloved victim:

> The comedy of manners generally contains an expulsion of the socially undesirable which insures the continued happiness of those remaining. Similarly, the detective novel features two expulsions of "bad" or socially unfit characters: the victim and the murderer. Because only unlikeable characters are made to suffer permanently in comedy, pains are taken to make the victim worthy of his fate: he must be an exceptionally murderable man.... The victim of *The Murder of Roger Ackroyd* is a *senex iratus* who forces an engagement on his stepson, impeding the path of true love and earning his doom. Old General Fentiman is murdered in Miss

Sayers' *The Unpleasantness at the Bellona Club* because he has made a bad will. Sigsbee Manderson in *Trent's Last Case* dies because he is much older than his wife, and a brute besides.... All of these victims have hindered the natural course of events, chiefly by obstructing the path of true love. Such obstruction in any form of comedy means eventual defeat or exclusion: and in the exacting code of the detective novel, that exclusion means murder.[2]

In an obligatory nod in the direction of realism, more recent puzzlers tend to feature middle-class communities in a realistic facsimile of Sussex rather than weekend bashes in never-never land, but their universally unpopular victims remain true to type. The murdered bigamist in Ruth Rendell's *An Unkindness of Ravens* (1985), for example, is an advanced case of that familiar "thriller of manners" victim, the bounder or cad.

Rub out the victim, and rub in nearly as many motives as there are spectators on the scene. The remote island, the hotel full of strangers, becomes suddenly a claustrophobic place and, for some, an intimate one. The corpse has brought these characters together, linked their destinies, and given them something to share. They ought almost to be grateful to the murderer, and probably would be, if fear didn't get in the way. Just about all of them stand to benefit from the foul play, whether the measure of their gain is money or vengeance, the thrill of being part of a mystery, or merely the smug superiority that a survivor feels toward a dead rival resented, envied, or despised. In death, the victim has done everyone a favor. The pity of it is that someone has to be found guilty, has to be unmasked in the end, when the detective convenes the cast of suspects and astounds them with his revelations.

The corpse, wrote W. H. Auden, "must shock not only because it is a corpse but also because, even for a corpse, it is shockingly out of place, as when a dog makes a mess on a drawing room carpet."[3] The incongruity of the corpse on the drawing room carpet is its shock value. On the other hand, once our eyes get used to the sight, the result turns out to be a domestication of homicide. Perhaps, wrote Walter Benjamin, the scene of the crime acquires rather than loses its Edenic properties with the discovery of the corpse. Benjamin had in mind the lavishly furnished "bourgeois interior of the 1860's to the 1890's":

The soulless luxuriance of the furnishings becomes true comfort only in the presence of a dead body. Far more interesting than the

Oriental landscapes in detective novels is that rank Orient inhabiting their interiors: the Persian carpet and the ottoman, the hanging lamp and the genuine Caucasian dagger. Behind the heavy, gathered Khilim tapestries the master of the house has orgies with his share certificates, feels himself the Eastern merchant, the indolent pasha in the caravanserai of otiose enchantment, until that dagger in its silver sling above the divan puts an end, one fine afternoon, to his siesta and himself.

The typical living room Benjamin describes—"tremulously awaiting the nameless murderer like a lascivious old lady her gallant"—"fittingly houses only the corpse."[4]

In some detective novels, particularly those that stress the psychological drama, the corpse is, in effect, brought back to life as the complexities of his character slowly and steadily reassemble themselves in the detective's mind. For Simenon's Maigret, this amounts to a first principle. "I will know the murderer when I know the victim well," Maigret remarks in one of his earliest cases. Probably no detective novelist has given greater weight to the victim than has the British writer P. D. James. According to Hitchcock's law, the more interesting the villain, the better the film.[5] Substitute "victim" for "villain" in that clause, and you arrive at James's *modus operandi*. Her victims may top everybody's hit list, but they never lack the power to interest us. Violent death has given a new dimension to the enigmas of their lives.

"The victim was central to his death," says Adam Dalgliesh, James's series detective, in *A Taste for Death* (1986); and in the murdered baronet of that book he confronts an enigmatic and fascinating specimen. Sir Paul Berowne, a minister of the crown, had been widely regarded as "the next prime minister but one." But that was before he renounced his political ambitions, having had a vision of God in a humble Paddington church—where, weeks later, his body turns up, throat slashed from ear to ear. There are plenty of suspects to go around, and much that seems incriminating in Berowne's past must be dug up. But it is the man's apparently self-abnegating personality that holds the key to the case. Though it's an old detective standby that a character's bookshelves proclaim his identity, Berowne's look curiously impersonal, like "the library of a private club or a luxury cruise ship." His was the room of a man who felt he had no right to be there, a man who felt he was "a harbinger of death."

In a crucial sense, Berowne's corpse proclaims his own guilt as well as that of his executioner; Berowne can almost certainly be seen as an accomplice in his own murder. That his corpse is found together with the murdered body of an obscure tramp hammers home the egalitarianism of this universe of death: Murder makes even stranger bedfellows than politics does, linking the high and the low and contaminating all sectors of society. And that the corpses are found in the vestry of a Romanesque basilica makes, for James, a further point about the kind of detective novel she favors. "Setting and theme should be one," James has said, adding that the apparent incongruity of the setting goes far to explain the appeal that domestic murder mysteries make to women. "If you think of a special kind of English crime, 'malice domestic,' there's no doubt [women] think of Christie first, Dorothy L. Sayers, Ngaio Marsh, Margery Allingham, Ruth Rendell," James told a *Newsweek* reporter. "It may be that women have a sense of security within the formality of the genre or that women—who have much more to lose by violence and therefore are more frightened by it—use the detective story to exorcise the fear or distance themselves from it."[6] The dead body in the library or the drawing room represents the nearness of violence and underscores the reader's vulnerability. At the same time, the surroundings domesticate the violence and negate its threat.

Gallup surveys confirm one's intuitive sense that women would be more likely to favor classic puzzlers, psychological thrillers, or urbane metropolitan murders without bloody messes, while men in equal numbers go for the guys with the guts for graphic violence, Mickey Spillane on the low end, Jim Thompson for the more sophisticated reader.[7] James herself paraphrases Auden: "I think on the whole that women agree ... that a single body on the drawing-room floor is more horrible than a dozen bullet-ridden bodies down Chandler's mean streets."[8] That assumption is no longer quite the truism it may once have been. In fact, James's own practice is far more complicated—and bloodier—than her male-female paradigm would suggest. In *Death of an Expert Witness* (1977), for example, she situates the murder in a forensic laboratory—at the very place where the science of detection has set up shop: hardly a locale associated with "malice domestic." Other contemporary authors have, in the slang of the day, "gendered" their fictions in ways that make the whole question of sexual difference—and how it translates into reader allegiance—trickier to answer. The appeal of a Sara Paret-

sky or a Sue Grafton is one made to female readers but in a deliberately hard-boiled idiom. What's more, the hard-boiled private eye
in many state-of-the-art examples—by male as well as female authors—has become a paragon of the unisex Yuppie ideal, talking
designer-name products and working out at the local fitness center;
where there's machismo, it is usually without the misogyny.[9] Grant
all this; grant, too, that the best authors in any category are beloved
by the best readers, whatever their gender. And still the sense of a
natural sexual division won't go away. Not the least of the differences between the classic whodunit as exemplified by Agatha
Christie and the hard-boiled novel Raymond Chandler championed
rests in their quarrel over the proper milieu for the corpse on page
one. And what else is the difference between Christie's Orient Express and Chandler's mean streets but a clash between a traditional
female sensibility and its male counterpart? The hard-boiled
animus toward the classic whodunit would seem to go hand-in-
glove with a violent distrust of the feminine. "Put the blame on
Mame," sang Rita Hayworth in *Gilda* (1946), describing just what
the hard-boiled sleuth of the period tends to do. The leading lady
is the focus of all his anxieties. He must renounce her for the sake
of his existential freedom: "I won't play the sap for you." After all,
the last detective who fell for this particular dame turned up in the
morgue, an exemplary victim. In the world according to Sam
Spade, the detective must aim not merely to solve the riddle of the
corpse but to avoid coming to the same dismal end: the fate of a
"sap."

2

---◆---

The Birth of a New Hero

*T*he detective is a prophet looking backwards.
—ELLERY QUEEN, *The Chinese Orange Mystery*

"It is very curious," Gertrude Stein wrote in 1936, "but the detective story which is you might say the only really modern novel form that has come into existence gets rid of human nature by having the man dead to begin with the hero is dead to begin with and so you have so to speak got rid of the event before the book begins." Stein went on to point out that "in real life people are interested in crime more than they are in detection, it is the crime that is the thing the shock the thrill the horror but in the story it is the detection that holds the interest and that is natural enough because the necessity as far as action is concerned is the dead man, it is another function that has very little to do with human nature that makes the detection interesting."[1] These statements are remarkably suggestive. As Stein sees it, the modernity of the detective story as a narrative form is bound up precisely with the conscious belatedness of its action and the retrospective nature of its exposition. It begins where the traditional narrative might conclude, with the death of "the hero." If the hero, in a novel by Tolstoi or Stendhal, acts on his destiny, defines his character, develops and changes, and if the novel itself is a record of these changes, that possibility is denied

13

from the outset in the detective novel. The detective story's initial corpse signifies that human nature is fixed, absolute, beyond revision, and hence, to all intents and purposes, beyond redemption. Like a literal rendering of *nature morte,* the French idiom for "still life": dead nature.

Stein raises more questions than she answers, but they all point in the same direction. Why is it so important, so essentially "modern," to "get rid of human nature," as the detective novel does? Is it because, as Thomas De Quincey argued, there is something "abject" in "human nature" at its most basic? Or is it because, at the late stage of our culture that is punctuated by the detective story's appearance, optimistic assumptions about the perfectibility of human nature no longer obtain? Must "human nature" be seen, therefore, as barbaric, incorrigible, the human animal having once and for all divided itself into two classes of being, victim and executioner? Is this what the detective novel is saying with its initial corpse?

Put it this way: A homicide stands for "human nature," Cain murdering Abel. The dead "hero" is the corpse of Romanticism with its worship of the noble savage. We can fix the time of death with some exactness, since it had to have happened before April 1841, the month in which Poe's "The Murders in the Rue Morgue" appeared in *Graham's Magazine* in Philadelphia. Surely it's no accident that in this, by common consent the world's first detective story, the culprit turns out to be a ghoulishly transmogrified version of the noble savage. The wicked deeds in that closed-shuttered, fourth-floor room in the nicely named Rue Morgue were committed, we learn, by a murderous orangutan—the id on a monstrous rampage, primitive energy uncontrolled, Romanticism gone haywire.

There are those who will quarrel with this sense of the detective novel as an expression of despair over the broken promises that Romanticism made to the poets and artists of the early nineteenth century. It might be argued that the detective genre is nothing if not Romantic in the value it attaches to the creative mind, the intuitive intelligence. Poe would seem to insist on this. His detective, C. Auguste Dupin, is both a poet and a mathematician, a blend of "the creative and the resolvent" faculties. This is not very different from what Coleridge meant by the imagination, and it's this as much as his confident rationalism that sets Dupin apart. "The fact is," Richard Wilbur writes, "that Dupin's logic, proceeding with a charmed arbitrariness toward the solution which seems to justify it, has what Poe called an '*air* of method,' but is really intuition in disguise.''[2] Only through a retroactive act of imaginative intuition—call it *deduction,* a word the detective story has curiously redefined—can Dupin reconstruct and thus somehow rescue a corrupt reality. This would seem to be the very epitome of a Romantic project: the use of the imagination as a species of will, the notion that experience can be saved through the agency of something resembling imaginative hindsight. Coldly superior, Dupin emerges as a superbly Byronic figure, world-weary yet defiant, in retreat from society and in despair of it yet sure of his own powers. He is the exception in the social order, the outsider looking in, the Romantic individualist par excellence. You would never take him for an organization man.

But Romanticism's cheerful faith is what's missing from Poe's picture of Dupin in his armchair, puffing on his pipe in the dark, eyes shut, contemplating local atrocities. The corpse on page one has changed everything; murder most foul has upstaged—as how could it not?—the holy "spots of time" Romantic poets dwelt on. One could say that the detective story participates in a Gothic tradition that came to fruition in the Romantic era but is fundamentally at odds with the primary Romantic impulse. Neither the indicative tense of affirmation nor the subjunctive mood of "as if"—two tenets of the grammar of Romanticism—will suit the spirit of the Gothic; its syntactical condition is that of the irrevocable past. In its world, the catastrophe has already happened and will happen again and again; no vision or revision can save the day.

"Beauty is truth, truth beauty," Keats declared in "Ode on a Grecian Urn," but the detective story sees truth in quite another light. It's the dread fact beneath a surface of lies and half-truths and misleading assumptions, and it's always incriminating, as the corpse on page one keeps reminding us. To the imagination of "The Murders in the Rue Morgue," nature in its raw state can no longer be considered a source of innocence, as it was for Rousseau with his noble savage or for Wordsworth with his blessed babe. Still less is it a source of moral instruction. It is no longer to be understood, in Wordsworth's terms, as a pristine "impulse from a vernal wood" or a sublime landscape that fills us with awe and confirms "our cheerful faith, that all which we behold / Is full of blessings." No, the setting that best exemplifies the state of nature in detective novels is that of *The Hound of the Baskervilles*: the Devonshire moors, a wilderness primordial and prehistoric, on which the spectral hound, appearing to fulfill an ancestral curse, leaves real footprints in its wake. Nature is "red in tooth and claw," and human nature is an extension of this bloody truth. Let nature be our teacher and out will come the beast beneath the skin.

Darwin's theory of evolution soon gave an explicit scientific form to the threatening undercurrent of Poe's first "tale of ratiocination." When Dupin points to the orangutan as the culprit in "The Murders in the Rue Morgue," in effect he's making a nineteenth-century translation of the Sphinx's riddle that Oedipus solves: The correct answer, in both cases, is man. Man, evolved from the apes, is no more than a toilet-trained ape or, as a character puts it in Eric Ambler's *Journey into Fear* (1940), "an ape in velvet." Narcissus, awakening from unquiet slumber, has dragged his body to the pool, looked at his reflection, and recoiled in horror from the monster that stares back at him. He is right to be shocked. The murderer is his double. There are two William Wilsons in Poe's story of that title, two Dorian Grays in Oscar Wilde's tale; inside every Dr. Jekyll there's a Mr. Hyde struggling to get out. The poor devil may try to control the homicidal urges that betray his simian ancestry, but they are not so easily repressed or repressed without a price. The greater the struggle to control them, the greater the chances of a hyperbolic release. Man—the creature of the riddle who walks on four legs, then two, then three, in his cycle of days—never did get too far from the brutishness of his four-legged existence.

Go back once more to "The Murders in the Rue Morgue" and examine what the orangutan was up to just before it murdered Mme. L'Espanaye and her daughter. "Razor in hand, and fully lathered, it was sitting before a looking-glass, attempting the operation of shaving, in which it had no doubt previously watched its master through the key-hole of the closet." What else was it trying to do but ape its master and assume the countenance of a civilized man? In its hands, however, the razor turns into a deadly weapon. The ape can't help itself; the very accoutrements of domestic civilization have become, in its hands, instruments of torture. Startled by its master and terrified of his whip, it flings itself onto the street. A lighted apartment catches its eye, and it must break and enter. Mme. L'Espanaye's fear drives it wild, as does the first blood it draws from her skin. Far from acting as a restraint, a primitive sense of conscience—fear of its master's wrath—causes it to compound the bestiality. It's in a vain attempt to conceal the crime that the daughter's corpse is shoved up the chimney. And what of the hapless sailor to whom the orangutan belonged? In the very act of trying to prevent the horror, he has hastened it along and can only stand by helplessly and watch. The superego has tried to modify the behavior of the wanton id but, in the absence of a mediating ego, has turned things from bad to worse. No wonder Dupin tells the sailor that, while "innocent of the atrocities," he is "in some measure implicated in them."

By calling his first collection of stories "Tales of the Grotesque and Arabesque," Poe specified his native element. *Grotesque* and *arabesque* are like Gothic inversions of *imagination* and *fancy*; they suggest delusions, distortions, wild caprices—caricatures of the Romantic sublime.[3] The terror in Poe's tales is not the morally uplifting kind that Wordsworth felt in the presence of cataracts and crags, but the product of an exaggeration. Poe spells it out in one of his letters: "the ludicrous heightened into the grotesque, the fearful colored into the horrible, the witty exaggerated into the burlesque, the singular wrought out into the strange and mystical." Everything in Poe's "tales of the grotesque and arabesque" proceeds from, and confirms, the hysteria latent in such a vision. The "tales of ratiocination"—"The Murders in the Rue Morgue," "The Mystery of Marie Roget" and "The Purloined Letter"— don't so much repudiate this vision as try to counterbalance it. They come in the form of a wished-for antidote, as if in response to the madman's earnest plea in "The Black Cat": "Hereafter, perhaps, some intellect may be found which will reduce my phantasm to the common-place—some intellect more calm, more logical, and far less excitable than my own, which will perceive, in the circumstances I detail with awe, nothing more than an ordinary succession of very natural causes and effects." "Poe invented the detective story," in Joseph Wood Krutch's impressive and much-quoted formulation, "in order that he might not go mad."

The doomed "hero" in Poe's tales of terror is sometimes the victim ("The Pit and the Pendulum"), sometimes the murderer ("The Cask of Amontillado"), and sometimes, most terrifying of all, the murderer who's also somehow a victim ("The Tell-Tale Heart," "The Black Cat"). In Poe's detective stories, these heroes are "dead to begin with," to use Gertrude Stein's phrase. They have succumbed to what Poe calls "the imp of the perverse," to demons of malice or of conscience, and they die their deaths offstage. Poe needs a new hero to replace them, an exemplar of the human mind rather than of frail human nature, since that has already been eliminated. He gives us Dupin, the archetype of all the Great Detectives from Sherlock Holmes on. The new hero, as Poe prescribed him and Doyle perfected him, represents logic and intuition in alliance, scientific method in name if not always in deed. His mission: to investigate the circumstances surrounding his predecessor's death.

———◆———

The extraordinary elevator sequence in Brian De Palma's movie *Dressed to Kill* (1980) would seem to spell out the logic whereby the death of "the hero" represents the occasion for the true hero's emergence. The character played by Angie Dickinson has been, so far as the viewer can tell, the movie's heroine. We have followed her adventures in a museum, a taxicab, and a man's apartment, which she leaves after some very casual sex. She enters the elevator, takes it downstairs, realizes that she has forgotten her wedding ring, and rides back up—to her doom. When the elevator stops, the killer enters and slashes her to death. And when the elevator stops again, seconds later, on a different floor, who should be waiting for it but the character played by Nancy Allen, henceforth the movie's protagonist? Significantly, Allen enters the picture but not the chamber of death; she sees the body on the floor and the killer's reflection in the elevator mirror, and she flees to safety. And suddenly we understand that Dickinson, the putative heroine, was a victim all along—the director only fooled us into thinking otherwise. The movie has punished her for her adultery; hence the emphasis on the forgotten wedding ring. As her successor—in the killer's mind and the camera's eye—Allen is better equipped to succeed. It is she who is the film's true heroine, for whom the other served as an annunciation and a study in contrasts.

There are crucial differences, of course, but in this one sense at least, Nancy Allen's relation to Angie Dickinson approximates that of the detective to the victim in a crime novel. The discovery of the corpse signals a transition from one "hero" to another, a figure antithetical to the first and thus better suited for survival. The scene of the crime is the locus of this transition, the place where "dead nature" confronts the new hero. It's as though the death of one made the other's life possible. And the image of the killer in the elevator mirror, distorted, disguised, seems an apt metaphor for what the detective sees—if only in his mind—when he starts to reconstruct the case.

The fictional detective was from the start a creature of intellect rather than will, an expression of the human mind rather than human nature. Nature was conceived to be a savage beast or a mutilated corpse, and corrupt in either case; mind was conceived to be in opposition to nature. Calm where nature was turbulent, it was capable of reducing the wildest phantasm to an orderly flow of effects and causes. The hero of the mind would naturally be a confirmed rationalist. For the Romantic poet's transcendent "spots of time," he substitutes the prosaic inquiry: "where were *you* on the night of the twenty-ninth?" Yet his endeavor has upstaged the crime under investigation, however lurid its details.

No longer is it, in Stein's words, "the crime that is the thing the shock the thrill the horror, but in the story it is the detection that holds the interest." And detection as a form of heroic action is unique in that it directs itself upon the past. Sherlock Holmes calls it "the Science of Deduction and Analysis." But T. H. Huxley came nearer the mark when he spoke of "retrospective prophecy as a function of science."[4] Prophecy? Yes, because its object is "the apprehension of that which lies out of the sphere of immediate knowledge." And it is "retrospective," wrote Huxley, in that it involves reasoning "from an effect to the pre-existence of a cause competent to produce that effect," as from the discovery of the corpse back to the reconstruction of the deed. It is always a backward process—it always comes as a sequel to events that transpired before page one.

Ellery Queen's early case, *The Chinese Orange Mystery* (1934), is a marvelous footnote to Huxley's definition of detection as "retrospective prophecy." The foreword to the case—which "might well have been subtitled: The Crime That Was Backwards"—adverts to a definition of the detective as "a prophet looking backwards." And the pages that follow convert this dictum into an elaborate and inventive conceit. Everything about the case, including the red herrings, has to do with things that go backward, are inverted, have been turned inside out or upside down. In the locked room where the corpse resides, the chairs and tables have been upended, the paintings face the wall, and the victim's clothes are on backwards. Elsewhere in the house, a set of valuable Hebrew books has been stolen, and it's vital that they are Hebrew books, since that language reads from right to left. Among the suspects is a confidence woman who calls herself Llewes—her real name, Sewell, spelled backwards. And there's a good deal of commotion about a rare Chinese postage stamp—rare because of a printing error that resulted in an inversion. One solution makes sense of all these diversions, for diversions they are, meant to obscure the essential fact that the dead man habitually wore his collar back to front. It is the corpse of a priest. The whole elaborate if impromptu plan is the handiwork of an artistic murderer, who evidently preferred to turn everything upside down rather than simply reverse the give-away collar. This is a murderer who has taken pains to make a point about detective logic's backward motion.

If mind-reading, backward-reasoning investigators of crimes—sleuths like Dupin or Sherlock Holmes—resemble prophets, it's in the visionary rather than the vatic sense. It's not that they see into the future; on the contrary, they're not even looking that way. But, reflecting on the clues left behind by the past, they see patterns where the rest of us see only random signs. They reveal and make intelligible what otherwise would be dark, and they depend not on supernatural guidance but on their superior ability to reason back from effects to causes—their version of scientific method. The figure of the sleuth becomes a metaphor for the intellectual hero.

The first literary exposition of "the science of deduction" preceded the creation of Sherlock Holmes by a century and a half. It is the method of the eponymous hero of Voltaire's *Zadig* (1749), a man whose study of nature has enabled him to discern "a thousand differences where other men see nothing but uniformity." In the third chapter of that work, Zadig identifies the queen's missing spaniel, and then the king's runaway horse, in accurate detail both times, without ever having set his eyes on either. He can tell that the horse, for example, "is five feet high, with very small hoofs, and a tail three feet and an half in length; the studs on his bit are gold, of twenty-three carats, and his shoes are silver of eleven penny-weights." How does Zadig know? The king's retainers suspect sorcery, but it is really the magic of science at work. Zadig makes it all sound elementary:

> I observed the marks of a horses's shoes, all at equal distances. This must be a horse, said I to myself, that gallops excellently. The dust on the trees in a narrow road that was but seven feet wide was a little brushed off, at the distance of three feet and a half from the middle of the road. This horse, said I, has a tail three feet and a half long, which, being whisked to the right and left, has swept away the dust. I observed under the trees that formed an arbor five feet in height, that the leaves of the branches were newly fallen, from

whence I inferred that the horse had touched them, and that he must therefore be five feet high. As to his bit, it must be gold of twenty-three carats, for he had rubbed its bosses against a stone which I knew to be a touchstone, and which I have tried. In a word, from a mark made by his shoes on flints of another kind, I concluded that he was shod with silver eleven deniers fine.

What we have here, Huxley argued in his essay "On the Method of Zadig" (1880), is nothing less than the basis of paleontology, archaeology, and geology—of science considered as a systematic habit of detection.

The Great Detectives feel obliged to imitate these feats of Zadig, which amount to a rite of passage. In performing them, the sleuth gives proof of his or her prowess and claims scientific legitimacy. Holmes, the world's most famous amateur chemist, gives frequent demonstrations of the method of Zadig. Shortly after meeting Watson in *A Study in Scarlet,* the 1887 novel that introduced the two to each other and the world, Holmes calmly announces that the "plainly dressed" stranger approaching his Baker Street digs must be a retired naval officer. Holmes is right, of course, and Watson is suitably startled by his matter-of-fact explanation. It was, says Holmes, a simple matter of putting two and two together from such evidence as the stranger's tattooed hand, side-whiskers, and air of self-importance. There ensues a Zadig-like example of reasoning, and then this memorable exchange: "'Wonderful!' I ejaculated. 'Commonplace,' said Holmes."

The demonstration that the Holmes-like William of Baskerville gives Adso, his chronicler and companion in *The Name of the Rose,* seems a deliberate echo of the wonders of *Zadig.* In the opening pages of the book, William and Adso are intercepted by "an agitated band of monks" as they approach the monastery where murder mysteries await them. William knows at a glance that the monks are hunting for "Brunellus, the abbot's favorite horse," which he describes unerringly on the basis of footprints and broken twigs and horsehairs left on brambles.[5] In Eco's novel as in *A Study in Scarlet,* this initial display of the detective's acumen doubles as a statement of his faith—faith that the universe is intelligible, faith in the legacy of Zadig, the magic of science. Yes, the sleuth acknowledges, signs and wonders do exist, in fact they're quite commonplace. They exist to be solved. The mysterious sign is really the giveaway clue to one who can read the book of nature.

All this brings us back to what Gertrude Stein supposed was true. The triumph of human mind over human nature, though always and only partial, is what the detective story was meant to glorify from the first. While it has a fatalistic view of history, it counters with a kind of ex post facto positivism: If we can't bring the corpse back to life, we can still find out how it got that way, and why. This is quite obviously true of classic detective stories, in which the detective relies on one or another permutation of the method of Zadig. With a scientific air, he proceeds from observation rather than from a priori premises, draws judicious inferences from scattered facts, and then frames hypotheses to agree with the evidence—making imaginative leaps where necessary. Though in American private eye novels, by contrast, the detective trusts his wits rather than his reasoning powers, it is still a matter of mental equipment; it isn't only his ability to take a punch that sees the hero through. The detective's job is to see the past and see it whole, starting with the corpse and then figuring out how it got that way. It's a case of mind (the detective) over dead nature (the corpse), and to say that the confrontation of the two results in a puzzle or intellectual parlor game is scarcely to malign the impulse. To the extent that the detective novel resembles a puzzle or game, it involves the reader as an active participant—it's as though, going along for the ride, the reader is consulted on which way to turn. "Not only is the detective story the great popular instance of working backwards from effect to cause," wrote Marshall McLuhan, "it is also the form in which the reader is deeply involved as co-author."[6] The two propositions go together.

3

◆

Mysteries and Myths

I suspect that the typical reader of detective stories is, like myself, a person who suffers from a sense of sin.

—W. H. Auden, "The Guilty Vicarage"

Both Gilbert K. Chesterton and Gertrude Stein—a happily fortuitous conjunction of names—emphasized the detective novel's modernity in their briefs on its behalf. Stein called the detective novel "the only really modern novel form"; Chesterton hailed it as "the earliest and only form of popular literature in which is expressed some sense of the poetry of modern life."[1] The genre's claim to modernity may seem less assured to contemporary readers. Proponents of crime fiction tend to speak of its old-fashioned literary virtues. They like pointing out that a good detective novel will serve up pleasures sometimes eschewed in straight fiction that is self-consciously modern or experimental. Crime novelists depend heavily on tight plot construction, surprise and suspense, reversals and recognitions. The narrative line proceeds in gradual stages from mystification to revelation, a teleological progression toward the truth. The good survive and prosper. The evil are isolated and carted off. We are promised a happy ending, or something that resembles one. In these and other ways, the genre would seem to conform to the most ancient storytelling traditions.

Paradoxically, the detective novel's claim to be a "really modern" form rests in its ability to connect with ancient myth or tradition. The formal elements and conventions of the genre seem to lend themselves remarkably well to the exposition of thoroughly modern myths—such as the story of Oedipus Rex—which turn out to be, often enough, the old myths reinterpreted or debunked. In fact, detective novels behave like the avatars of post-modernism. They constantly feed on themselves, raiding their predecessors, invoking rules and conventions if only to violate them—as when, in a reversal that dates back to *Oedipus Rex*, the killer turns out to be the detective.

Chesterton characterized the detective novel as the folktale of the modern metropolis. The analogy between fairy tales and detective novels has never ceased to apply, though the genre's attitude toward the modern metropolis seems to have changed over the years since Chesterton himself celebrated the exotic enticements of Edwardian London in *The Man Who Was Thursday* (1908) and *The Club of Queer Trades* (1905). In detective novels as in fairy tales and dreams, the same characters and props constantly reappear in new combinations: the Watson figure, the locked room puzzle, the least likely suspect, the damsel in distress who turns out to be a femme fatale, the remote country mansion. Each recurrence means something different; detective novels are as full of symbolic resonance as dreams. They evoke our anxieties and then relieve them the way fairy tales do.

Let a paraphrase of the story of "Elijah's Violin" suggest the extent to which fairy tales depend upon a reintegration of familiar motifs. Start with a king and his three daughters, each of whom is granted a wish. Alone of the three, the third daughter wishes for the right thing: Elijah's magic violin. To win the prize for her, her father must travel to a distant kingdom and free a princess from the stone in which she's encased. After accomplishing this mission, the king presents the violin to his daughter, who makes a prince appear when she plays it alone in her room. Her sisters—half out of envy, half out of curiosity—misuse the violin in her absence, bringing harm to the phantom prince. The princess must therefore embark on a quest for her wounded paramour. Her adventures bring her to the woods, where she falls asleep under a tree and is serenaded by the birds, whose language holds no mysteries for her. From them she learns that a map to the palace appears on the leaves of the tree, and sure enough nature herself guides her through the labyrinthine forest and out into the promised land. Emerging in the kingdom where her prince lies ailing, the princess knows exactly what she must do. She presents herself to the court disguised as a man, claims to be a physician, and promises to heal the prince—knowing that she'll be put to death should she fail. At last, in the presence of the wounded prince, she remembers something that a mysterious old woman had told her when she left home. The princess burns three strings of Elijah's violin, and the act restores the prince to life and health. This happened once upon a time; they marry and live happily ever after.

"Elijah's Violin" is a specifically Jewish fairy tale, but in how many others do these same elements figure. We have met the same three daughters often enough to know beforehand that the third has been favored by destiny and that her sisters are likely to be spiteful and cruel. We've met the other characters, too—the wounded prince, the sagacious old woman, the imprisoned princess, the noble father—and we've been through these same woods, gotten lost on the way, and had to depend on the kindness of strange birds to set us straight. We've embarked on quests that result in trials, and we know that the death penalty awaits us should we fail. We've disguised ourselves, pretended to be somebody or something we aren't, shedding an identity to recover a truer one. And how often has an enchanted artifact—a lamp to be rubbed, a violin whose strings we must burn—saved the day for us? In the parenthesis between "once upon a time" and "happily ever after," the history of our childhood has occurred, like a collective dream.[2]

Something very similar is true of the detective story, the spell it casts on us and the way it returns us, over and over again, to primal scenes and archetypal characters. In detective novels we meet with talismans as strange and seemingly enchanted as Elijah's violin itself—only on our haunts they're likely to take the form of a piece of string tied in knots at equal intervals, a rare coin, or a piece of avian statuary allegedly encrusted with jewels beneath its black enameled surface. Here, too, are happenstances as apparently magical as the benevolent birds of instruction in the fairy-tale forest's deep darkness: Doubles roam in our midst, letters are purloined, false identities are assumed and shed like so many expedient disguises, corpses lie concealed in snowmen, and the photograph of a long-deceased murderess in a manuscript submitted to a publisher turns out to be a photograph of the publisher's wife. We even have our version of the betrayed princess embarking on her quest: He is, in the world of detective fiction, the wrong man, framed for crimes he hasn't committed, a man with every reason to be paranoid or to turn himself into a criminal in self-defense. As Father Brown puts it in Chesterton's "The Sins of Prince Saradine," "It isn't only nice things that happen in fairyland."

———◆———

A narrative form that restricts itself to the aftermath of events presumed to have already taken place must indeed be considered peculiarly modern—if a condition of modernity is a feeling of belatedness, of having arrived on the scene at the tail end of something that's over and done with. Fundamental to modern literature is anxiety—the author's or the protagonist's—about having come too late. There is the sense of beginning not in the middle of things, as Homeric epics do, but after they have already run their course. The detective novel internalizes this anxiety and presents it (or disguises it) as a formal convention: the corpse on page one. The past, which can be neither forgotten nor undone, will return to haunt us, try though we will to repress it. See, there it is, staring us in the face from under a dead man's eyelids. The past is the problem that the present must solve. We live in the valley of the shadow of the deceased.

The conscious belatedness of the action in a detective story is perfectly consonant with the modern view of human development— the view that suggests that the definitive episodes in a person's life occurred somewhere in the past, are accessible to the memory only by a strenuous feat of detection, and can only be "solved," never undone. Not by accident did the detective novel flourish as never before during the first decades of the twentieth century, at the same time that psychoanalysis took hold as an explanation of the human mind.

Consider the detective story in the context of Freud's model of the human mind, and what else is the sleuth but the ego striving to mediate between an implacable superego and an uncontrollable id? The battle of wits between sleuth and culprit can be seen in many ways, but one of them is surely as a dramatization of the constant strife and periodic reconciliation between the ego and the id. Nor is it a mystery that sleuth and culprit should exert a mutual attraction on one another. In the culprit the sleuth encounters his doppelgänger: a contorted picture of himself, what Dorian Gray sees in the portrait he keeps hidden. This sense of doubleness is built into the very structure of the detective story, with its emphasis on mirror images and disguises, betrayals and identity confusions. The detective story's eternal triangle, a version of Freud's family romance, is doomed from the start. Rub out the victim, and the triangle becomes a straight line, at whose opposite ends stand the sleuth and culprit. To solve the murder, the sleuth must narrow the distance between them until they meet at the vanishing point of resemblance. The sleuth must, in effect, be able to read the culprit's mind in order to say how or why the murder was committed. That's one reason both Dupin and Sherlock Holmes are introduced to us as mind readers, capable of guessing quite accurately the thought patterns of their companions. What the culprit did in the past, the sleuth must duplicate—albeit in a purely conceptual sense—in the present. By an act of imagination, the sleuth becomes the culprit's double, and his reconstruction of the crime is like the recollection of a repressed trauma during a psychoanalytic session.

It's easy to see how Holmes's brand of mind reading resembles Freud's. No doubt it's this, as much as the two men's shared fondness for cocaine and tobacco, that tempts writers and filmmakers to smuggle Freud into Holmes's fictive life, and vice versa. Reading Freud on the meaning of a literary motif—the theme of the three caskets in *The Merchant of Venice,* say—we feel we're in the presence of a superior detective. The motif in question is laid out as though it were a mystery that needs elucidation, a cipher that begs to be decoded, a clue that needs to be restored to its context. And the text on which Freud performed his most brilliant feat of critical detection is not only a parable of psychoanalysis—the slow but inexorable process of bringing the fearsome darkness to light—but a parable bearing a profound resemblance to the incidents and methods of a detective novel. Think of it this way: Freud is the sleuth who cracked the Oedipus case wide open.

In classical literature, the paradigmatic murder mystery is Freud's central myth, a patricide and a parable about the universality of guilt and incestuous desire. (In the Bible, by contrast, the paradigmatic murder mystery is the slaying by Cain of his brother Abel, a fratricide and a parable about human conscience and divine omniscience.) According to myth, Oedipus solved the riddle of the Sphinx; like a latter-day Oedipus, Freud solved the riddle of the Theban king who slept with his own mother after slaying his father without ever being aware of who he was or of what he was doing. Oedipus, according to Freud's solution, embodied the guilty secret of all men in all ages. Guilt is the awareness of repressed desire, and the tragedy of *Oedipus Rex* charts the stages of the hero's growing self-awareness—culminating in his recognition that he himself is the culprit of the drama as well as its sleuth.

Freud was attracted not only to the content, manifest and latent, of Sophocles' tragedy but equally to its "process of revealing"—"a process that can be likened to the work of a psychoanalysis," as Freud wrote in *The Interpretation of Dreams.* The "process of revealing" is one way of describing the work of a detective. The structural similarities between *Oedipus Rex* and what you might call a generic detective story are, in fact, remarkable. The issue of the play is an unsolved murder that antedates the start of the play. The initial corpse, as in a detective novel, bequeaths a pervasive sense of guilt; the slaying of Laius, though it took place in the past, accounts for the plague on the land that Oedipus must act to remove. Oedipus becomes a sleuth, determined to find out who assassinated the old king at "the place where three roads meet." As a detective, Oedipus is relentless, unshakable in his resolve, undeterred by those who plead with him to give it up. It's a role that suits him well; he established his right to the kingdom of Thebes—and to the bed of his queen—precisely by his skill at solving mysteries.

It was Oedipus who provided—and embodied—the correct answer to the riddle of the Sphinx. What is the creature that has four legs at dawn, two at high noon, and three at dusk? Man is the answer: Man is the creature that crawls on four legs, then walks on two, then resembles an awkward three-legged beast negotiating his movement with a cane. The solution to the murder of Laius is Oedipus, which is—as Freud made us see—another way of answering the Sphinx's primal riddle. Oedipus is man, all men; the cycles of man are enacted in his career. Oedipus the banished infant, unable even to crawl because his legs are bound, returns as the strong man of midday, capable of supplanting his father in his mother's bed, and becomes in the end the old, blind, decaying, self-exiled king of *Oedipus at Colonus,* who needs his daughter to support him while he walks. And so the murder mystery arrives at its terrifying denouement when the tragic hero recognizes himself as the antagonist he has tracked down. The detective's investigation proceeds with a gradual sense of disclosure, climaxing in revelation. The culprit and sleuth have converged—with a shock heard round the world—in the single identity of Oedipus.

In practice, psychoanalysis is a form of sleuth work, and it's tempting to pursue the parallel a little, as John Cawelti does in his book *Adventure, Mystery, and Romance* (1976). Here's his summary of the analogy between the analysis of dreams and the ratiocination of crimes: "A brilliant investigator (Dupin, Freud) is confronted with a series of material clues (footprints, tufts of hair, dream symbols, slips of the tongue) that if properly intepreted are signs of a deeply hidden and disturbing truth. By a combination of method and insight, the investigator overcomes the confusion that attends these clues (the criminal's plot, psychological displacement) and reveals the hidden truth (solves the crime, interprets the dream)." To Cawelti, the analogy suggests "a common concern with hidden secrets and guilts that may reflect a cultural pattern of the period": guilt as a universal psychological condition, whether projected onto an external character, as in the crime novel, or traced to the dreamer's own mind.[3] No fictional detective has been more decisively influenced by Freud's theories than Lew Archer, the sleuth in Ross Macdonald's novels. *The Chill* (1964), *The Goodbye Look* (1969) and *The Underground Man* (1971) feature elaborate oedipal riddles in Southern California, an all-pervasive sense of guilt, and plots "which opened up gradually like fissures in the firm ground of the present, cleaving far down through the strata of the past." This simile, from *The Chill,* is entirely characteristic of Macdonald, who underwent a successful course of psychotherapy in the late 1950s and brought the experience to bear in the novels he wrote thereafter.

In Macdonald's deterministic universe, the book's initial corpse completes or extends a chain of events that date back to remote, long-repressed origins. "The web of causality is almost infinitely exact," Macdonald told an interviewer in 1971. "There are no coincidences in life."[4] There are certainly no coincidences in a Lew Archer mystery. Murder here represents the return of the repressed; it is the inexorable consequence of a guilty past. Every homicide occurs in a series. It is the product of the murderer's compulsion to repeat, and it can be interpreted as a variation of the oedipal myth. How often Archer's cases involve the disappearance of a child or parent—and a search undertaken by a parent or child of the opposite sex. In *The Chill,* for example, a college-age woman named Dolly Kincaid disappears; her mother was killed ten years earlier and her—false—testimony was instrumental in convicting her father of the crime. Why Dolly lied and who really shot her mother are questions crucial to Archer's investigation of the murder of Dolly's *teacher,* who had a pretty powerful "father fixation" herself. The culprit is, as so often in fairy tales and detective stories, the third in a sequence of three: a woman who was introduced to us as the college dean's mother—but is, we learn in the end, the man's wife. Freud, Macdonald once remarked, "made myth into psychiatry, and I've been trying to turn it back into myth again in my own small way."[5]

Extrapolating from the Ross Macdonald model, we might consider the psychoanalytical implications of detective novels that are less overtly Freudian in their aims or concerns. The paradigmatic corpse found facedown can stand for the parent we secretly wished dead. Repressing the memory with a guilty shudder, we nevertheless mistake the wish for the deed in our dreams and other necessary fictions through which the psyche disguises, expresses, and escapes from its fears. Geraldine Pederson-Krag, in an influential article published in *Psychoanalytic Quarterly* (1949), linked the discovery of the corpse to "the primal scene" of parental intercourse and went on to spin out the comparison in these succinct terms: "The victim is the parent for whom the reader (the child) had negative oedipal feelings. The clues in the story, disconnected, inexplicable, and trifling, represent the child's growing awareness of details it had never understood, such as the family sleeping arrangements, nocturnal sounds, stains, incomprehensible adult jokes and remarks. The criminal of the detective drama appears innocuous until the final page. In real life he was the parent toward whom the child's positive oedipal feelings were directed, the one whom the child wished least of all to imagine participating in a secret crime."[6]

◆

A dead parent or a dead god: The corpse on page one can be understood as either. The detective story's conventions can support a religious myth as easily as one based on the family romance: The story's original crime, the one buried in the past in Ross Macdonald's novels, simply becomes a secular version of original sin. If the book's central event, the murder, is an antecedent of the plot, it follows that we're dealing with a historical universe in which the self is not an existential hero capable of choosing his destiny but a spectator at his own trial. Guilt, preceding birth, is a foregone conclusion, and the drama concerns the possibilities of absolution and redemption. The reader has moved from the psychiatrist's couch to the confessional. Like the sailor in "The Murders in the Rue Morgue," he doesn't have to perpetrate the atrocity in order to be implicated in it. Afflicted as he is with the consciousness of guilt, he may worry that his own sinful secrets will come out, but he's also willing to wager, with suitably crossed fingers, that the Great Detective will absolve him of wrongdoing. And he *is* absolved, at least for the time being. The detective novel has been his confessional. "I like to think," wrote Robert Lowell in the essay "Art and Evil," "that Plato was a reader of thrillers, and after banning Homer from his Republic, he would have declared thrillers innocent of Original Sin and given them the key to his Athens."[7]

The corpse on page one points us in two directions, like a scarecrow. It is found at the crossroads of the past and future, and it initiates not one but two narrative sequences, parallel tracks that meet in the infinity of the detective's mind: the story of the murder and the story of the investigation. The narrative occurs in two different time zones. Murder, the discovery of a corpse, marks the end of one narrative and the beginning of another. This is how Dennis Porter puts it in his essay "Backward Construction and the Art of Suspense" (1981): "From the point of view of the art of narrative, the functional value of the discovery of a corpse is that it often represents the most brutal of reversals—murder, in spite of its repetition in detective novels, is always produced as a surprise—and the deadest of dead ends. After a death the investigative task often has to begin again."[8]

Just as the body represents the last link in a forgotten chain of events, it also warns of further violence to come. The "law of progressive homicide" ensures that more victims will follow, and part of the reader's guilty pleasure comes from guessing just who among the suspects will be terminally eliminated from suspicion. Since in many cases we get to meet them in their living state, the second and third corpses in a detective novel are generally more likeable than the first, and the effect is a heightened sense of guilt. "The murderer," wrote Auden in his characteristically prescriptive way, "should start with a real grievance and, as a consequence of righting it by illegitimate means, be forced to murder against his will where he has no grievances but his own guilt."[9]

Despite his belligerence toward detective stories and their fans, Edmund Wilson conveyed a shrewd insight into the genre's "law of progressive homicide'' and its promise of ultimate absolution. Unlike some who praised the genre but made few claims for its seriousness, Wilson disparaged it despite discerning in it something resembling a religious need fulfilled: relief from guilt. How else to account for the genre's great popularity between the world wars? Not by analogy to crossword puzzles, said Wilson. Here's his answer in "Why Do People Read Detective Stories?":

> The world during those years was ridden by an all-pervasive feeling
> of guilt and by a fear of impending disaster which it seemed
> hopeless to try to avert because it never seemed conclusively possible
> to pin down the responsibility. Who had committed the original
> crime and who was going to commit the next one?—that second
> murder which always, in the novels, occurs at an unexpected moment
> when the investigation is well under way; which, as in one of the
> Nero Wolfe stories, may take place right in the great detective's
> office. Everybody is suspected in turn, and the streets are full of
> lurking agents whose allegiances we cannot know. Nobody seems
> guiltless, nobody seems safe; and then, suddenly, the murderer is
> spotted, and—relief!—he is not, after all, a person like you or me.
> He is a villain, known to the trade as George Gruesome—and he has
> been caught by an infallible Power, the supercilious and omniscient
> detective, who knows exactly where to fix the guilt.[10]

To obtain the desired effect, a single corpse may suffice in a story, but in a novel only a succession will do. "I admit that a second murder in a book often cheers things up," says the artless Captain Hastings in Christie's *The A.B.C. Murders.* "If the murder happens in the first chapter, and you have to follow up everybody's alibi until the last page but one—well, it does get a bit tedious."

Murder repeats itself, as do religious rituals. Admit another allegorical reading: the full-fledged theological interpretation of detective stories proposed by C. Day Lewis. Lewis, who became England's poet laureate in 1968, wrote some estimable poems, but it's no slander on his name to say that the detective novels he wrote as Nicholas Blake may be his most lasting accomplishment. Having given the world Nigel Strangeways, a sleuth whose personality was loosely based on W. H. Auden, Nicholas Blake was prepared to argue the case for the murder mystery as a modern substitute for a religious myth. Imagine an anthropologist a century hence, Blake wrote. "When a religion has lost its hold upon men's hearts, they must have some other outlet for the sense of guilt," the anthropologist will say—and will seize upon the detective story as fulfilling this requirement:

> He will call attention to the pattern of the detective-novel, as highly formalised as that of a religious ritual, with its initial necessary sin (the murder), its victim, its high priest (the criminal) who must in turn be destroyed by a yet higher power (the detective). He will conjecture—and rightly—that the devotee identified himself both with the detective and the murderer, representing the light and the dark sides of his own nature. He will note a significant parallel between the formalised dénouement of the detective novel and the Christian concept of the Day of Judgment when, with a flourish of trumpets, the mystery is made plain and the goats are separated from the sheep.[11]

The analogy between Christian mystery and the crime-novel kind is a two-way street. "The women who visit Christ's tomb on Easter morning and find the body gone," writes Elliot Gilbert in his study of the mystery genre, "are participating in what could be called, without disrespect, the greatest locked room story ever told."[12]

Push the religious parallels a little further, and you arrive at an analog for the case of the spurious corpse—the corpse that won't stay dead—that we come across now and again in detective novels. Sometimes it's a ruse contrived to look like a supernatural event, as when the murderer stands accused by his victim in Poe's "Thou Art the Man"—the corpse has become a ventriloquist's dummy. Or sometimes the corpse enjoys his posthumous existence by having, when alive, hatched a nasty postdated surprise, as in Blake's *Thou Shell of Death*. Dimitrios, in Eric Ambler's *A Coffin for Dimitrios* (1939), that brilliant hybrid of the spy and detective novels, is less fanciful: He cheats death by staging a drowning and slipping his passport into the dead man's pocket. The posthumous "life" of such corpses can be seen as a kind of ironic echo of the theme of rebirth and resurrection—if you're willing to push the analogy between detective stories and vegetation myths or medieval romances.

C. Day Lewis writing as Nicholas Blake emphasized "the guilt-motive" in readers of detective novels. So did Auden, who spoke of the detective story as the "mirror image" of "the Quest for the Grail."[13] In fact, the hard-boiled novel in the Hammett-Chandler tradition behaves very much like a quest romance. (The Agatha Christie puzzle novel is, by contrast, a version of pastoral.) The world according to Raymond Chandler features an ironic brand of modern knight-errantry, damsels in distress, a spate of misleading appearances, and a plot consisting of a series of trials and tests of the hero's mettle, all of which he passes, though not without some bruises along the way. But note this difference: The hard-boiled gumshoe's saga, unlike the medieval quest romance, takes place in an age of anxiety, collective guilt, skeptical disbelief. Consider the spurious corpse in Chandler's *The Lady in the Lake* (1943). The title alone invokes the land of Arthurian legend, as does the book's most important plot surprise, which looks an awful lot like the miraculous revival of a drowned woman. In Chandler country, however, miracles are criminal deceptions, magic a matter of murder, and revelation a form of reversal. The puzzle in *The Lady in the Lake* concerns a missing woman (Crystal Kingsley) and a dead one (Mildred Haviland). The solution: The latter has killed the former and then assumed her identity, having given herself a perfect alibi, since everyone thinks *she's* the lady in the lake.

Chandler and Dashiell Hammet withheld the promised absolution from guilt—it is one of the ways they broke with detective story tradition. Perhaps nowhere is the change more evident than in their mythifying portrayal of women, the way they transmogrify the classic whodunit's romantic heroine into a vixen or tramp. In hard-boiled novels, every *femme* is more *fatale* than the last. The private eye proves his mettle by resisting or renouncing her charms. Where Lord Peter Wimsey in *Strong Poison* (1930) acts to exonerate the wrongly accused Harriet Vane, Sam Spade in *The Maltese Falcon* (1930) turns the guilty Brigid O'Shaughnessy over to the police. Spade even takes a sardonic pleasure doing so. "If they hang you," he tells her, "I'll always remember you." There, in a nutshell, is one critical difference between the two genres. The hard-boiled detective's investigation is a proof of universal guilt rather than a vindication of feminine innocence. The hostility toward women in the novels of Hammett and Chandler is fierce but complicated, all mixed up with fear and desire. Eve is named in the indictment of Adam; Jocasta hangs herself in the Oedipus murder mystery.

All through Chandler's work we find the same pronounced ambivalence toward leading ladies that we associated with *film noir* style. Like the lady in the lake, "Little Velma"—the object of Moose Malloy's pursuit in Chandler's *Farewell, My Lovely* (1940)— is a lethal enchantress. Moose finds more than he bargained for when he finally catches up with his "former sweetie." She now goes by the name of Mrs. Lewin Lockridge Grayle and greets him by plugging five bullets into his belly. The romantic or erotic heroine is the instrument of violent death, but just to make sure we realize what's at stake Chandler takes the trouble of making "Grayle" a part of her acquired name.

The Maltese Falcon's Brigid O'Shaughnessy, in John Huston's film as in Dashiell Hammett's book, remains the foremost example of the type: the seductress whose fatal embrace tempts as it threatens the tough-guy sleuth. An acquired cynicism saves Sam Spade from succumbing to her romantic lure, which is that of Eros enhanced by Thanatos—and to which he is profoundly drawn. And here, too, though Hammett doesn't merge the themes, the sought-for Grail turns out to be yet one more deception on top of so many others. The sculpted black bird, for whose possession so much blood has been shed and so many confidences betrayed, is revealed to have been a worthless fake all along. The jewels and gold ostensibly concealed beneath the bird's black enameled exterior fail to materialize when the paint is scraped off. Yet even when the imposture is revealed to the characters, their disappointment lasts for only a moment and doesn't deprive them of their illusion—and their dedication to continuing the hunt for their Grail. If the plots of books and movies have an afterlife, surely the fat man (as played by Sydney Greenstreet) and Joel Cairo (in the person of Peter Lorre) will sail the far seas eternally in search of the "dingus," as Sam Spade (Humphrey Bogart) calls it with a happy sneer. As the fat man says to the hired gunsel he has decided to betray: "Well, Wilmer, I'm sorry indeed to lose you, and I want you to know that I couldn't be any fonder of you if you were my own son; but—well, by Gad!—if you lose a son it's possible to get another—and there's only one Maltese Falcon."[14]

Like Poe's Raven, with its insistent refrain of "Nevermore," the Maltese Falcon has acquired a mythic or symbolic significance that no single interpretation can quite exhaust. The history of the Maltese Falcon, as related by the fat man, is the testament of an ancient plunder, a tyrant's booty hijacked by pirates centuries ago. The black bird can be said to belong legitimately to no one, hence its elusiveness is essential to its character. To Steven Marcus, the spurious falcon suggests an allegory of the progress of wealth: wealth as the residue of crime. In Marcus's ingenious interpretation, the Falcon "turns out to be and contains within itself the history of capitalism. It is originally a piece of plunder, part of what Marx called the 'primitive accumulation'; when its gold encrusted with gems is painted over, it becomes a mystified object, a commodity itself; it is a piece of property that belongs to no one—whoever possesses it does not really own it. At the same time it is another fiction, a representation or work of art—which turns out itself to be a fake, since it is made of lead. It is a *rara avis* indeed."[15]

Perhaps, after all, Hammett does merge the themes of the lethal enchantress and the spurious Grail. If Sam Spade, in Ross Macdonald's words, is playing "for the highest stakes available, love and money, and loses nearly everything in the end," the falcon represents half of his losses and Brigid O'Shaughnessy represents the other half. Macdonald hazards other guesses, too, about the Maltese Falcon's mythic significance, but these seem rather fanciful. "Perhaps the stakes and implied losses are higher than I have suggested," he writes. "The worthless falcon may symbolize a lost tradition, the great cultures of the Mediterranean past which have become inaccessible to Spade and his generation. Perhaps the bird stands for the Holy Ghost itself, or for its absence." Well, perhaps.[16]

What is certain is that the Maltese Falcon inspires an all-consuming passion in its seekers. Above all, its story is a parable about desire and obsession—about desire that transcends its object. The falcon really is a "dingus," when all is said and done—it is valueless except as a projection of either greed or a shared obsession transcending greed. That's why the Fat Man and Joel Cairo leave it conspicuously on the hotel-room table when they make their getaway—it's now devoid of meaning and can be cast aside like the broken guitar in the rock concert scene in *Blow-Up* (1966), fought over avidly by the crowd but no sooner had than tossed away by the film's enigmatic protagonist. *The avian statuette on the hotel-room table can't have been the true Maltese Falcon, for it would cease being such the moment it was possessed!* The object of desire is necessarily a fake, yet we go on wanting it, pining away for it, or actively pursuing it, despite the knowledge that we've been hoaxed once already. This is the kind of sleight-of-hand trick that makes *The Maltese Falcon* so fascinating and exemplary a work. Hammett produces the symbol of a quest romance only to explode it, and we're left where we began, with the guilt and the doubt that preceded the corpse on page one.

4

———◆———

Murder Considered
as a Fine Art

*H*e told me frankly he was not fool enough to attack me there
in the labyrinth, knowing I had a loaded revolver, and that
he ran as much risk as I. But he told me, equally calmly, that he
would plan my murder with the certainty of success, with every
detail developed and every danger warded off, with the sort of
artistic perfection that a Chinese craftsman or an Indian
embroiderer gives to the artistic work of a life-time.

—G. K. CHESTERTON, "The Curse of the Golden Cross"

The culprit in Agatha Christie's *Curtain* (1975), known until his
final unmasking as "X," is diabolically clever but not entirely original. X is "a murder addict." He (it could as easily be she) manages
to bring out the "potential murderer" in other people, having no
other motive than schadenfreude: malicious joy or spiteful glee. He
doesn't commit murders, he instigates them, waging a brand of
psychological warfare so subtle that his all-too-vulnerable surro-
gates never realize they're being worked on. He is always equipped
with an alibi; you'll never find his fingerprints on the smoking gun.
Thus, he is guilty not only of pure murder—murder for its own
sake—but of seemingly foolproof crimes. If this sounds familiar,

it's because Shakespeare got there first, delineating X's *modus operandi* in that one of his characters who most nearly approaches absolute evil. Hercule Poirot, who has read *Othello*, knows exactly whom he is up against. "Iago is the perfect murderer," Poirot explains in the postdated letter to Captain Hastings that sets forth the solution to this, their final case. "The deaths of Desdemona, of Cassio—indeed of Othello himself—are all Iago's crimes, planned by him, carried out by him. And *he* remains outside the circle, untouched by suspicion—or could have done so." X, in short, is what Iago would be if Iago lived within the precincts of a detective novel. The salient difference between the plot of *Othello* and that of *Curtain*, leaving aside all questions of literary quality, is simply that there's a detective in the latter to foil the villain. That, and the handkerchief. "For your great Shakespeare, my friend, had to deal with the dilemma that his own art had brought about. To unmask Iago, he had to resort to the clumsiest of devices—the handkerchief—a piece of work not at all in keeping with Iago's central technique and a blunder of which one feels certain he would not have been guilty." To unmask X, nothing so clumsy is needed, not with Poirot's "little gray cells of the brain" at work. We can pardon Poirot his preening; *Curtain* is his last time on stage.

The motiveless murderer turns up elsewhere in detective fiction, most commonly in the form of the psychopathic killer, though occasionally as a romantic experimentalist, as in Hitchcock's movie *Rope* (1948). Hitchcock also harnessed the idea of the surrogate murderer in *Strangers on a Train* (1951) and rode it for all it was worth. But it was Christie who combined the types to arrive at an emblematic version of the perfect murderer. The perfect murderer, like Iago, resembles an invisible playwright, who designs the set on which the drama of detection plays itself out. Having cloaked himself in invisibility, he can admire from a safe distance his malevolently bloody creation. He acts as our surrogate, inasmuch as, in providing a corpse, he does our bidding. However transparent his motives, there must be something essentially gratuitous in his actions, some element to his plan, or his execution thereof, that can't be explained by reference to motive alone. Call it, as De Quincey did, murder as a perverse species of art. It is an aesthetic phenomenon to the precise extent that it resembles a gratuitous and self-delighting performance that strives for the critic's approval and demands the audience's applause. G. K. Chesterton insisted that crime be understood in this aesthetic light. "A common thief would have been thankful for the warning and fled; but you are a poet," says Father Brown, all admiration, before he reconstructs Flambeau's daring stratagem in "The Flying Stars." Or again, in the much-later story "The Curse of the Golden Cross," a character reports that his antagonist "told me, equally calmly, that he would plan my murder with the certainty of success, with every detail developed and every danger warded off, with the sort of artistic perfection that a Chinese craftsman or an Indian embroiderer gives to the artistic work of a life-time." A crime "is like any other work of art," Father Brown says in "The Queer Feet," summing up the case. "Don't look surprised; crimes are by no means the only works of art that come from an infernal workshop."

Of the perfect murder conventionally understood—the murder that will forever escape detection—we'll find few examples in the works of our favorite mystery writers. It's a rule of the game according to Doyle that the culprit does get caught, though he be ever so ingenious, just as Christie's X is caught and punished at the end of *Curtain.* In fiction, however, the perfect murder is not the one that goes unsolved but the one that most strenuously taxes the detective's imagination. To paraphrase what a Freudian psychiatrist once said about his profession, the crime has to be not only impossible but also very difficult. It's an exercise in the incredible, a puzzle that appears to yield no rational solution yet, incredibly, does. The closer it approaches the truly inexplicable, the more nearly perfect it will seem. Often enough, as in Chesterton's stories and John Dickson Carr's novels, there's an element of the uncanny about it, the illusion of some supernatural agency at work. But even when it's a matter of the improbable rather than the almost inexplicable, it calls for an intricate design, for huge reserves of guile under pressure, and it makes the successful sleuth seem like a miracle worker. What's more, it has usually been embellished in some fanciful way; the perpetrator has prepared it with all the trimmings of a labor of love. The perfect murder is, in short, a work of art, diabolical in its ends and entertaining in its means—a riddle and a cipher.

Everyone has a list of favorite examples. In Michael Innes's *Hamlet, Revenge!* (1937) there is an example of the perfect murder, dramatic. It requires split-second timing: The actor playing Polonius in an amateur production of *Hamlet* is shot to death a moment after the stage Polonius is stabbed behind the arras by Hamlet; the murder weapon, a revolver, is hidden in Yorick's skull. In Edmund Crispin's *The Moving Toyshop* (1946), the scene of the crime itself disappears. A young man discovers a corpse in an Oxford toyshop, runs off to fetch help, and returns to find both the corpse and the toyshop missing—a grocery store has, it seems, always been there. Innes is arch, Crispin more so; their idea of the perfect murder comes awfully close to high-spirited farce. The opposite impulse is on display in Edward Candy's charming *Words for Murder Perhaps* (1971), in which a subdued, self-conscious, middle-aged adult education instructor—a character straight out of Philip Larkin—becomes the leading suspect in a series of literary murders, perfect pranks. The book's title—echoing Yeats's *Words for Music Perhaps*—gives a fair hint of what's to come. A "lethal literary lunatic" with an ear for famous elegies finds an Arthur Hallam to poison, an Edward King to stab to death, and somebody's cat to drown. The killer leaves behind notes on which he has typed, respectively, lines from "In Memoriam" (Tennyson's elegy for his friend Arthur Hallam), from "Lycidas" (Milton's elegy for his Cambridge classmate Edward King), and from Thomas Gray's "Ode on the Death of a Favourite Cat, Drowned in a Tub of Gold Fishes."[1]

If the perfect murder were a synonym for the impossible crime, the undisputed master would be John Dickson Carr. The homicidal puzzles he designs seem to challenge our belief in rationality itself—they imply that laws we thought immutable, such as the law of gravity, exist to be broken by perfect murderers. In *The Crooked Hinge* (1938), for example, the only person capable of the crime would have had to be able to turn himself into a midget—and back—within a matter of minutes. (It can be done.) We know we're in the presence of a grand master of the impossible when, early in Carr's *The Three Coffins* (1935), we come across a circus magician named Fley, whose props fit into "a box the size of a coffin." The man is, it seems, obsessed by coffins. A fellow performer, "Pagliacci the Great," asks him why. "Three of us were once buried alive. Only one escaped," says Fley. "And how did you escape?" asks Pagliacci. "I didn't, you see. I was one of the two who did not escape." The exchange is a fitting prelude to the murder of Fley in the middle of a dead-end London street some chapters later. Three reliable witnesses see everything—and nothing. They hear the shot ring out. They see the body fall. But no one sees the murderer. The shot could only have been made from close up—and could not have been self-inflicted. Yet on that snow-covered street only the victim's footprints appear.

A perfect murder must entertain us before it does anything else—we enjoy it before we understand it, and it's important that our pleasure come first. It's easy to see why we can never enter fully into the detective's consciousness, nor ever really want to, for that would let the cat out of the bag prematurely. The longer we remain in the dark, the greater our pleasure; the culmination of our pleasure will also mark its demise. Yet paradox prevails. Rather than savor our mystification, we keep turning the pages compulsively, devouring them rapidly, though we know that the end of our reading will come as a letdown. It must, for then the game will be over and our craving for fresh excitement will start anew. We, too, are "murder addicts," indulging our vice without paying the price, keeping our hands unsullied just as X in *Curtain* aims to do. Our disappointment when we reach the last page will be all the more acute, our addiction the more pronounced, where the crime is puzzle-perfect. For no solution, however convincing, can quite measure up to the riddle it unravels, any more than an *explication de texte* can take the place of the text itself. In Ellery Queen's *The Chinese Orange Mystery,* for example, the reason the dead man's clothes have been turned inside out is guaranteed not only to surprise the reader but to arrest him with the force of its inevitability; no one will have cause to complain of any lack of ingenuity. Yet here, too, that familiar feeling of disappointment sets in. Yes, the solution has done its job, reassuring us that even our choicest conundrums admit of an answer; it's a happy ending in more ways than one. Still, it was the mystery that kept us going, and we're sorry to see it end.

The inevitable superiority of the puzzle-perfect crime to its solution is beautifully illustrated by Chesterton's Father Brown story "The Honour of Israel Gow." Why, in the mansion of a recently deceased rich miser, are there found candles without candlesticks, jewels removed from their settings, prayer missals from which all instances of "the great ornamented name of God" have been removed? Why, in those same missals, are the halos missing around the head of the infant Jesus? Why, finally, does the corpse that's buried in the backyard lack its head? The explanation is brilliant: The rich man's servant, a lunatic in his literal-mindedness, has been willed all the gold of his master, to which with painstaking thoroughness he has helped himself. He has removed the gold teeth from his late master's skull, the gold leaf from his manuscript pages, and the gold of his jewelry with a fine disregard of the things to which they've been attached. So splendid an example of a logical lunatic is a sufficient reward for the reader. The solution here has the added virtue of simplicity—and it helps make a very Chestertonian point, warning us against attributing man-made phenomena to supernatural causes. Yet inevitably there is something anticlimactic about the explanation. This is, we can't help feeling, merely one possible solution to a puzzle that, spun out as a poetic conceit, implies wonders not so easily explained away. The ending has done its work, has tied up all the loose strings, but it has also made us forfeit the pleasures of metaphor in favor of a dull, prosaic truth about greed and human nature. The corpse without its head and the prayer book without God: The conjunction promises metaphors more interesting than a coincidence of gold.

———◆———

Perfect murders must be judged by the degree of their difficulty and by the artfulness of their contrivance, and that puts the matter in the appropriate aesthetic light. What we're dealing with is a genre that regards the spheres of ethics and aesthetics as at times incompatible, at times mutually exclusive. The detective novel takes the most fundamental of transgressions, removes it from the sphere of morality, and treats it instead as the basis for a sport, a contest, a game, or a theatrical event. For all the talk about Iago, this is as true of the nefarious X in Agatha Christie's *Curtain* as of the frankly beneficent villains we sometimes come across. In detective novels, murder becomes a branch of the fine arts, and individual cases are to be judged by criteria that wouldn't be inappropriate in a discussion of painterly technique or poetic craft.

Within this aesthetic sideshow, values must be assigned with a real or affected disregard for moral principles and premises; an aesthetically pleasing act may well be a purely immoral one. Chesterton, with his love of paradox, was quick to grasp the point. "The criminal is the creative artist; the detective only the critic," says Valentin, who is identified as "the head of the Paris police and the most famous investigator of the world" in Chesterton's first Father Brown tale, "The Blue Cross" (1911). Chesterton cherished the *frisson* such a statement would produce in his ideal reader, but this shock effect doesn't diminish or deny the significance of the analogy. What the murderer creates, the sleuth interprets, much as a literary critic, analyzing a poem, will plumb it for meanings beyond those that the author intended. What Chesterton neglected to add was what Oscar Wilde had already proclaimed: The critic is himself a type of artist. In his guise as Great Detective, he is half poet, half scientist, an artist by temperament, a critic by trade. He's a connoisseur of crime, as others of his class and station may have become connoisseurs of Venetian art. He is both the culprit's nemesis, foiling him in the end, and the culprit's double, matching him stroke for stroke in cunning. It's natural, therefore, that contradictory impulses should be fused together in his person. He practices ratiocination, but that is sometimes just a fancy word for playing a hunch. A crime, if it is exceptional enough, will concentrate his mind wonderfully and impel him to expend vast quantities of energy, but he is naturally an indolent fellow. It's safe to presume that he's on the side of the angels, but like any responsible critic he must own up to his dependence on a prior creation—in his case, the work of art that is the original crime.

The detective in the classic tradition is, in other words, as much "a murder addict" as Agatha Christie's X. He is hooked on homicide, it determines his whole reason for being; he is never more alertly alive than when a fresh corpse beckons. To such a man, murder may be a moral violation, yes, but first it's an intellectual problem, something to solve rather than someone to punish. However much he affirms a code of justice, he remains an aesthete at heart, a dandy by the very nature of his calling, with a dandy's appreciation of the grotesque and the perverted. Not for nothing is Philip Trent, in E. C. Bentley's *Trent's Last Case* (1912), identified as "a painter and the son of a painter," an arty chap who compulsively quotes poetry—it's perfectly in keeping with his appetite for perfect murders. Trent is the model of all the dilettante crime solvers that would soon populate the literature: patrician fops like Wimsey and Ellery Queen, imported elves like Hercule Poirot, oversize curmudgeonly wizards like Gideon Fell and Nero Wolfe.[2] Nor should it surprise us that Trent—like the detective in Carr's *The Crooked Hinge*—is content to finger his culprit without bringing him to justice. Once the problem has been solved, the detective's duty is done with, and besides, he may have some lingering admiration for the fellow whose dark stratagems he has brought to light. Admiration? Yes, for didn't the man create a memorable diversion and provide a source of mental refreshment?

The motif of the unmasked but uncaptured culprit occurs too often in detective stories for its significance to be denied. It's usually, though not always, arranged by the simple expedient of painting the putative villain in an attractive light, endowing him with charm and resourcefulness, and letting him escape, at the moment just prior to discovery, overseas. Thus, in Nicholas Blake's *The Corpse in the Snowman* (1941), which is set in England during the early days of World War II, our unmasked murderer signs off in a letter mailed from abroad in which he sounds rather like Sydney Carton at the end of *A Tale of Two Cities*: noble, self-sacrificing and intent on making amends in a grandly romantic gesture of farewell. The tone itself tips us off. "Good-by to everyone," we read on the last page. "I shall not 'give myself up to justice,' preferring a more productive end to a sadly unproductive life. By the time you get this, I shall be in Germany—I know quite a few ways of getting in. There, I shall do as much damage as I can before they find me out. I have friends who will be working with me. Salud." The letter writer intends to take on the Third Reich from within— an act of selfless heroism not usually associated with a killer. But then, this is no ordinary murderer. This is a murderer whose victim, a menace and a heel, was as universally despised as any in the genre. What's more, this is a murderer with a keen sense of artistic detail—though he modestly attributes his clever stratagems to expediency rather than the demands of "an artistic gesture." What he committed was the homidical equivalent of a poetic conceit: Having dispatched his victim, a malicious purveyor of "snow" (already a synonym for cocaine), he disposed of the body by burying it upright in the figure of a snowman outside Easterham Manor, the quintessential country mansion where the novel is set. No wonder the author elected to free him from the fate of ordinary justice. A pity that the American title of this book gives so much (but not too much) away; the British version was titled simply *The Abominable Snowman*.

"There will be time to murder and create": T. S. Eliot's line in "Prufrock" does double service thanks to its singular infinitive. In detective novels, the culprit and sleuth perform as though in concert, dramatizing how to "murder and create" in one motion or, rather, as two halves of the same act. To solve the crime, the detective must first unravel it, then reconstruct it. The perfect murder would be unfinished if the detective weren't on hand to solve it; he completes it as a literary critic explicating a text completes the text. But the Great Detectives—the ones who mean the most to us, Dupin and Holmes and Poirot and the rest—are critics of a highly specialized order. The Great Detective is, in Oscar Wilde's phrase, "the critic as artist." To offset his scientific genius, he has, invariably, an artist's temperament and sensibility: deviant, intense, eccentric.

5

---◆---

De Quincey's Irony

*P*eople begin to see that something more goes to the
composition of a fine murder than two blockheads to kill and
be killed, a knife, a purse, and a dark lane. Design, gentlemen,
grouping, light and shade, poetry, sentiment, are now deemed
indispensable to attempts of this nature.

—THOMAS DE QUINCEY, "On Murder Considered as One of the Fine Arts"

The aesthetic rationale for the detective story was put forth, in
advance of the fact, in a pair of remarkable essays by Thomas De
Quincey. In the famous "On the Knocking at the Gate in *Macbeth*"
(1823), the self-described opium eater and connoisseur of murder
made *Macbeth* sound like a precursor of crime fiction. The terminally horizontal "attitude" of the murder victim, De Quincey
wrote, "would little suit the purposes of the poet." The poet reserves his "sympathy of comprehension" (as opposed to "a sympathy of pity or approbation") for the murderer: "In the murderer,
such a murderer as a poet will condescend to, there must be raging
some great storm of passion—jealousy, ambition, vengeance, ha-
tred—which will create a hell within him; and into this hell we are
to look." The corpse stands for dead "human nature,—i.e. the divine nature of love and mercy." The murderer expresses "the
fiendish nature" that has taken its place. And what De Quincey

called a "sympathy of comprehension" is precisely what will link the culprit and the detective in fiction. A master detective is only as impressive as the criminal he must foil. Hence Hitchcock's law: The more interesting the villain, the better the film.

De Quincey wrote about murder in the abstract—and about specific cases, literary and historical—as though it were a new species of aesthetic entertainment and he were its Aristotle. As far as he could see, "the final purpose of murder, considered as a fine art, is precisely the same as that of tragedy in Aristotle's account of it; viz, 'to cleanse the heart by means of pity and terror.'" Detective stories don't quite live up to that description. But they are unquestionably a practical consequence of the habit or custom of treating murder as an aesthetic spectacle with rules and conventions, and subject to strict evaluative criteria. De Quincey described the habit—and furthered it—in his proleptic essay "On Murder Considered as One of the Fine Arts" (1827). In the London of his time, he noted, "the tendency to a critical or aesthetic valuation of fires and murders is universal." If that is the case, and if a high murder rate is a fact of the industrial jungle, why not make the best of a bad business, transfer murder from the ethical to the aesthetic realm, and see if you can cultivate a taste for it?

"On Murder Considered as One of the Fine Arts" is a masterpiece of wicked irony that would have served as a defense of detective stories—if detective stories had existed at that time. In a parody of academic form, De Quincey tells us he is delivering "the Williams lecture," named after the notorious murderer John Williams. (De Quincey's fascination with the man's misdeeds would not subside; to the original essay, he later added a lengthy postscript in which he jovially examines "the immortal Williams murders of 1812.")[1] The essayist directs his "sympathy of comprehension" to Williams, not his victims. To this "epicure in murder," as De Quincey depicts him, one could attribute the notion that murder has or should have rules, in the sense that an art form or a game can be said to have rules: "For he seems to have laid it down as a maxim that the best person to murder was a friend, and in default of a friend, which is an article one cannot always command, an acquaintance, because, in either case, on first approaching his subject, suspicion would be disarmed, whereas a stranger might take alarm and find in the very countenance of his murderer elect a warning summons to place himself on guard." It's by savvily applying Williams's "maxim" that Sam Spade solves the murder of his partner, Miles Archer, which is the one formal problem posed in *The Maltese Falcon*. The culprit had to have been Brigid O' Shaughnessy, alias Miss Wonderly (Spade reasons), for with no one else—least of all a gunman like Floyd Thursby—would an experienced operative like Archer have gone into the fatal alley. With the beautiful Brigid, however, a philandering gentleman's "suspicion would be disarmed"—and was.

Let no one underestimate the importance of such and sundry other maxims in the evolution of the detective genre. If they can be seen to figure in *The Maltese Falcon*—that archetype of the hard-boiled novel with its disdain of received conventions and rules—they amount to a code of law in the classic whodunit. More than one "Golden Age" practitioner took pains to describe what was cricket and what wasn't. Thus, S. S. Van Dine offered "Twenty Rules for Writing Detective Stories" in 1928 ("There simply must be a corpse in a detective novel, and the deader the corpse the better"). A year later Ronald Knox laid down "A Detective Story Decalogue" that was alternately whimsical ("No Chinaman must figure in the story") and exact ("The stupid friend of the detective, the Watson, must not conceal any thoughts which pass through his mind; his intelligence must be slightly, but very slightly, below that of the average reader"). Initiates into the London Detection Club, founded in 1928 and consisting of the day's most distinguished crime fictioneers, had to take a solemn oath affirming "never to conceal a vital clue from the reader."[2] The game's afoot, and what's a game without rules? When Agatha Christie allegedly played unfair with readers of *The Murder of Roger Ackroyd* (1926), she stirred up the noisiest debate in detective novel history. Many readers felt that there either was or should have been a rule prohibiting the culprit from serving as the book's narrator; Christie had, by breaking the convention, dramatized its importance. The idea of a noisy debate about the proprieties of murder itself illustrates the genre's essential paradox: It is possible to play fair with foul play—if you treat murder not as the gravest of ethical transgressions but as an aesthetic spectacle.

De Quincey's irony, in "On Murder Considered as One of the Fine Arts," prefigures the paradox. Whatever else it may imply, his irony bears witness to the detective story's bill of divorce separating morality from aesthetics. How else to account for the extravagant praise De Quincey lavishes on the murderous John Williams, "this patron of gravediggers"? Williams, he writes, is "a sort of martinet in the scenic grouping and draping of the circumstances in his murders." He might be regarded, indeed, as "the most aristocratic and fastidious of artists": one who pursues murder "as an end for itself." What justifies this outlandish display is De Quincey's only half-facetious argument that murder as a fact makes a mockery of all morality. A dig at the "categorical imperative," the cornerstone of Immanuel Kant's moral philosophy, clinches the case. Kant had argued that truth telling is an absolute virtue—even when one is speaking to a murderer. Here is De Quincey's scathing comment: "So far from aiding and abetting him [i.e., a murderer] by pointing out his victim's hiding-place, as a great moralist of Germany declared it to be every good man's duty to do, I would subscribe one shilling and sixpence to have him apprehended,— which is more by eighteenpence than the most eminent moralists have hitherto subscribed for that purpose."

There's a real moral quandary being satirized here, and its overtones are unsettling. If telling the truth to a killer may abet his homicidal plans, all common sense militates against it, and then what happens to the idea of truth telling as a moral absolute? What happens to the idea of moral absolutes themselves? Murder becomes a drastic metaphor for the great "is" that stands in the way of any "ought," the stubborn resistance of human nature to self-government by any prescriptive moral code. De Quincey's irony expresses the bitter awareness that human nature is "fiendish," not divine, and that therefore, prescriptive "natural laws"—unlike, say, the law of gravity—cannot be presumed to exist. Every murder proves that the ten commandments lack any binding force, just as every suicide disproves the "law" of self-preservation—an argument made by the philosopher A. G. N. Flew, who used an episode in Raymond Chandler's *Farewell, My Lovely* to illustrate the point.[3]

"Everything in this world has two handles," De Quincey asserts. "Murder, for instance, may be laid hold of by its moral handle (as it generally is in the pulpit and at the Old Bailey), and *that,* I confess, is its weak side; or it may also be treated *aesthetically,* as the Germans call it—that is, in relation to good taste." Presume the murder already to have been committed, put it in the past tense. We have tried our best to stop it, to no avail:

> Why, then, I say, what's the use of any more virtue? Enough has been given to morality; now comes the turn of Taste and the Fine Arts. A sad thing it was, no doubt, very sad; but *we* can't mend it.

Therefore let us make the best of a bad matter; and, as it is impossible to hammer anything out of it for moral purposes, let us treat it aesthetically, and see if it will turn to account in that way. Such is the logic of a sensible man; and what follows? We dry up our tears, and have the satisfaction perhaps, to discover that a transaction which, morally considered, was shocking and without a leg to stand upon, when tried by the principles of Taste, turns out to be a very meritorious performance. Thus all the world is pleased; the old proverb is justified, that it is an ill wind which blows nobody good; the amateur, from looking bilious and sulky by too close an attention to virtue, begins to pick up his crumbs; and general hilarity prevails.

Where virtue failed, let connoisseurship take over. Let the ironist and the aesthete be one, and it becomes possible to speak of "a fine murder." "People begin to see that something more goes to the composition of a fine murder than two blockheads to kill and be killed, a knife, a purse, and a dark lane. Design, gentlemen, grouping, light and shade, poetry, sentiment, are now deemed indispensable to attempts of this nature."

———————◆———————

De Quincey's star example was hardly worthy of the encomia that the writer tosses his way. De Quincy compares Williams—who "exalted the ideal of murder"—to Aeschylus, to Milton, to Michelangelo. However, the actual John Williams was artful in no sense of the term. It took no Great Detective to find him out. A bloodthirsty butcher, he relied not on clever devices but on daring and brute force. He was cold blooded but not immune from panic; he furnished no alibi for himself and left enough clues to beat a path straight to his door. But if the historical John Williams belied De Quincey's thesis, the villains who emerge to do battle with the Great Detectives prove De Quincey a prophet. The criminals in detective novels are often in some perverse sense artists, aesthetes of crime, perfect murderers. They almost have to be, in order to stand any chance of gaining a hearing.

The Great Detectives are, you see, nothing if not jaded. Ennui, not injustice, is their true enemy, as indifference rather than hate is the true antonym of love. When Sherlock Holmes solves the riddle of "The Red-Headed League," Dr. Watson is all agog with admiration. "You are a benefactor of the race," he exclaims. That's as may be, Holmes replies in his shoulder-shrugging way. But he has already tipped us off to his real motive. "It saved me from ennui," Holmes says, not even bothering to stifle a yawn. "Alas! I already feel it closing in upon me. My life is spent in one long effort to escape from the commonplaces of existence. These little problems help me to do so."

With his fits of melancholia and his love of cocaine, Sherlock Holmes has all the traits of the Romantic rebel as personified in the poetry of Charles Baudelaire.[4] It was Baudelaire who identified the affliction from which Holmes suffers. Among the monsters evoked in the keynote poem to *Les Fleurs du mal,* one stands out as the "ugliest" and "cruelest" of the whole "infamous menagerie": "It is Ennui!—weeping with involuntary tears / And dreaming of hangings as he puffs on his hookah." This personified vice can serve as an image of the man who would be a dandy if he weren't as addicted to solving murders as he is to his needle. Only a case can rouse Holmes from his customary boredom and inertia. Only a crime—and only an extraordinary one, at that—can give his life meaning, and then only for a brief interval between vast stretches of ennui.

It's a point Watson makes over and over again in telling us about his friend. "The outbursts of passionate energy when [Holmes] performed the remarkable feats with which his name is associated were followed by reactions of lethargy," Watson remarks in "The Musgrave Ritual." During these periods "he would lie about with his violin and his books, hardly moving, save from the sofa to the table." There is this famous exchange between Holmes and Watson in *The Sign of Four:*

"Which is it today," I asked, "morphine or cocaine?"

He raised his eyes languidly from the old black-letter volume which he had opened.

"It is cocaine," he said, "a seven-per-cent solution. Would you care to try it?"

. . .

"May I ask whether you have any professional inquiry on foot at present?"

"None. Hence the cocaine. I cannot live without brainwork. What else is there to live for? Stand at the window here. Was ever such a dreary, dismal, unprofitable world? See how the yellow fog swirls down the street and drifts across the dun-coloured houses. What could be more hopelessly prosaic and material? What is the use of having powers, Doctor, when one has no field upon which to exert them?''

De Quincey's addiction to opium, Poe's dependence on alcohol and Holmes's on cocaine add up to more than a superficial point of resemblance. All three may be described as murder addicts. Dupin and Holmes are romantic rebels who would keep the ''hopelessly prosaic'' world at bay. They reject the ''dreary'' commonplace in favor of perverse pleasures—flowers of evil. As such they participate in a tradition that at first glance may seem foreign to the very premises of the detective story: the tradition of aestheticism and decadence that Baudelaire initiated and that bore its strangest fruit in the 1880s, the same decade that witnessed the creation of Sherlock Holmes.

Consider a couple of crucial convergences. Both *The Sign of Four* and Oscar Wilde's *The Picture of Dorian Gray* were written on commission for *Lippincott's* magazine, the result of one inspired night's work by the American publisher—a dinner party in London in 1889, at which both Wilde and Conan Doyle were present.[5] *A Study in Scarlet,* Holmes's first adventure, had appeared two years earlier, in 1887, or just three years after the publication of J-K. Huysmans's *Against the Grain,* which Arthur Symons called ''the breviary of the Decadence'' and which the hero of *Dorian Gray* reads with rapt devotion. These historical conjunctions are far from merely fortuitous, as we'll see if we examine the Duc Jean des Esseintes, Huysmans's wealthy protagonist, with Holmes in the back of our mind. Des Esseintes has withdrawn from society. He suffers from world-weariness, bad nerves, hypersensitivity, boredom raised to a metaphysical ideal. His decaying teeth point ironically to the moral decay of which he is the consummate product, but his malaise goes hand in hand with a sense of his personal superiority. Disgusted with the bourgeois notion of the family, he is avid— to the extent that this adjective consorts at all with his languid disposition—for new sensations and perverse pleasures. He is a great armchair traveler, not deeming it necessary to visit a place in order to enjoy the experience of being there, since to his way of thinking an act of imagination will always surpass a banal actuality. He has some shrewd things to say about Poe and Baudelaire, who translated Poe, their ''common poetic inspiration'' and their radically differing ''emotional concepts.'' (Baudelaire's ''ruthless passion" is played off against Poe's "chaste, ethereal amours.") To "the imp of the perverse" as depicted by Poe, Des Esseintes affirms his allegiance. An elegant aesthete, he prizes artificiality and excess in all things and cultivates a deliberately eccentric style of behavior, just as he cultivates only those flowers that seem most exotic, least natural, most monstrous even, in their substance and shape. His orchids are, of all evil flowers, the loveliest and the most alluring.

Compare him to Holmes in his bachelor digs, with his cocaine, his fiddle, and his tobacco stashed in his Persian slippers. Holmes is as obsessive in his nature as Des Esseintes, as bored with the prosaic facts of existence, as extreme in his defiance of social niceties and bourgeois norms. He has a penchant for indoor target practice: A bullet-pocked V salutes Queen Victoria on the wall above his fireplace, and that is only the most visible sign of his eccentricity. Like Des Esseintes, he has Poe on the brain, though this way of conceding an obvious debt is singularly ungracious. "No doubt you think that you are complimenting me in comparing me to Dupin," he tells Watson in *A Study in Scarlet*. "Now, in my opinion, Dupin was a very inferior fellow."

To the concept of mental travel that Des Esseintes espouses in *A Rebours,* Holmes would not be unreceptive. "It is a singular thing," this "armchair lounger" remarks in *The Hound of the Baskervilles,* "but I find that a concentrated atmosphere helps a concentration of thought. I have not pushed it to the length of getting into a box to think, but that is the logical outcome of my convictions." It remains for Holmes's brother, Mycroft, to embody the ideal of the armchair detective, but Sherlock himself leads as isolated an existence as that of Des Esseintes, and by choice. He may know everything there is to know about the manifold varieties of tobacco ash, but to the common pursuits of happiness his indifference is complete. One of the first things we're told about him in *A Study in Scarlet* is that he has no real interest in the solar system as such—and is proud of his ignorance, real or feigned, of the Copernican theory. "What the deuce is it to me?" he thunders. Nothing, in fact, that does not contribute to "the detection of crime" can possibly concern him. Between crimes, he welcomes no society but Watson's, which he irritably tolerates, while he waits for the wished-for messenger who will bring him the glad tidings of some new mischief afoot.

Holmes in his perversity differs from Des Esseintes in one critical way. He has transmuted his manic obsessiveness into something socially useful, the solution of crimes rather than their commission; he is, though that is not where his ambition lies, "a benefactor of the race," as Watson proclaims. In short, Holmes is a Des Esseintes who goes against the grain of decadence without quite repudiating it as a style and an attitude.[6] In his occupation as the world's first "consulting detective," Holmes at once participates in and transcends this decadent tradition. Yes, he concedes a lot to the malaise of the age—you can see it as much in the demonic energy he unleashes during a case as in the lounging ennui he exhibits at all other times. But he has also developed a style to transmute that malaise, to redeem it, and to reconcile it with the characteristics of the English gentleman, which he always remains. His idiosyncrasies are a necessary part of his make-up, a reminder that his heroism is fraught with irony—a variant of the irony that prompted De Quincey to consider murder as one of the fine arts.

6

No Police Like Holmes

*T*hough he might be more humble, there's no p'lice like
Holmes.

—E. W. Hornung

"Clearly," Howard Haycraft wrote in 1941, the year of the detective story's first centennial, "there could be no detective *stories* (and there were none) until there were *detectives*. This did not occur until the nineteenth century."[1] Subsequent historians of crime fiction concede Haycraft's point, adding embellishments. "As long as the officially practiced, universally accepted means of crime detection was torture, the detective story was impossible," writes Aaron Marc Stein. With the nineteenth century, organized police forces "responsible only to the law" had effectively supplanted "the agents of the king who had been responsible only to the royal will." Crime solving thus became synonymous with a species of disinterested detection, while crime itself began to lose its romantic aura. With "the emergence of free societies"—or, what amounts to the same thing, the general perception that society was constituted to preserve the individual's freedom under the law—no longer could crime be thought unequivocally glamorous, a blow struck by Robin Hood, "the man who dared to stand up to tyrannical authority," on behalf of underdogs everywhere. The detective

55

could supplant the criminal as a popular hero—but only now that detectives had come into being, and only after the scientific and political ideals of the Enlightenment had paved the way.[2]

No detective stories without real-life detectives to occasion them—the theory has more than its simplicity to commend it. Where it goes astray is in its failure to allow literature a sufficient amount of autonomy from historical circumstance. On the art-follows-life theory it would follow that the first literary detectives would be professional policemen, modeled on exemplary types that surfaced in the news of the day. But that is far from what happened. The exploits of the Bow Street Runners, London's police force until the creation of Scotland Yard, turned up in fiction here and there but excited no new literary genre into being. Neither did the plain-clothes force organized in 1829 by Sir Robert Peel, from whom "Bobbies" got their name and Scotland Yard its mandate. The figure of Sherlock Holmes was inspired not by a policeman but by an Edinburgh "consulting surgeon" named Joseph Bell. The fictionalized memoirs of Vidocq, the reformed criminal who became the first chief of the Paris Sûreté in 1811, made a powerful impression on both Poe and Conan Doyle, and he was clearly the model for Chesterton's Flambeau in the Father Brown stories. But Father Brown and not Flambeau is Chesterton's hero; the classic detective is ever an amateur, be he fastidious or dissipated, rugged or effete; he is nearly always the exception, only rarely the legally constituted authority. If this is true of Chesterton, who liked putting his paradoxes at the service of pieties, with how much greater subversive force does it apply to the tales of Dupin and of Holmes? For all that they owe to the Enlightenment confidence of Voltaire's Zadig, our first fictional detectives owe very nearly as much to a Romantic backlash against Enlightenment ideals. They are, though aligned with the forces of righteousness, rebellious personalities, and their nominal alliance with the police is either strained or it gives way to open competition. The detective is precisely a fictional alternative to the real police, who are, in turn, represented in detective stories chiefly as figures of fun—like the hapless Inspector Lestrade of the Holmes adventures.

Part of the sleuth's mythic appeal rests right here, in his independence from historical prototype, his pronounced difference from any cop you'd have been likely to meet. Like his quarry, he is somehow beyond the law, just as his behavior stamps him as having gone beyond the accepted social norms. The example of Wilkie Collins's

The Moonstone (1868), in which Sergeant Cuff of Scotland Yard is the detective hero, will be pressed against this claim, for Collins did model Cuff after a real-life policeman: Scotland Yard's Inspector Whicher, whose most celebrated case was Constance Kent's murder of her small brother. The fictional Cuff, however, is not your ordinary man from Scotland Yard. He is marked by an eccentricity: His all-consuming passion for the cultivation of roses is a running gag in *The Moonstone*. It's significant, too, that Cuff enters the scene only after the local constable—a much more representative figure of the professional policeman in classic detective fiction—has made a hash of the affair, badly antagonizing everyone and failing even to recognize the all-important clue left near the scene of the crime. Finally, Cuff himself is plainly wrong about who took the jewel, and how, and why. Cuff knows enough to study the smear on the freshly painted ornamental door leading to Rachel Verinder's bedroom, where the theft took place, but reality in this case is stranger than his interpretation of the evidence allows. To solve the crime, committed as it was during an opium trance, one would have to reenact the deed; to do that, one would need to wipe out the repressive mechanisms of the mind; one would need to trust the drug to induce the unwitting culprit to repeat what he has repressed; one would, indeed, need to be something of a lawbreaker oneself. Holmes the cocaine addict would have got it right, as Ezra Jennings the opium addict does in *The Moonstone*. Freud, another cocaine addict, would have had no trouble explaining it all.

The crime in *The Moonstone* is solved, then, but with little thanks to Cuff and his methods; two cheers are about as much as the genre usually allots for our official guardians of the peace. As E. W. Hornung, the creator of Raffles and brother-in-law of Arthur Conan Doyle, put it, "Though he might be more humble, there's no p'lice like Holmes."[3] Humble, prosaic, oafish, well-meaning, slow—these are some of the adjectives called to mind by the policemen that populate detective stories. Invariably they get it wrong: No greater record of futility exists than the one chalked up by Lieutenant Tragg and District Attorney Ham Burger in the Perry Mason mysteries—over seven dozen cases and never a conviction!—and that's just the most blatant instance of the ridiculing of officialdom in murder mysteries. Few detective novelists ever went broke by underestimating the intelligence of the local police force or by overstating its vanity and sometimes its venality.

The depiction of policemen in mainstream crime fiction became a great deal more complicated when the stream diverged and one tributary ran to such burgs as Dashiell Hammett's "Personville" (pronounced "Poisonville"), where the cops and robbers are more alike than different. For Hammett and his like-minded followers, the traditional type could no longer serve; the convention smelled archaic. The hard-boiled idiom, predicated as it was on a view of crime as endemic to urban society, required that the cops be depicted, with exceptions, as mean and corruptible, each man with his price. This transmogrification of the cop marked a major departure from the classic whodunit form; Hammett and Chandler sought to tap the genre's capacity to serve as an instrument of social commentary. But the idea of an implicit antagonism between sleuth and cop—sometimes manifesting itself as a more-or-less friendly competition, sometimes as a nasty feud—long preceded the appearances on the scene of Sam Spade and Philip Marlowe. It is one of the detective story's oldest and most durable traits, and that fact alone compels us to revise Haycraft's theory about the provenance of fictional detectives.

The real reason that the classic detective story would be inconceivable without the prior existence of professional policemen is that they constitute a negative example, human fallibility personified. They're straight men who come to scoff and stay to clap—or rush out to take the credit they don't deserve. Ultimately, they look dopier than the whole roll call of Dr. Watsons. Nor is their inadequacy attributable entirely to shortcomings of intelligence; they lack, as we're told in "The Purloined Letter," imagination. In a word, they are philistines—men of rectitude, in some cases, but hopelessly bound by the limits of conventional wisdom and customary practice, which detective stories from the start call into doubt. Where the detective criticizes the culprit in the sense that a literary critic interprets a text—with, that is, a suitable amount of appreciation—his criticism of the police is more nearly a matter of indignation, scorn, or condescension. As Nigel Strangeways, Nicholas Blake's Auden-inspired sleuth, gleefully says in *The Beast Must Die*: "You had better start reconciling yourself to the idea of being foiled again, Chief-Inspector Blount."

———◆———

It is true that the policeman is sometimes a more complex and sympathetic figure than the standard ineffectual inspector or crooked cop. Chief Inspector Jules Maigret of the Paris police, an introspective pipe smoker, patrols the rainy precincts of Paris in Georges Simenon's novels. The hero in Friedrich Dürrenmatt's *The Judge and the Hangman* is the old and ailing Hans Barlach, police commissioner of the Swiss city of Berne. Both are among the most fully developed characters in detective fiction, experts at psychological detection. Upon inspection, however, such police-protagonists are sleuths first and policemen only secondarily, as a plot convenience. They are depicted not as representative figures but as exceptional ones. They don't play by the book; they rely on intuition and deduction rather than on orthodox police procedures. To all intents and purposes, their relation to the police as an abstract idea or organization is that of the traditional go-it-alone detective.

Chesterton in his "Defence of Detective Stories" (1901) spoke as the champion of "the romance of police activity." With the flair for paradoxes that prompted an anonymous *Time* magazine writer to dub him a "paradox-hund," he wrote:

> When the detective in a police romance stands alone, and somewhat fatuously fearless amid the knives and fists of a thieves' kitchen, it does certainly serve to make us remember that it is the agent of social justice who is the original and poetic figure, while the burglars and footpads are merely placid old cosmic conservatives, happy in the immemorial respectability of apes and wolves. The romance of the police force is thus the whole romance of man. It is based on the fact that morality is the most dark and daring of conspiracies. It reminds us that the whole noiseless and unnoticeable police management by which we are ruled and protected is only a successful knight-errantry.[4]

Nevertheless, it's a rare reader of *The Man Who Was Thursday* who comes away more impressed with the book's ultimate vision of order than with the extravagant acts of anarchy along the way.

The genre of the police procedural, in which the hero works for the police and follows accepted police routine, endorses Chesterton's position far more straightforwardly than do Chesterton's own stories and novels. The police novel has come a long way from the days when taciturn Scotland Yard detectives—such as Inspector French in Freeman Wills Crofts's novels—broke alibis by methodically cross-checking railway timetables and clocks. The form was not only revitalized but virtually reinvented by the American Ed

McBain, its greatest practitioner, in his 87th Precinct novels, now more than three dozen strong. Though McBain authenticates his books by describing actual police procedure, the crimes he offers are anything but routine; they tend to be sensational enough for a tabloid's front page, and as puzzles they are artfully contrived, difficult to solve. The setting is a fictional translation of New York City. McBain exalts a conglomerate hero, the cops of the 87th Precinct, who succeed through their diligence and perseverance in catching the repeat rapist or the ax-wielding lunatic or the anti-abortion terrorist. There are a few rotten apples in the squad room, but for the most part, the officers are a sympathetic lot—decent, compassionate, fair, with wives and girl friends to keep them honest. The squad's success would seem to be a way of confirming, in McBain's words, "our faith that a society of laws can work."[5]

Still, the natural antagonism toward the police (always exempting certain individual members of the species) does not die easy in crime novels and films. The very Hollywood movies most ideologically receptive to the idea of the policeman as hero—the Dirty Harry movies in which Clint Eastwood overmatches hoodlums and punks and long-haired terrorists—undercut the tendency. Harry's stormy relationship with his superiors on the police force pretty much replicates the angry opposition between the sleuth and the police in Chandler's novels. In one of the movies, Harry turns in his badge and goes it alone; in another, he frustrates a group of vigilante assassins led—he finds out—by his boss. The point is that Dirty Harry is in but not *of* the police. He's too independent, too bull headed. He's like a hard-boiled hero who happens to sport a badge, and he's destined to remain at odds with his fellows because they're corrupt or because they're lily-livered bureaucrats.

Among recent and contemporary British masters, there is less reluctance than formerly to cast the heroic sleuth as a Scotland Yard detective. It is a concession to realism—the knowledge that private detectives, in real life, do not investigate murders—and also a concession to the Scotland Yard mystique. (There's nothing comparable in the United States.) The detective hero often remains an outsider nevertheless; the differences between him and his fellow cops are usually more evident than the similarities. Take Commander Adam Dalgliesh of Scotland Yard, the sleuth in P. D. James's novels. He is exact in following approved police procedure. He has, working around him, a constellation of well-defined assistants in whose lives the reader gets steadily more involved. But what an unlikely policeman is Dalgliesh; how odd it is to think of him as such. He is introspective, brooding, mournful. Though he now suffers from writer's block, he has won some acclaim for his published poetry—and is perfectly capable of tracking down a recondite literary clue. The decisive event in his life was the death, in childbirth, of his wife and son. This is the burden of pain he brings to his job, and it helps account for the depth of his response to murder and its aftermath. Dalgliesh is characteristically severe in his self-description. From *A Taste for Death:* "The poet who no longer writes poetry. The lover who substitutes technique for commitment. The policeman disillusioned with policing."

Unlike James, Ruth Rendell makes no attempt to simulate actual police routine in her novels of straight detection. Her Scotland Yard men are Chief Inspector Reginald Wexford of Kingsmarkham in suburban Sussex and his sidekick, Mike Burden. Essentially they're a variant of the Holmes and Watson partnership. In Rendell's story collection *Means of Evil* (1979), we learn that Wexford is "a tall, ungainly, rather ugly man who had once been fat to the point of obesity but had slimmed to gauntness for reasons of health." Nearing sixty, he is sane, shrewd, happily married, a devoted father. Burden, twenty years younger, is a "sartorially immaculate" widower with a pronounced puritanical strain. Together the two resemble "a tramp and a Beau Brummell," with the difference that in this case "the dandy relied on the tramp, trusted him, understood his powers and his perception." Their very presence on the scene is meant to reassure us; we know that the perpetrators will get what's coming to them.

In Rendell's Wexford novels, the policeman is finally as benign and paternal a figure as the uniformed officer on the street during Gene Kelly's rendition of "Singin' in the Rain." It's precisely this quality of reassurance that Rendell withholds in her non-Wexford tales, which is why many readers prefer them. What Rendell offers at her best is the universe of the detective story *minus the detective.* She offers a vision of what life would be like if we lived without the protection of the common law—in a place, that is, where the superego has stopped working and where the police are largely irrelevant, because they never arrive in time to avert the inevitable calamity. Rendell's natural talent is for disturbing her readers rather than consoling or assuaging them. She specializes in the cunning final twist and in the reasonable madman, and her psychological thrillers, such as *The Killing Doll* (1984), *A Fatal Inversion* (1987, under the pseudonym Barbara Vine), and *Talking to Strange Men* (1987), communicate an almost palpable sense of impending disaster.

Rendell's novels are studies in psychological terrorism. They are especially unnerving when two apparently unrelated plots intersect—or when one slightly mad person gets in the path of another. A teenage boy plays at necromancy and, in time, outgrows it—but the sister who brought him up never quite loses her belief in his power to alter lives. A woman suffering from "postnatal insanity" kidnaps a baby and thinks she's done nothing wrong. Or the boys at rival prep schools organize themselves into enemy intelligence outfits. Each side employs ciphers and code names, safe houses, drops: all the paraphernalia of the spy thriller. A solitary, pathetic plant-store proprietor stumbles on a coded message, thinks he's uncovered a criminal ring, and tampers with the message—with the effect that one of the juvenile operatives is thrown into the path of a convicted child molester. In these novels and stories, every fatality is seen, in retrospect, as inevitable. All psychology is abnormal psychology, since most madmen believe that they're sane. And there's nothing the police can do to help.

Rendell shows what happens when the police—considered as the external symbols of the moral authority governing our social lives—simply disappear: when ordinary people are mastered by their own obsessions. Jim Thompson went further and showed what happens when the policeman is of all parties the last we should entrust with our safety. *The Killer Inside Me* (1952), a pulp fiction masterpiece, is remarkable for the ferocity with which Lou Ford, the book's narrator, explodes the image of the benevolent cop. Lou Ford is the deputy sheriff of "Central City," a little town in Texas. He is also a killer, a first-person killer; we see everything from his warped point of view. He is demented, but he takes pains to present himself as reasonably as possible. He hangs a man in his jail cell, makes it look like suicide, tells everyone about his deep and undying friendship for the man he murdered, and almost convinces himself. A sadist and a misanthrope, he puts out a cigar butt in a beggar's hand and likes beating a girl up before going to bed with her. While he doesn't enjoy sex, he can't help himself: "Tell a hophead he shouldn't take dope. Tell him it'll kill him, and see if he stops."

Besides killing people, Lou Ford has devised a novel means of torturing people. He corners somebody in conversation and clobbers him with clichés:

"Well, it's like this," I said. "Now, I've always felt we were one big happy family here. Us people that work for the country . . ."

"Uh-huh. One big happy family, eh?" His eyes strayed again. "Go on, Lou."

"We're kind of brothers under the skin. . . ."

"Y-yes."

"We're all in the same boat, and we've got to put our shoulders to the wheel and pull together."

His throat seemed to swell all of a sudden, and he yanked a handkerchief from his pocket. Then he whirled around in his chair, his back to me, coughing and strangling and sputtering. I heard his secretary get up, and hurry out. Her high heels went tap-tapping down the corridor, moving faster and faster toward the woman's john until she was almost running.

I hoped she pissed in her drawers.

Lou Ford puts all his aggression and all his low cunning into the linguistic games he plays with people. He tells a psychiatrist that he occasionally feels persecuted. "I can't say that it doesn't bother me, but—." "Yes? Yes, Mr. Ford?" "Well, whenever it gets too bad, I just step out and kill a few people. I frig them to death with a barbed-wire cob I have. After that I feel fine."

We have come across other first-person killers—notably in the novels of James M. Cain, *Double Indemnity* (1936) and *The Postman Always Rings Twice* (1934)—but Lou Ford does more than any of the rest to subvert the conventions of the detective novel. A compulsive put-on artist, he is just smart enough to know what we will fall for, and he'll say anything to ingratiate himself with us. At an advanced point in the narrative, for example, he tells us that he's been diagnosed as a paranoid schizophrenic. We have his word for it—but what good is that? The more startling possibility is that he's conning the reader—and that what he calls "the sickness" is another name for a type of moral anarchy or evil that cannot be so easily explained.

In making us doubt his narrator's reliability without offering an alternative version of events, Thompson links his vision of moral chaos to a condition of epistemological anarchy. Ultimately, the plot reaches a nihilistic orgasm when Lou Ford, like Samson in the temple of the Philistines, blows up his house with himself in it as his enemies come to get him. It is a vision of utter destruction, and it follows the logic of the story Lou Ford pauses to tell us about the successful businessman who came home one day and killed his wife, his children, and himself. "He'd had everything, and somehow nothing was better."[6]

When the forces of nihilism are as extreme as that—and the police are part of the problem, not part of the solution—there is no substitute for the Great Detective.

———◆———

Dupin and his descendants are mental supermen, emblems of the aristocratic intellect lording it over the prosaic bourgeois brain. Their exploits may constitute a criticism of crime, but they are also and more immediately a criticism of the commonplace, of all the habits of behavior and mind that the police represent. The canonical example is "The Mystery of Marie Roget," the second of Poe's three Dupin stories, in which the detective never visits the scene of the crime (except, of course, in the sense in which Des Esseintes visits exotic lands while remaining in his armchair in *A Rebours*). Dupin relies exclusively on newspaper accounts of the case, developing his solution in precise opposition to the sensational and superficial theories of the press and the police. These avatars of the public mind are limited, Dupin asserts, to "the range of ordinary expectation." For them, what is past is necessarily prologue, but for Dupin the unforeseen, being always upon us, must enter into the calculations. Dupin recognizes his solution for what it is: a triumph of the imagination. "It is no longer philosophical to base, upon what has been, a vision of what is to be," he remarks. "*Accident* is admitted as a portion of the substructure. We make chance a matter of absolute calculation. We subject the unlooked for and unimagined, to the mathematical *formulae* of the schools." Beyond his abstract interest in "the cause of truth," Dupin has an ulterior motive in tackling the case of Marie Roget: to show up "the extreme remissness of the police."

If the detective story meant an end to the Robin Hood romance, in which the criminal is the hero, the old myth refused to go away. Dupin is no Robin Hood—he doesn't steal from the rich to give to the poor—but his alienation from the officially sanctioned forces of law and order is very nearly as complete. The prefect is Dupin's enemy in the sense that one's chess opponent is one's enemy (which is qualifying it some but not much). The appeal of Dupin is, in part, the appeal of the outlaw. Where Dostoyevski's Raskolnikov,

say, goes outside the law in the act of committing gratuitous murders, Dupin goes outside the law in performing acts of gratuitous
detection—with the added difference that Dupin gets, in effect, to
realize his Napoleonic superiority, at which project Raskolnikov so
ignominiously fails in *Crime and Punishment.*

Dupin's idiosyncrasies immediately establish his status as an outsider—and as an idealized stand-in for his creator, a vehicle for
Poe's wholly imaginary victory over the disastrous circumstances
of his life. Dupin is Poe as Poe would like to see himself: effortlessly
superior, haughty, aristocratic in temper if not in title, vindicated
in the end by those who may once have disparaged him—the almost
bitterly aloof man of intellect. By affixing the blame where it belongs in "The Murders in the Rue Morgue," Dupin not only clears
an innocent man accused of murder; he also asserts his own superiority, succeeding where others have demonstrably failed. The case
would not have intrigued him so much had it not provided an opportunity to administer a defeat to the functionaries "at the *bureau*
of the Prefect of Police." In them we see an image of the conspiracy
of mediocrity that confounded Poe, as he saw it, in his literary career. And in Dupin he found a way to strike back.

Dupin has what Poe himself never enjoyed: enough of an inheri-
tance to make it unnecessary for him to join the workaday world.
He is free of the exigencies of making a living, free to indulge his
genius only when and if it pleases him to do so. The contradictions
in Poe's nature are raised to the level of paradox in Dupin, whose
tone is very much that of Poe the critic. Despite his bohemian manner, he boasts a fiercely disciplined mind. Though he is the creation
of an author who held that rationalism was the enemy of all beauty,
he himself holds a brief for the rational intellect. His feats of deduction prove his eminence, just as they affirm, if only in the realm of
wish fulfillment, the belief that intelligence can prevail over any
and all adversity. This was, in Poe's imagination, a losing battle,
and it's significant that he dropped Dupin after only three stories.

The closest character to Dupin in Poe's nondetective fiction is
Roderick Usher in "The Fall of the House of Usher," that gothic
nightmare of decadence and decay. When we first meet Dupin in
"The Murders in the Rue Morgue," we can't help noticing the
resemblance. Like Usher, Dupin is allergic to daylight; he smells of
decay as Lear's hand smelled of mortality. We're told that he inhabits "a time-eaten and grotesque mansion, long deserted
through superstitions into which we did not inquire, and tottering

to its fall in a retired and desolate portion of the Faubourg St. Germain''—an image that would scarcely be out of place in ''The Fall of the House of Usher.'' The difference, of course, is that Usher cannot escape from his personality, has yielded to solipsism, and is condemned to sit immobile and friendless as his reverie masters him. Dupin, on the other hand, is saved from madness by his detective avocation. A case concentrates his mind wonderfully; otherwise he would surely sink into decay as Usher does—just as Holmes would be a lethargic opium eater if all of London's criminals ever decided to take an extended holiday.

Dupin's behavior becomes a matter of eccentricity, not madness, and his eccentricity is exemplary; it subverts the drearily prosaic and material world, the know-nothing world of the guardians of public morality. With his Watson figure, the nameless narrator, Dupin enacts a harmless *folie à deux.* He is said to be ''enamored of the Night for her own sake; and into this *bizarrerie,* as into all his others, I quietly fell.'' A cultivated taste for *bizarrerie* is an essential ingredient in his personality. It's pleasant to conjure up the image of Dupin snoozing in his dark eyeglasses while the prefect rehearses his theories in ''The Mystery of Marie Roget.'' In that single image of nonchalance and disdain lies the detective story's central comment on the institutions of the law.

Many of Dupin's descendants are as colorful and as outrageous as their precursor, though they mightn't have as rich a basis in their authors' psychohistory. The common rule is that they must be uncommon; they are the products of an exaggeration, different from you and me. From Sergeant Cuff's ruling passion for roses to Nero Wolfe's infatuation with orchids, that symbol of the decadent imagination, is an easy step for the detective novel to take. (Lawrence Block, parodying Nero Wolfe, goes one step further: His detective, Leo Haig, repairs to an aquarium full of black sharks instead of a hothouse for orchids.) By their amiable or outrageous eccentricities we shall know them: the retired Sherlock Holmes keeping his bees on Sussex Downs, available for emergency service but otherwise in retreat from society; Father Brown, the anomalous priest in an age of disbelief, with his cape and umbrella and his maddening cheerfulness; the British dilettante Philip Trent and the affected Americans cast in his image, such as Philo Vance (who, wrote Ogden Nash, ''needs a kick in the pants'') and Ellery Queen. Lord Peter Wimsey with his monocle is the elegant fop favored by birth; Hercule Poirot is the dandified foreigner, with his waxed mustache, his sartorial starchiness, and his everlasting vegetable marrows. Sir Henry Merrivale, the sleuth in the novels John Dickson Carr wrote under the name Carter Dickson, speaks in "a gentle growl," drops the final *g* in participles, favors odd exclamations ("Lord love a duck!") and, we're told, once managed to win a courtroom case despite having begun his address to the jury with "Well, my fatheads." There are sleuths whose great girth would make them stand out in any crowd: Nero Wolfe tops a surprisingly long list of grotesquely overweight crime solvers—the joke being that these giants of intellect dwell in oversize but functionally useless bodies.

No detective writer had more fun exploiting the mind-body dichotomy in his work than did Rex Stout. In the detective tag team of Nero Wolfe and Archie Goodwin—and this is one reason for their formidable appeal—the necessary division of labor between sleuth and sidekick translates into a division between mind and body. Wolfe, weighing in at a seventh of a ton, is purely cerebral, incapacitated by his size from any physical activity more strenuous than lifting a glass of beer or inspecting his prize orchids in his rooftop greenhouse. (It is irresistible to imagine that Rex Stout invented Nero Wolfe as a play on his own name: *Rex,* the Latin word for king, became the Roman emperor Nero, and *Stout* suggests the detective's dominant physical feature.) Wolfe needs Archie to do his bidding for him in the world at large—to do the living for him, one can almost say—for Archie embodies all those all-too-human traits that Wolfe forfeits as the price of his genius. They're a match of opposites, the original odd couple, and their mutual attraction owes everything to the fundamentally irreconcilable differences between them. Smuggle them into an absurd universe, and they would look an awful lot like Hamm and Clov in Beckett's *Endgame*—the one cannot sit, the other cannot stand up. "Every man his speciality," says Hamm.

Why do all such Watson-Holmes partnerships seem a virtually inexhaustible source of narrative energy for writers of detective novels? The simple answer is that they provide the means for an expedient solution to the problem of narration. As Dorothy Sayers explained: "By describing the clues as presented to the dim eyes and bemused mind of Watson, the author is enabled to preserve a spurious appearance of frankness, while keeping to himself the special knowledge on which the interpretation of those clues depends. This is a question of paramount importance, involving the whole artistic ethic of the detective-story.''[7] The presence of the Watson figure keeps the reader in his place, which is in the dark. In the discrepancy between his and the sleuth's understanding of events is all the room for suspense the author needs, and all his justification for withholding information from us.

Beyond this indispensable narrative function, the partnership between eccentric sleuth and amiable narrator allows for rich possibilities in characterization. This was one way that Conan Doyle bettered his necessary precursor, Poe. Sayers was moved to exclaim ''how the sturdy independence of Watson adds salt and savour to the eccentricities of Holmes, and how flavourless beside it is the hero-worshipping self-abnegation of Dupin's friend.''[8] Holmes and Watson are complementary figures—not the twin selves of an ego at war with itself but friends who support and sustain one another. They're a harmonious fusion of opposites, dichotomize them as you will: Call Holmes an emblem of air and mind, Watson an emblem of earth and sense, or say that the former's fearless self-confidence is well matched by the latter's loyalty and pluck. The Sherlock Holmes adventures are the chronicle of a partnership as much as they're the record of a Great Detective.

In the tension between two such fully realized characters as Holmes and Watson is the gist of a modern myth of friendship, one that invokes—and revises—the paradigmatic literary friendship founded on stark opposition: the friendship between Don Quixote and Sancho Panza. What is changed is the proportion of satire to romance in the equation. The Great Detective meets the requirements of a Don Quixote who can successfully tilt at windmills. He can play the quixotic part without ever seeming quixotic—without that rush of fervent idealism that would make him look ridiculous. In this world, the common sense of a Sancho Panza can go only so far. The intellectual prowess needed to crack a case is lodged in the arrogant misfit, the aristocrat who survives the fall of his class—a figure as anomalous in our time and as deliberately archaic as Don Quixote was in his. But the Don needs his Sancho Panza to humanize him and connect him to the big busy world from which, because of his incorrigible eccentricities, he always seems estranged. And Sancho, whether he is called Watson or Archie Goodwin, remains a source of vital comic energy. A Holmes or a Wolfe would be insufferable without a friendly, mediating voice between him and us.

Whatever else they may signify, the Great Detective's eccentricities give casual evidence of his genius, which is largely a matter of temperament and superior intellect. Contrary to Thomas Alva Edison's definition of genius as 1 percent inspiration and 99 percent perspiration, hard work scarcely enters into it. Nero Wolfe's way of working up a sweat is to lean back in his chair with his eyes shut tight and his lips moving rhythmically out and in. Not for him are the all-nighters and hard knocks that a hard-boiled shamus must put up with; not for him the tiresome routines doggedly pursued by Inspector Cramer, the cop whom Wolfe regularly outwits. Wolfe solves crimes the way Dupin solves "The Mystery of Marie Roget": in an armchair preferably, and certainly without leaving his house. The posture, or the pose, suits Wolfe well. He is as idiosyncratic as Dupin, as indolent, and as subject to fits of ennui—a man, to paraphrase Oscar Wilde, without any occupation save that of his genius.

For any legwork that needs doing, Wolfe has Archie Goodwin, who translates the notion of a Dr. Watson across the divide of a century and an ocean. Like Watson, and unlike either Wolfe or Holmes, Archie is a confirmed ladies' man—though Watson is the marrying type and Archie isn't. Both are content with their subordinate role and both are fiercely loyal—though Archie is paid for his services while Watson is motivated by friendship alone. The good-natured Watson is Holmes's link to the prosaic world of everyday life while at the same time his presence on the scene accentuates Holmes's essential remoteness. The same goes for Archie and Wolfe. Both are highly competent—good men to have along if you're expecting trouble. Archie may grouse where Watson is all admiration and wonderment; he's more dashing, too, than his archetype, and the New York he knows is a far cry from Watson's London. But these are minor if entertaining variables in the equation. Like Watson—like us—Archie is always several moves behind the resident mastermind, and this makes him a perfect narrator. Let Archie present himself to us as to the testy client on the first page of *Too Many Women* (1947): "I told him I was Archie Goodwin, the heart, liver, lungs, and gizzard of the private detective business of Nero Wolfe, Wolfe being merely the brains. He asked sarcastically if I was a genius too, and I told him no indeed, I was comparatively human."

7

The Legacy
of Edgar Allan Poe

"*B*ut if you're going to analyze impossible situations,"
interrupted Pettis, "why discuss detective fiction?"
"Because," said the doctor, frankly, "we're in a detective story,
and we don't fool the reader by pretending we're not. Let's not
invent elaborate excuses to drag in a discussion of detective
stories. Let's candidly glory in the noblest pursuits possible to
characters in a book."

—JOHN DICKSON CARR, *The Three Coffins*

Literary forms do not usually spring full-born into existence; they
evolve gradually, by trial and error, in one generation's revolt
against its elders or in collective acts of homage and adaptation,
the development of a set of novelties into a recognizable style. Poe's
invention of the detective story seems to belie this truth; it comes
as close to a clear-cut case of literary parthenogenesis as any we
have on record. Nearly all the conventions of the classic whodunit—from locked rooms to least likely culprits, eccentric sleuths
and their admiring companions, dullard cops, and wrongly accused
bystanders—originate with Poe. The rules of detection, the crime
involving a cipher that needs decoding, the theme of the murderous

double, the city as a criminal landscape, the identification of the man in the crowd as "the type and the genius of deep crime": All date back to a handful of Poe's tales.

In introducing the motifs that soon entered the public domain as the fixed conventions of a new genre, Poe revealed the originality that makes his literary achievement seem like a succession of prophecies that history has contrived to fulfill. Originality is one word for it; intuition is another—a remarkable intuition about the spirit of his age and the emerging future. It's not so much that Poe's tales of ratiocination single-handedly accomplish a synthesis of elements found in inchoate form in a handful of predecessors, though a case to that effect could be made. Rather, it's that the prophetic Poe, collaborating with his zeitgeist, arrived at the distinctive signs and symbols of a universal nightmare—and devised in the form of the detective story a means of keeping the nightmare at bay. Poe may not have been the literary artist Kafka was, but as a fantasist he stands in a similar relation to the dreamscape of his age. It seems incredible to recall that Poe's stories were once thought, as Joseph Wood Krutch put it, to "bear no conceivable relation, either external or internal, to the life of any people." It was, Krutch felt, "impossible to account for them on the basis of any social or intellectual tendencies or as the expression of the spirit of any age."[1] Exactly the reverse is true, though evidently it took some distance from the phenomenon for the recognition to be made. So assuredly does the phantasmagoria of Poe's tales draw us into our own nightmarish fantasies that his very idiosyncrasies have come to seem our common literary property. Harold Bloom, no ardent fan of Poe, grudgingly gives him his due: "Emerson, for better and for worse, was and is the mind of America, but Poe was and is our hysteria, our uncanny unanimity in our repressions."[2]

Cavil as literary critics might about Poe's stylistic lapses, there's no getting around his sheer power to terrify us. To linger overlong on the infelicities of his prose is fruitless. For it's not as a literary artist but as a literary mythmaker that Poe speaks to us, and it's a property of myth that it transcends the terms of any given expression to which it gives rise. Poe is that rare writer whose central achievement survives any number of literary faults, from questionable diction to awkward syntax. And because the recurrent elements of his myth are so easily detachable from his prose style, he not only survives but often gains from translation—whether from English into French, thanks to Baudelaire, or from English back into English, via the paraphrases proffered in passing by the poets Daniel Hoffman and Richard Wilbur in their critical writings on Poe.

People are forever exclaiming over Poe's dual paternity of detective stories and French symbolism, but the link between these two literary developments shouldn't escape our notice; they are both modern in the same way. The symbolist poet, like the literary detective, is a prophet looking backward. Like the detective story, the symbolist poem places its emphasis squarely on the consequences of an action rather than on the action itself. Mallarmé's aesthetic injunction, *peindre, non la chose, mais l'effet qu'elle produit*— paint the effect of a thing rather than the thing itself—follows a principle propounded in Poe's "Philosophy of Composition." This work begins with the reminder that William Godwin wrote *The Adventures of Caleb Williams* (1794), that early avatar of the detective novel, by starting with the climactic second volume and working his way backward. Poe says that he, too, prefers "commencing with the consideration of an *effect*," a word he always italicizes. He recommends that the writer keep "the *dénouement* constantly in view" in order to "give a plot its indispensable air of consequence, or causation." Let the denouement come first. Long live the corpse on page one.

There is a sense in which the whole history of detective stories may be regarded as yet another series of translations of Poe's work. Like his horror stories, Poe's tales of ratiocination are the stuff of dreams, and their recurrent motifs function as variable metaphors, to be combined and recombined endlessly in ever-changing patterns. The incidents and situations Poe presents—the hermetically sealed chamber in "The Murders in the Rue Morgue," for example, or the villain above suspicion in "Thou Art the Man"—are eminently repeatable because they exist independently of the specific plots in which they figure. They are charged with a metaphorical significance that goes well beyond their purely narrative function, and so they invite adaptation, interpretation, translation. A basic and almost definitive procedure of French symbolism—the substitution of metaphor for metonymy as the governing principle of a poem's organization—derives directly from their reading of Poe, and perhaps Poe's tales should be approached as symbolist poems in a narrative disguise.

Some words about these rhetorical terms are in order. If the action in a poem is necessarily figurative, it can work either by the

principle of metonymy or by the principle of metaphor. The metonymy is the rhetorical device that bids us to identify the whole from
one of its attributes or parts. In a poem written according to the
logic of metonymy, what you see on the poem's surface is the tip
of the iceberg, an increment of reality in the form of a single representative instance: "of many, one." The metaphor, by contrast, is
the rhetorical figure of substitution; we see not the object itself but
some other object it suggests—not the actual pears, say, but the
nudes they resemble. In a poem written according to the logic of
metaphor, what you see on the poem's surface is a symbolic transfiguration of reality, an allegory with—or, in some cases, without—
a key. Wordsworth's poems furnish textbook illustrations of the
logic of metonymy. An encounter with a beggar, a leech gatherer,
an old man in search of a wounded son is "of many, one" (the
phrase is his). The same goes for a moment of awe occasioned by
the glimpse of a crag from a rowboat or by the vista from the sum-
mit of Mont Blanc. These and other "spots of time" are isolated
but paradigmatic incidents, whose moral value depends upon their
representative nature.[3] For Baudelaire, on the other hand, and yet
more so for Rimbaud and Mallarmé, the events in a poem need not
be representative in this sense at all; they may point not to a condition of external reality but to the mind of the maker—not an actual
tree, observed and remembered, but the tree as the product of the
imagination. "Every landscape is a state of mind," said Paul Verlaine, and it follows that the people we meet against this landscape
are metaphorical extensions of the poet's consciousness.

Poe's tales serve better than his poems to illustrate the logic of
metaphor as a governing principle of poetic organization. In Poe,
every landscape exists in metaphor and every action corresponds
to an inner conflict. His stories translate his states of mind into
particular narrative sequences. Like the products of a dreamer's
compulsion to repeat himself, the same motifs occur over and over
again. In his essay "The House of Poe," Richard Wilbur dwells on
the compulsively recurrent motif of "circumscription":

> The heroes of Poe's tales and poems are violently circumscribed by
> whirlpools, or peacefully circumscribed by cloud-capped Paradisal
> valleys; they float upon circular pools ringed in by steep flowering
> hillsides; they dwell on islands, or voyage to them; we find Poe's
> heroes also in coffins, in the cabs of balloons, or hidden away in the
> holds of ships; and above all we find them sitting alone in the

claustral and richly furnished rooms of remote and mouldering mansions.

Convinced that "Poe's use of architecture is so frankly and provably allegorical," Wilbur attends to "the mouldering mansion and its richly furnished rooms"—a crucial metaphor in Poe, and a cornerstone of the classic whodunit. The remoteness of Poe's "typical building" suggests to Wilbur the poet's withdrawal from the world of material reality; that the house is generally in a state of decay Wilbur takes not as "an indication of necrophilia" but as "a sign that the state of mind represented is one of almost pure spirituality."[4]

The prevalence of this motif in Poe's work, the symbolic weight it assumes, suggests a Romantic tendency taken to completion: the notion that the imagination affords an exotic refuge from the spiritually impoverished world of material reality. Solipsism is both the danger and the wished-for end of such an approach, and Poe's imagery, operating on an unconscious or subconscious level, implies a critique of the very tendency he was doing so much to advance. Spirituality involves the mind's retreat into a hypnagogic state, like that of a dreamer teetering on the edge of sleep. But the dreams of a divided self inexorably turn nighmarish; the pursuit of spirituality ends in an image of disaster. The dilapidated and teetering mansion of Roderick Usher houses the labyrinthine paths of reverie. It is, as Wilbur says, the habitat of "the visionary hero," who has "very nearly dreamt himself free of his physical body, and of the material world with which that body connects him."[5] At the same time, however, this place of disembodied reverie is the living tomb of Usher's sister, who has suffered the fate of Antigone; she has been buried alive. It's as though, in "The Fall of the House of Usher," Usher's spiritual freedom requires the premature burial of his sister. The imagination, through whose agency reality is redeemed, itself leads to an imprisonment as cruel and terrifying as that from which it was meant to liberate the hero. The ghastly specter of death-in-life will populate the place forever. Such are the consequences of solipsism.

The pattern keeps recurring in Poe. Closed confines, much as they may be wished for, have a habit of turning into torture chambers, as in "The Pit and the Pendulum," or scenes of murder, as in "The Murders in the Rue Morgue." Surely it's significant that Poe, whose architecture is nearly always allegorical, made his first

detective story a locked-room puzzle—a transfiguration of the motif of the premature burial, a metaphor for a state of mind. An
architectural reading of "The Murders in the Rue Morgue" confirms some of our suspicions about its author and gives rise to
others about the genre it commenced. The three domiciles in the
story correspond to the three indispensable players in any murder
mystery: the sleuth, the victim, and the culprit. Where they live
links them and their destinies. Each of the three places is secluded;
as Wilbur remarks, "even when Poe's buildings are situated in cities, he manages to circumscribe them with a protective desola-
tion."[6] Each houses a pair of persons, and the relation between
each pair bears notice. Dupin and his companion, hero and sidekick, live in one; Mme. L'Espanaye and her daughter, the victim
times two, live and die in the second; in the third we find the sailor
and his murderous pet—an inept Prospero and his unleased Caliban. Look closer. All three apartments are on the fourth floor; all
are dark; the rooms in each are massively shuttered. Wilbur provides a helpful gloss toward an allegorical interpretation: "The
three secluded ménages of the story are telescoped into one, the
three buildings becoming a single structure which signifies the re-
integrated and harmonized consciousness of Dupin."[7]

———————◆———————

If the reading of a detective novel is like the interpretation of a
dream, few of the genre's conventions can have a finer symbolic
resonance than the locked room. What are we to make of it, this
death chamber that seemingly affords neither entrance nor exit?
What makes it the archetypal problem, the quintessence of the classic whodunit—so much so that with the inarguable recent decline
of locked-room mysteries per se, discussants sometimes use the
term to encompass any detective story featuring an "impossible"
crime?

Begin with the most obvious implications of the metaphor. To the
extent that the detective story is always and ever an epistemological
riddle, a progression toward the truth by way of questioning our
sources of knowledge, the locked room stands for the imprisonment
of meaning. It is the emblem of an action undertaken in secret, in
private, behind the shut doors of the impenetrable past. Within the
hermetically sealed chamber, silent as death, truth takes the form
of an enigma shrouded in a mystery of false clues. The doors were
locked, the windows securely latched, no one was seen entering or

leaving the premises, and the snow outside is undisturbed—yet the body of a dead man lies inside. The absence of a weapon compounds the problem and almost makes the murderous deed seem the work of a ghost or demon. The corpse is necessarily silent about his fate; the detective extracts his story nevertheless. The detective unlocks the meaning of events; he discerns in them the logic of a homicidal intention, shows where the plan went astray (if it did), explains what happened and how and why. He alone possesses the magic key.

The locked room is also neutral territory, the battlefield on which sleuth and villain tangle. In Poe's paradigmatic case, the locked room is a point of intersection, the place where doubles and twins collide. That is its significance in narrative terms, but it owes that significance to its power as a metaphor. Locked rooms conjure up a primal trauma of imprisonment and claustrophobia, a nightmare in which the walls move inexorably forward to crush the condemned man over whom time's pendulum swings to and fro. The nightmare comes in many forms and has many applications. It served Sartre's conception of hell as a room of *No Exit,* in his play of that title. It also served Luis Buñuel's rather more sardonic vision of inferno, the church that no one is able to leave in his film *Exterminating Angel.* It stands, finally, for death, for the threat of death, or for death in life: an estrangement from reality, a paralysis of the will. An alternative to gothic horror, the locked-room mystery as Poe fashioned it admits of solution. To solve the puzzle is to end the nightmare, to escape from the infernal trap. Subtract the sleuth from the equation, however, and you get horror unalleviated: the nightmare of the man who was buried alive.

Paradoxically, it is the sleuth's capacity for solipsism—his ability to will himself from afar into the room without exit—that allows him to crack a locked-room case. It's as if to say: Man must will himself into a locked room in order to be able to escape from it. In Jacques Futrelle's "Problem of Cell 13," among the most famous of locked-room stories, an imprisonment is undergone voluntarily so the hero can demonstrate his ability to escape stone walls and iron bars. The hero of this "inverted" tale, also known as "the Thinking Machine," makes good on his wager to escape from a prison cell, no matter how closely guarded, strictly by the use of "his brain and ingenuity." The detective faced with a locked-room murder is also an escapist, if in a less literal sense. In solving the case, he, too, must abstract himself from reality—he must enter a metaphorical cell, hear the key turn in the lock behind him, and stare up at barred windows before he can envisage his escape. From his armchair, with shut eyes that shut out the world, he wills himself into the secret chamber of the dream, and plucks out the heart of its mystery, just as Dupin transports himself, by an imaginative leap, from one massively shuttered room (the one in which he lives) to another (the one in which the two women were killed), or as Chesterton's Father Brown solves the locked-room mystery of "The Oracle of the Dog" without ever having to leave his quarters.[8]

The armchair detective, like the locked room, is a compelling idea because it takes a tendency to an extreme—in this case, the notion that the heroic mind can solve the riddles of material reality without needing to come into contact with it. Dupin and his companion suggest the type: They favor darkness, silence, and "the twofold luxury of meditation and a meerschaum" in their accustomed armchairs, which they do not need to vacate in "The Mystery of Marie Roget." By a strict definition, there are really only two armchair detectives—sleuths who make a career of heeding Pascal's advice and staying in their rooms. The first is Sherlock Holmes's older brother, Mycroft, who is introduced to us in "The Greek Interpreter." Mycroft can never overcome his fatigue with the world. He is too fat and lethargic to actively employ his talents, which, we are assured, far exceed those of his brother. "If the art of the detective story began and ended in reasoning from an armchair, my brother would be the greatest criminal agent that ever lived," says Sherlock. "But he has no ambition and no energy." Mycroft is a precursor of Rex Stout's equally obese Nero Wolfe, whose reluctance to leave his brownstone amounts almost to a phobia. But if there are few pure examples of armchair detection, there's a sense in which nearly all the Great Detectives illustrate the concept. At a crucial point in the investigation, a Wimsey or a Wolfe, a Dupin or a Maigret, will withdraw into his own mind, appear in a state of distraction, and engage in a form of stationary travel or long-distance thought. It is amusing to intercept one of them in the act of thinking; their bodies proceed as though the minds that usually direct them are elsewhere—as they are. It happens in *Murder Must Advertise* at that point in the narrative when Wimsey, seeing the light at last, lets his fingers build "a lofty tower" out of the sugar cubes on the kitchen table. It happens in the Nero Wolfe novels when that imperial soul leans back in his armchair with his eyes shut and his lips moving rhythmically out and in. Baroness Orczy's Old Man in the Corner ties and then unravels complicated knots on a line of string; Maigret chomps on his pipe. (Were Philip Marlowe a character in a classic whodunit, he'd lose himself over the chessboard.) Each is oblivious, impervious to interruption. Each has retreated to the locked room of his mind.

The best locked-room murders go beyond all this. They offer us the lure of the impossible, the illusion of a miracle. They are perfect murders not simply because they are nearly insoluble but because they stretch our belief in reason almost to the breaking point. We are brought to the brink of the incredible, having no rational explanation for events, until a tiny, overlooked flaw in the criminal contraption enables the sleuth to bring the whole thing noisily down. In the realm of the impossible, Chesterton and John Dickson Carr stand supreme. Chesterton specialized in the construction of crimes that could not happen but did—a tradition happily extended by Carr, whose singular brilliance at devising and solving locked-room puzzles makes him the Houdini of whodunits.

Carr's debt to Chesterton is clear and clearly acknowledged. He patterned his oversized sleuth, Dr. Gideon Fell, after the physical contours of Chesterton himself; the bald and bespectacled aristocrat Sir Henry Merrivale, the detective in the series Carr wrote under the pseudonym Carter Dickson, is likewise a man of considerable bulk. An epigraph from Chesterton's "The Blue Cross" obliquely announces the puzzle that Fell must unravel in the final section of *The Crooked Hinge* (1938): "There was one thing which Flambeau, with all his dexterity of disguise, could not cover, and that was his singular height." In *The Crooked Hinge*, naturally enough, Fell goes up against a culprit who appears to be capable of altering his height at will.

In his devotion to the locked-room form Carr stood alone. Surely there are no better locked-room mysteries than Carr's *The Three Coffins* (1935) and Dickson's *The Judas Window* (1938)—no stratagems better calculated to defy any solution but the one we are belatedly given. The latter makes the macabre suggestion that every room in London has "a Judas window which only a murderer could see"—a way of entering a locked room without unsealing it. The former contains Gideon Fell's definitive "Locked-Room Lecture," in which the numerous varieties of locked-room puzzles are cataloged, described, and explained. Both novels owe their success not merely to the ingenious variations they play on the locked-room form and not merely to the fact that they conclude with convincing solutions to the problems they pose. "It was murder, but an incredible murder"—this, from *The Three Coffins*, is Carr's signature sentence. How could a man kill his victim in the middle of an empty street, with watchers at either end, and escape undetected, leaving no footprints in the snow? Such puzzles captivate us beyond the pressure of ordinary suspense. They transport us from the realm of the merely improbable to the intoxicating realm of the frankly impossible. "The effect is so magical," Fell remarks, "that we somehow expect the cause to be magical also." Fell isn't at all abashed by the charge that the locked-room puzzle is the baroque elaboration of a conceit, a problem in logic that very neary defeats logic. "A man escapes from a locked room—well? Since apparently he has violated the laws of nature for our entertainment, then heaven knows he is entitled to violate the laws of Probable Behavior!"

Any locked-room puzzle conveys a measure of reassurance to the reader, since it must get solved in the end, but Carr offers something besides reassurance, something at odds with it: a quiet hysteria, the feeling of danger that threatens at every step to undermine the foreordained happy ending. Everything in *The Three Coffins*, from the first victim's cryptic last words to the extra overcoat in his hall closet, contributes to this effect. Carr plays with a full deck of Tarot cards; his chapter titles themselves announce the way stations of a recurrent dream: "The False Face," "The Seven Towers," "The Breaking Grave," "The Blood on the Coat," "The Murder by Magic," "The Clue of the Church Bells," and (of course) "The Impossible." So strong is the sense of the supernatural that the magic seems to linger even after the concluding pages in which the murders are shown to be the work of human hands after all.

The effect is the same in Carter Dickson's *The Reader Is Warned* (1939), notwithstanding the absence of a locked-room puzzle per se. Here again the villain violates the laws of nature for our entertainment; here again, chance and design intersect uncannily to make the unbelievable seem real. The crime in *The Reader Is Warned* has apparently been achieved by "teleforce"—purely mental concentration—by a culprit seemingly capable of being in two places at the same time. "Every organ of the deceased's body was sound," and it is impossible to determine the cause of death. A man with a perfect alibi—witnesses will swear they saw him far from the scene of the crime—takes credit for the murder. How could he have done it? How, indeed, could anyone have? And we're given the further riddle of "the revived corpse": How can a man be dead and alive at the same time? "Up to now I always believed I lived in an ordered, ordinary world where nothing much ever happened," says an incidental character in *The Reader Is Warned*. "In actual fact, nothing much has changed. I still eat and sleep as usual. All the wall-paper looks the same, and I don't get any more money. But I feel I've stepped over into a new kind of world where anything can happen."

It's in Carr's *The Burning Court* (1937) that the incredible receives its perfect exposition. The novel begins with a publisher on a train looking over a manuscript about arcane murders. He peruses the first chapter, about a nineteenth-century murderess who specialized in arsenic and was guillotined for her crimes. He learns assorted facts of interest—that, for example, gastroenteritis exhibits some of the same symptoms as arsenic poisoning. Upon completing the chapter he turns the page, and there is a photograph of that infamous murderess: "He was looking at a photograph of his own wife." With this singular sentence ends the opening chapter of *The Burning Court*. In the next chapter, the publisher feels queasy, and almost misses his stop. He arrives home, greets his wife, climbs the stairs to wash up, returns downstairs, looks in his briefcase, and notices that the photo is missing. The doorbell rings. In steps our hero's neighbor, scion of a wealthy family, whose uncle has just died. Of gastroenteritis, naturally.

Nor does Carr stop there. Uncle Miles's corpse is missing from the sealed crypt. In the bed in which he died, "a piece of string tied into nine knots" at precise intervals had been found under the pillow. And that is exactly what appears in the otherwise empty coffin. By the time the novel ends, criminology and witchcraft seem to overlap perfectly; we learn, for example, that "the tying of nine knots in a string is believed to put on the victim a spell which places him entirely in the power of the sorceress." We reach a rational solution. The culprits are named, their schemes foiled— and then an epilogue spells out an alternative solution, one that explodes our happy confidence that all natural phenomena are subject to rational laws. Thus the author has his cake and eats it, too— his books affirm the triumph of reason but leave an aftertaste of mystery and doubt.

8

---◆---

No Mask Like Open Truth

*N*o mask like open truth to cover lies,
   As to go naked is the best disguise.

CONGREVE, *The Double Dealer* (1694)

Any theory of detection resting on Poe rests on a paradox. Two seemingly contradictory propositions must be kept in mind. The first is that the evidence of our senses is not to be trusted. What seems and what is are often opposed, since appearances deceive and witnesses tend to be unreliable. But it is not enough to discount appearances; one must also see through them. One must learn to decipher the hieroglyphics of everyday life. "The world speaks to us like a great book," William of Baskerville says in Umberto Eco's *The Name of the Rose*. Books, however, speak only to those who are able to read them. A literary detective is needed to interpret the surface rhetoric of reality. The codes, ciphers, and secret messages found in detective stories ever since Poe's "The Gold Bug" merely cast this notion in its most explicit form. An extra overcoat in the hall closet, the subsequent disappearance of the same, a clock in a jeweler's window that's forty minutes fast, an ambiguous sign hung upside down on the wall—such clues as these (taken from John Dickson Carr's *The Three Coffins*) disclose what they conceal but only to an adept codebreaker, who sees signs and symbols where others see merely riddles.

The truth, we are meant to understand, exists at a critical remove from the visible. So goes the first of our propositions derived from Poe. But no sooner have we made it an article of faith than we're stopped in our tracks by a warning voice. This is what it sounds like in Kenneth Fearing's *Dagger of the Mind* (1941): "The only reason I didn't have the answer right now was that it was too glaringly simple, too obvious. One can never see the thing that lies directly under his nose, although he can see everything else." The theme has been restated numerous times since its perfect exposition in "The Purloined Letter." "Perhaps the mystery is a little *too* plain," Dupin tells the prefect of police even before the latter has had a chance to explain the problem that has given him and his men such trouble. "A little *too* self-evident," Dupin adds. We can well understand the prefect's discomfort upon hearing these words, for they go counter to all he has been taught—and we, as readers, are in a similar predicament. Just when a diet of detective stories has conditioned us to lift the veils of the ordinary and cross-examine false appearances, a counterexample will come along to cross us up. And so, our second proposition: The truth often lies on the surface, or close to it, and yet is no less hidden for that.

Put "The Murders in the Rue Morgue" and "The Mystery of Marie Roget" in the first category and "The Purloined Letter" in the second. In the first two stories, the detective needs to extrapolate an entire cause-and-effect scenario from a handful of clues. Dupin's method is to eliminate all impossibilities; then whatever is left, no matter how improbable, must be the truth. The more *outré* a crime, the easier it is to solve. By this criterion, "The Murders in the Rue Morgue" are relatively easy to solve, since Dupin can simply isolate the incongruous elements and use them as the key to the larger mystery. Its very ordinariness makes "The Mystery of Marie Roget" more difficult, if by far less memorable, than "The Murders in the Rue Morgue." But in both stories, the underlying logic of Dupin's method is the same. The murderer, though intent on concealing his identity, is bound to leave enough traces behind to give himself away, and Dupin must extrapolate from these partial clues the whole of the dark scenario. The clues are like the visible intimations of a buried truth. For it *is* buried—prematurely buried, like so many victims in Poe's stories—and the fact of its concealment should be enough to arouse our suspicions. We are advised to scrutinize all appearances rather than accept them on trust. Reality wears a mask; remove it and another mask takes its place. The detective must recognize the face behind the mask, as Sherlock Holmes in "A Scandal in Bohemia" can tell—at a glance, naturally—that the tall visitor in the astrakhan coat and black mask is none other than the prince of Bohemia.

For suspense, it's essential that we start by suspecting the wrong man—a maxim that Alfred Hitchcock turned into a central operating principle in his masterly parables of justifiable paranoia. In *Saboteur* and *Spellbound,* in *North by Northwest* and *Vertigo,* the wrong man is either a victim of false identification or somebody's convenient fall guy, framed for a crime he hasn't committed or set up for an even crueler fate. He is our stand-in, the character whose point of view is our own. An innocent in some but not all senses, he has been thrust—as have we, the moviegoers—into the middle of someone else's drama. He is always caught between two tasks: In order to clear his name, he needs to divide his attention between eluding his relentless pursuers and making his own inquiry into what really happened. Yet whether it is chance or a villain's evil design that has singled him out, there is a sense in which the wrong man is right for the role he has to play. Events have uprooted him, torn him from his customary surroundings, stripped him of his usual props and cards of identity, forced him to rely on his own wits, prompted him to wonder about his values. He is being tested and judged, and only he can save himself. The predicament is like the perfect cinematic equivalent of a career man's existential crisis.

The real murderer in *Spellbound* is not the spurious psychiatrist played by Gregory Peck, though he thinks himself guilty and all appearances point accusingly at him. The real murderer is a benevolent-looking father figure, and we'll suspect him only if we're wise to the ways of the genre. He is an example of the generic least likely suspect: a cold-blooded culprit with an instinct for survival, who takes pains to cover himself with an airtight alibi and often provides not only a corpse but a fall guy to take the heat. The least likely suspect tends to be a worthy villain, being generally clever and subtle and always villainous in the extreme; he bears false witness, perjures himself, and otherwise compounds his initial offense where that is the expedient thing to do. The efficacy of the type depends on our willingness to suspend our distrust—or on our capacity for being duped, which comes to the same thing.

As a convention of the genre, the culpable least likely suspect reminds us that respectability is a sham virtue, since the citizen above suspicion may have the most to hide. In "Thou Art the Man," the first known instance of the species, Poe gives his unlikely culprit a name—Goodfellow—that is itself a blatant lie. It's as if a shadow has fallen between the word and what it is supposed to designate, as if the language itself offers no safeguard against duplicity but, on the contrary, allows the wicked but self-styled "Goodfellow" in our midst to camouflage his crimes. Low cunning has taught this type of villain that the best defense is a strong offense, so he appoints himself the leader of the forces of righteousness, the grand inquisitor. The lesson for the detective is to take nothing on faith, least of all a display of piety. The appearance of innocence can be seen to vary inversely with the actuality of guilt, as in "Thou Art the Man." A flamboyant display of rectitude can almost suffice to convict a man of fraud, as in Wilkie Collins's *The Moonstone*.

We're not to trust what's on the surface, then, and yet the greater danger lies in our overlooking it. Appearances are all that we have, as detective novels keep reminding us; they demand that we interpret them, not ignore them. We are especially apt to overlook the thing in front of us—we're like the logician who deduced by a series of elaborate propositions that his misplaced eyeglasses were on his face. "There is such a thing as being too profound," Dupin says in "The Murders in the Rue Morgue," and "The Purloined Letter" drives home the point.

Notwithstanding the absence of a murder, this, the third and last of the Dupin tales, is also the best of them—the one that has achieved the status of an epistemological parable. It registers its impact on us precisely because it eschews the obvious trappings of mystery; it offers nothing so blatant as the cipher in "The Gold Bug." The absence of any *outré* elements in "The Purloined Letter" makes the crime the more difficult to solve, and the more instructive. A simple paraphrase is in order. A letter has been stolen "from the royal apartments"; we are never told what it contains, only that it compromises the honor of a lady "of most exalted station"; it must be recovered at any cost. The police know who took it but can't, though they search high and low, find it in the culprit's chambers. They're looking in the right place, but the trouble is that they're trying too hard. The culprit is the evil Minister D——, "an unprincipled man of genius" who has anticipated how the police will react and has devised his stratagem accordingly. He counts on their proceeding according to textbook plan; he knows they will look for hidden compartments in out-of-the-way places—will look for them exclusively—and so he opts to leave the letter out in the open, in "a trumpery fillagree card-rack of pasteboard," where it will be continually overlooked.

Dupin's solution to the case completes its fearful symmetry. Putting himself in his adversary's mind, Dupin understands that D—— has successfully read the minds of the police. Dupin is thus, in effect, a mind reader twice over. Having divined the minister's plan, he intuits the probable hiding place and then, rather than disclose his deductions to the police, proceeds to turn the tables. On the pretext of recovering the gold snuffbox he had left, with apparent carelessness, on a previous visit, Dupin insinuates himself into the villain's rooms. He has arranged for a noisy diversion: "a loud report, as if of a pistol," on the street. When D—— goes to the window to investigate, Dupin removes the stolen document and replaces it with a harmless look-alike. The letter has now been purloined a second time, the villain hoist with his own petard. The hiding place remains perfect, though now what it hides is the evidence that D—— has been found out. "I should like very well to know the precise character of his thoughts, when, being defied by her whom the Prefect terms 'a certain personage,' he is reduced to opening the letter which I left for him in the card-rack," Dupin says with satisfaction.

In one of several analogies Dupin rather surprisingly draws between his brand of detection and children's games, the selection of the perfect hiding place is likened to a sophisticated player's choice of a hard-to-find word on a detailed map or chart. "A novice in the game generally seeks to embarrass his opponents by giving them the most minutely lettered names; but the adept selects such words as stretch, in large characters, from one end of the chart to the other. These, like the over-largely lettered signs and placards of the street, escape observation by dint of being excessively obvious; and here the physical oversight is precisely analogous with the moral inapprehension by which the intellect suffers to pass unnoticed those considerations which are too obtrusively and too palpably self-evident. But this," Dupin snorts, "is a point, it appears, somewhat above or beneath the understanding of the Prefect."

"Most minutely lettered names," "over-largely lettered signs and placards"—the repetition of *letter* in these phrases can't be an accident. Nor should the multiple meanings of the word be overlooked. The author of "The Purloined Letter" is aptly described as a man of letters. *Letter* signifies literal truth, as when we speak of the letter of the law. A letter is both a typographical character and an epistolary document—the word refers both to the smallest component of a literary work and to the finished product, to language and its creations. This confluence of associations obliges us to discern, amid the actual mystery that Dupin solves in the story, another mystery that can't so easily be explained, because the terms themselves surround a void. The letter Dupin retrieves is said to confer power not on its reader but on its "holder." For all intents and purposes, it might just as well be characterless, a blank. We are asked to accept its importance on faith alone. Throughout the story it remains unread, its contents undisclosed; it is merely filched from one place to another, filched twice over. It's hard to credit the notion that its theft will prove, or has proved, disastrous.

The document in question is the very model of what Hitchcock called "the MacGuffin": a device or gimmick of alleged but undefined and hence spurious significance, which triggers off the plot.[1] The letter itself doesn't bear close scrutiny because it has no intrinsic meaning; its value derives from its use. We'll not go wrong if we regard it as a narrative convenience, a fiction designed to make fiction possible, a prop—though one upon which vast metaphorical constructions can be put.

The letter—like the fake Maltese Falcon in Hammett's novel and Huston's film—is the object of a fierce collective obsession despite being inherently worthless. The letter's very ordinariness makes it emblematic: It is so ordinary in appearance that it can be left out in the open and so inherently uninteresting that the bearer doesn't notice its loss. What does the emptiness of the letter signify? Since its meaning is to be guessed at and cannot be verified, its significance must be in some sense nearly arbitrary; the purloined letter, like paper money, is valuable only because people think it is. Does this render the letter a fit symbol for all linguistic (or semiotic) activity? Reduce literature to the inscrutable letters it comprises and you arrive at the last in a series of closed doors, the one that will not open: Is his the hidden message inscribed in the letter in invisible ink? Or did Poe achieve what he didn't intend, a parable of the writer who always means more than he can know or say, whose truths though concealed from himself are open to the world?

The possessor of the letter is said to have the power to compromise a royal personage or to save her honor; it has put some unexplained political power in the hands of Minister D——. But in truth police and politicians are as irrelevant to the true drama of the case as they are incompetent to solve it. The true drama is the clash of opposing wills and competing intellects, and it centers on the letter—that is, on language and writing: the product and symbol of intellect and will, the very means with which the human mind asserts its sovereignty. Perhaps that is the message inscribed between the lines of the twice-purloined letter. When a Dupin or a Holmes goes up against a Napoleon of crime, a Minister D—— or a Moriarty, the object in dispute need be nothing more substantive than a piece of paper. A will, a deed, a land survey, or a map, the basis of blackmail, incriminating evidence—the document itself is a pretext for the showdown of minds at the heart of the fiction. The letter has the function of the chessboard (the board itself, not the pieces on it) in a match between grand masters—only in Poe's case, what the antagonists are fighting for is supremacy in the world of letters. The actual letter can be left out in the open because the real struggle occurs on a metaphysical plane.

The plot of ''The Purloined Letter'' figures, though in a purely incidental way, in the first of Sherlock Holmes's adventures, ''A Scandal in Bohemia,'' where the master sleuth arranges a noisy diversion to permit him to recover a purloined, though conventionally hidden, photograph. Other writers, from Chesterton to the present, have played ingenious variations on Poe's theme. In ''The Invisible Man,'' for example, Chesterton translates the most obvious hiding place into the invisible culprit. The murderer here, seen by everyone but noticed by no one, is the mailman, an apparently ubiquitous Edwardian figure whose comings and goings are so banal as to escape attention. Again in ''The Dagger with Wings,'' the criminal disguises himself out in the open, so to speak, relying on the expectation that a man opening the door in his housecoat must be the master of the house. And in ''The Sins of Prince Saradine,'' a third Father Brown story, the eponymous sinner escapes detection by impersonating his own butler. There are, as well, many stories in which the murder weapon blends as invisibly into its surroundings as the purloined letter does in its pasteboard card rack. Of all of these—deadly icicles that melt, knives disguised as tent pegs, and the like—surely the most delicious example is the frozen leg of lamb in Roald Dahl's ''Lamb to the Slaughter.'' After dispatching her husband with the item in question, Dahl's murderess simply puts it in the oven and serves it to the nice policemen who come to visit her that evening.

Dorothy Sayers's "The Fascinating Problem of Uncle Meleager's Will," one of the more whimsical of the Lord Peter Wimsey stories, pays its homage to "The Purloined Letter" by offering a baroque elaboration of the most obvious hiding place. The document here has been hidden, in the form of a crossword puzzle, on the tiles at the base of the pool by the side of the mansion, where the characters spend their time when they aren't sleuthing. "Every book in the library had been scrutinized page by page, the walls and chimneys tapped for hiding places, the boards taken up, and so forth," Sayers tells us, and for that reason the search for Uncle Meleager's will has been as futile as the official police search in "The Purloined Letter." It takes a Great Detective, a Father Brown or a Peter Wimsey, to spot the emperor's true clothes, and that's as much a function of the nature of reality as a comment on our limitations as observers. Sir Winston Churchill once said, apropos of counter-espionage work, that in wartime the truth must be accompanied by a bodyguard of lies. Yet as Congreve wrote in *The Double Dealer* (1694), there's "no mask like open truth to cover lies,/ As to go naked is the best disguise."

Consider one last reprise of the purloined letter motif. In Kenneth Fearing's *The Big Clock* (1946), we find ourselves in a magazine empire that's a dead ringer for the house that Henry Luce built as a monument to "the American century." Earl Janoth, the genius of the place, whose creations include *Newsways, Commerce, Sportland,* and *Crimeways,* is guilty of murder. What could be more natural than for this masterly media manipulator to throw the blame on another man—the last man, save himself, to be seen with the victim? First, however, he must find his scapegoat, and so he organizes a searching party and appoints his crack investigative reporter, George Stroud, to head it. The catch is that Stroud is the man they're all looking for: The wrong man has been placed in charge of finding himself.

Fearing twists his knife a little further. He makes his plot hinge on Stroud's purchase of a Louise Patterson painting, and the painting does indeed compromise the innocent man; it is evidence of his marital infidelity, though not of murder. And there, hanging on the wall of Stroud's office, to which all his operatives must report, is another painting, in the same distinctive manner, by the same artist. In a twist altogether understandable to readers of "The Purloined Letter," this painting registers its significance on no one who enters Stroud's office except the painter herself; it's simply too obvious a part of the decor; they take it so for granted they don't even notice it's there. None of Stroud's operatives know Janoth's real motives in organizing the search—or suspect that Stroud is doing his best to subvert it—which gives a splendidly satirical edge to the book's depiction of how newsmagazines operate. Fearing's clever juggling of levels of awareness (through the device, lifted from Wilkie Collins, of multiple narrators), no less than his brilliant blending of the "purloined letter" and "wrong man" motifs, makes *The Big Clock* a performance to be relished.

9

---◆---

The Double

*B*oth in nature and in metaphor, identity is the vanishing-point of resemblance.

WALLACE STEVENS, *The Necessary Angel*

The test of a first-rate intellect, according to Scott Fitzgerald's famous aphorism, is its ability to hold contradictory ideas at the same time and continue to function smoothly. This formula for the dialectical imagination could have been composed with Poe in mind. In a kind of cerebral application of Newton's second law of mechanics, an idea or impulse in Poe's mind was likely to quicken an equal and opposite reaction. Few poets would assert, as Poe did, that the long poem "is simply a flat contradiction in terms"—shortly before embarking on "Eureka," his lengthy cosmological reverie, which he subtitled "a prose poem." Few authors insist so strongly on the importance of irrational impulses and uncanny occurrences while simultaneously professing confidence in the mind's ratiocinative powers. It seems logical to suppose that Poe unfurls the banners of scientific optimism and progress—as in the figure of the detective—precisely because his true element is terror, the terror of unknowing. Poe releases the terror in such pure products of gothic fantasy as "The Black Cat" (in which a man, possessed by "the spirit of perverseness," hangs his cat), "The Fall of the

93

House of Usher" (in which a man is haunted by the prematurely entombed body of his twin sister), and "William Wilson" (in which a man named William Wilson kills a man named William Wilson, his double or his second self). It is precisely this quality of gothic terror that the figure of the detective controls or neutralizes in Poe's tales of ratiocination. It's as though a tale of ratiocination were simply a tale of the grotesque and arabesque with one major change: the introduction of a detective.

The gothic theme of the double is structurally present in virtually all detective stories, since there is a sense in which every sleuth is every culprit's double. It's hard not to regard the detective story's archetypal constellations as projections of Poe's personality, and the opposition between the detective and the villain—the conflicting holders of power in a detective story—as like the two sides of a hopelessly split identity. The natural antagonism between them is augmented, or offset, by mutual attraction. They are foes to the death if need be, yet theirs is a mimetic relationship: One party seems to ape the other. The major difference between the tales of ratiocination and a tale of terror such as "William Wilson" is that, in the gothic imagination, contact with one's double is understood to mean the certain annihilation of the self. In the detective story, by contrast, the sleuth survives the necessary clash, his own identity strengthened by the encounter.

The theme of the double is made explicit at the start of "The Murders in the Rue Morgue," in which the narrator tells us that he "often dwelt meditatively upon the old philosophy of the Bi-Part Soul, and amused myself with the fancy of a double Dupin— the creative and the resolvent." Richard Wilbur, among the most gifted of Poe's interpreters, dwells meditatively on this fancy, having first enumerated some of the doubling patterns in Poe's nondetective oeuvre.[1] In "The Cask of Amontillado," Wilbur reminds us, both antagonists have nine-letter names, Fortunato and Montresor, that connote wealth and good fortune; in "A Tale of the Ragged Mountains," a character named Bedlo fantasizes the death of a man whose name, Oldeb, is the palindrome of his own. The emphasis in both cases is on the necessary enmity between twins—as if the torn ego reified itself and replicated itself in the form of fragmented beings sworn to each other's destruction. Wilbur makes much of the fact that Dupin is said to have two distinct speaking voices, one high and one low, in "The Murders in the Rue Morgue." They correspond to the two voices—"the one a gruff voice, the other much shriller''—that the gendarme heard coming from the murder chamber. Play detective with these clues, interpret them as a critic would, and you arrive at Wilbur's conclusion: The sailor and the orangutan are like the warring halves of a single personality, while Dupin, containing both their voices within him, has an integrated consciousness. Therein lies his allegorical triumph: He "uses his genius to detect and restrain the brute in himself, thus exorcising the fiend."[2]

De Quincey had suggested that the poet look at murder from the point of view of the culprit, not the victim. Poe, introducing his "double Dupin" into the equation, went one step further. Dupin is capable of seeing things from the culprit's point of view because the culprit is another side of himself. The identification of Self with Other is an effective investigative method because it is first a valid description of a psychological condition. The hunter and the hunted are one. Where the split in Dr. Jekyll or Victor Frankenstein means certain destruction, the detective in Poe's tales can contain his antagonistic double, in both senses of *contain*. What it takes is an act of self-recognition, which is also an act of self-abnegation. The detective must be able to enter the villain's mind, and to do this he must be able to escape from his own; the Self must become one with the Other before rejecting the Other. The process entails a degree of sympathetic identification—like that which links Dimmesdale and Chillingworth in Hawthorne's *The Scarlet Letter*. If the end result is the detective's triumphant assertion of his integrated self, that is possible only because he has successfully confronted his double. He has, in order to understand and thus foil the villain, looked in his own heart and found him. Pogo's words, in Walt Kelly's comic strip, fit the case: We have seen the enemy and it is us.

"The Purloined Letter" is Poe's fullest exposition of the theme of the double. With the dull-witted prefect of the Paris police, a man known by the letter *G*, Dupin has little enough in common. With the narrator, who lacks even an initial to distinguish him from pure anonymity, Dupin shares quirks and predilections, but it's the very differences in their mental makeup that make a state of friendship possible. But with Minister D——, who purloined the letter and has thus far foiled the police, Dupin shares more than the telltale first initial of his name. They share not only a *letter* but the vocation of men of *letters*. The narrator, whose function in purely narrative terms is to be several moves behind the Great Detective, tells us that Minister D—— is one of two brothers. The minister's brother has a reputation as a poet, he says, while the minister himself "is a mathematician, and no poet." Dupin corrects his friend immediately. "You are mistaken; I know him; he is both," Dupin says. For proof he offers the case of the purloined letter itself. "As poet *and* mathematician, he would reason well; as mere mathematician, he could not have reasoned at all, and thus would have been at the mercy of the Prefect."

Minister D—— is as much a fusion of "the creative and the resolvent," as close to an idealized image of Poe as his brother—who, we might reasonably suspect, is none other than Dupin himself. This makes the minister the most redoubtable—and therefore, in the aesthetic sense, the worthiest—of the foes that go up against Dupin in Poe's stories. The Minister is the artist, while Dupin is the artist and critic combined in an opposing self. They are two of a kind, and what separates them is never really articulated, perhaps because it's a distinction without a true difference. Minister D—— is "an unprincipled man of genius," says Dupin, who presumably does have moral principles, enough at any rate to serve the cause of justice, or chivalry, or whatever it is he's serving by retrieving the stolen document. But these principles remain tacit at best and seem to dissolve in the story's powerful atmosphere of decadence and gloom. Justice can't be Dupin's driving force. He admits as much when he lets on that the monetary reward has been an incentive and further reveals that he recovered the letter primarily to avenge himself on D—— for some personal grievance; vengeance in Poe always makes the most pressing claim. And, of course, Dupin enjoys tweaking the prefect's nose by solving so baffling a case with little labor and no sweat.

Dupin, knowing his nemesis, knows exactly how he must proceed in "The Purloined Letter." He illustrates his method by describing the schoolyard game in which a player, hiding some marbles in his hand, invites a second player to guess whether he holds an even or odd number of them. When the act is repeated, an educated guess becomes possible; guessing begins to acquire a semblance of logic, as divination slides into detection without altogether forfeiting its original character. The second player—call him the sleuth—must ask himself whether his opponent is a simpleton (in which case he will make "a simple variation from even to odd") or a somewhat more sophisticated character (who will resist "too simple a variation ... putting it even as before"). Dupin's interlocutor obligingly puts a name to this method. "It is merely," he says, "an identification of the reasoner's intellect with that of his opponent." "It is," agrees Dupin, with the air of a professor giving out a good grade. He then clinches the analogy, hammering its lesson home in the terms of a wise schoolboy's maxim: "When I wish to find out how wise, or how stupid, or how good, or how wicked is any one, or what are his thoughts at the moment, I fashion the expression of my face, as accurately as possible, in accordance with the expression of his, and then wait to see what thoughts or sentiments arise in my mind or heart, as if to match or correspond with the expression." Know thine enemy, know thyself. Study the mirror closely.

Films policiers put their own spin on the theme of the double. William Friedkin's *The French Connection* (1971), an outstanding example, suggests that the good guys and bad guys are morally linked. To the extent that they rely on similar methods and are locked in a *mano a mano* duel, cops and criminals begin to resemble one another until, as Wallace Stevens wrote, identity occurs at "the vanishing point of resemblance." But the film's texture is far more complicated that this statement implies. The cop in this case, named "Popeye" Doyle and played with admirable ferocity by Gene Hackman, is a shabbily dressed plainclothes man with an itchy trigger finger and a filthy mouth. The chief culprit, played with his customary suavity by Fernando Rey, is an elegant Parisian, a dandy with a cane, who seems to have stepped out of a Luis Buñuel dinner party. Popeye Doyle—a name that ironically merges a comic book hero with the creator of Sherlock Holmes—is seen, in one of the most affecting sequences in the movie, shivering on the sidewalk in the cold with a cardboard container of coffee. We see him from across the street, through the window of the posh French restaurant in which the elegant drug thief dines in style. The difference between antagonists, in manners and social class and nationality and mental ability, is complete. One is all brawn and physical energy, the other is full of wiles and disciplined self-control. They are opposites. Yet the contest between them has made each the other's double—inevitably, from the moment they first donned the parts of the pursuer and the pursued and Rey eluded Hackman on the subway. Both men are morally contaminated. It is with Hackman that viewers are coaxed into identifying themselves, and Hackman—obsessed with Rey and maddened by him—

is responsible for the violent death of a bystander, himself an ambiguous figure: a repulsive cop whom Hackman has reason to despise, perhaps because the resemblance between *them* is plain.

The empowering insight of such gothic works as James Hogg's *Confessions of a Justified Sinner* or Poe's "William Wilson" is that the self divided against itself cannot stand. The protagonist's confrontation with his double must lead to destruction and damnation, because the very existence of the double proves that the fatal split in human consciousness has already occurred. What Poe called "the imp of the perverse" implies no less. In the companion stories that dwell on this theme, "The Black Cat" and "The Imp of the Perverse," the ego is split between the self that commits unmotivated crimes and the self, as perverse in its own way, that cries out to be punished. Put another way, the ego is a casualty of "the twin irrepressible impulses *to do evil* and *to judge oneself*," as Daniel Hoffman says in his study of Poe.[3] These warring impulses, left unchecked, can lead only to suicidal nihilism.

Consider the case of William Wilson. There are two of him, twin irrepressible impulses made flesh. The William Wilson who tells the tale tells us he has been dogged all his life by a man who shares his name, his appearance, and his birthdate (which is also Poe's own: January 19, 1809). This "singular namesake," an embodiment of "conscience grim," is driven to judge his evil-doing double and exposes him as a card sharp. Wilson, who has already tried once to kill his better half, finally does so in a fit of hysterical passion, running his sword through his namesake. "At that instant some person tried the latch of the door"—there occurs a strategically prosaic interruption of the drama very much like the knocking-at-the-gate episode in *Macbeth*. Here as there, in Thomas De Quincey's words, the interruption signifies that "the human has made its reflux upon the fiendish; the pulses of life are beginning to beat again; and the reestablishment of the goings-on of the world in which we live first makes us profoundly sensible of the awful parenthesis that had suspended them." The instant passes, and Wilson returns to his "dying antagonist." What happens next is doubly startling. A mirror appears on the wall, which had been blank just an instant before. In the mirror is the image of the slain William Wilson, pronouncing his final judgment: *"In me didst thou exist— and, in my death, see by this image, which is thine own, how utterly thou hast murdered thyself."*

Where the gothic tradition and the detective novel intersect, a similar fate is in store for our hero. The search for a missing person ends in a shattered mirror in William Hjortsberg's *Falling Angel* (1978), which reads like a cross between *The Exorcist* and *The Big Sleep.* It's like a gothic alternative to the Oedipus myth: The detective, hunting for a man, belatedly realizes he is hunting for himself. Set in the New York of 1959, this hard-boiled homicide novel metamorphoses by degrees until its subplots involving satanic cults and voodoo sects take center stage, at which point the hero's vanquished double returns to destroy him. In literature more generally, the *doppelgänger* nearly always spells death, as in act 1 of Shelley's *Prometheus Unbound,* where we're told that "the Magus" Zoroaster "met his own image walking in the garden." The living themselves have ghosts, Shelley declares, shadow selves that roam apart "till death unite them and they part no more."

This is where the classic detective stands apart. As William Patrick Day puts it in his excellent study of gothic fantasy, *In the Circles of Fear and Desire,* the detective "can live comfortably with the fact that he has within him the potential to become something monstrous, that he belongs, in part, to the world he opposes. This acceptance of his own doubled identity frees the detective's powers of understanding and analysis." Day goes so far as to identify Sherlock Holmes as a fundamentally gothic character, aloof, clandestine, and at home in the wilderness of the Devonshire moors. Indeed, Holmes is precisely the type of "effective hero" that gothic fantasies from *Dracula* to *Frankenstein* lack:

> The Gothic fantasy lacks an effective hero, a character who through his own efforts can resolve the mystery and put an end to horror. The figure of the detective develops from the tension created by the lack of a true hero. He is, in effect, the hero the Gothic world needs but cannot sustain. The presence of such a character revises the balance and dynamics of the genre, focusing on the restoration of the order and meaning rather than on the steady disintegration of identity and the absolute instability of the world in which the characters live. Out of the Gothic fantasy's critique of the romance grows a revised version of the romance, and the romance quest hero returns in the guise of the detective.[4]

Where the gothic fantasy charts what Freud called the return of the repressed, the detective story relies on deliberate and artful repetition. Notice how Dupin in "The Purloined Letter" foils his foil. To turn the tables on his double, he has had to duplicate the villain's work; he purloins the purloined letter from Minister D——'s chambers, does so clandestinely, and leaves no traces of his work, substituting a letter similar in appearance to the one over which all the fuss has been made.

Conan Doyle, trying to kill off his immortal hero, provides the ultimate proof that a truly Great Detective can emerge unscathed from a fight to the finish with his double. In the prematurely titled "The Final Problem" (1894), Professor Moriarty wrestles Holmes right off the edge of the Reichenbach Falls. Both are said to die as a result, but Conan Doyle, giving in to a reading public that had gone into mourning, consented to bring his hero back while consigning the "Napoleon of crime" to oblivion. Alas, London is the drearier place, Holmes confesses in "The Adventure of the Norwood Builder" (1905), "since the death of the late lamented Professor Moriarty." And no wonder, since Holmes could have called Moriarty *mon semblable, mon frère.*

10

---◆---

Funerals in Eden

"*I*t seems to have been a queerly assorted house party to find under so conventional a roof," Georgia commented. "A trollop, an Anglo-Saxon squire, an American wife, a rolling stone, a fribble, and a quack."

NICHOLAS BLAKE, *The Corpse in the Snowman*

The classic whodunit is a bundle of paradoxes. You might reasonably call it an ambidextrous genre; to nearly every generalization you can make about it, you can tack on a qualifying "on the other hand." Consider some of its built-in ambivalences. It has a fatalistic view of human nature, yet it promises a happy ending. Its plot depends on an act of terminal violence, yet its characters frequently comport themselves with drawing-room decorum. This is a genre, moreover, that delights in sinister possibilities and uncanny coincidences, diabolical omens and mystifying clues. A spectral hound leaves very tangible footprints on the ground. A black retriever makes a peculiar wail when a walking stick is thrown into the sea. A sign in spidery script reading, "Vengeance is Mine, Saith the Lord," hangs upside down on the murdered man's bedroom wall. Such puzzles as these resonate with a significance that transcends explanation, lingering in the reader's mind long after he or she has forgotten the solution that so handily disposes of them. Yet this is also a genre that fundamentally exalts the rational intellect, succeeds in proving the world intelligible, and warns us against confusing divinity with dog "spelt backwards," as Chesterton puts it in "The Oracle of the Dog." As befits the double nature of the genre, the hero is at once an artist and a critic, a double man, whose apparently amoral bohemianism doesn't deny his commitment to the truth. Though his adventures are entertainments first and foremost, they may nevertheless promote a criticism of life, even if that phrase in this context can scarcely bear the moral weight that Matthew Arnold assigned to it.

To this list of paradoxes, add one more: Murder in the classic whodunit takes place more often than not in an idyllic setting; the scene of the crime is a version of paradise. In the murder mystery, wrote Auden, "Nature should reflect its human inhabitants, i.e. it should be the Great Good Place; for the more Eden-like it is, the greater the contradiction of murder. The country is preferable to the town, a well-to-do neighborhood (but not too well-to-do—or there will be a suspicion of ill-gotten gains) better than a slum."[1] Upon inspection, the Great Good Place turns out to be the epitome of a closed society. "I have always thought that murders may be divided into two classes, closed or open," says a character in Anthony Berkeley's tour de force, *The Poisoned Chocolates Case* (1929). "By a closed murder I mean one committed in a certain closed circle of persons, such as a house-party, in which it is known that the murderer is limited to membership of that actual group. This is by far the commoner form in fiction. An open murder I call one in which the criminal is not limited to any particular group but might be almost any one in the whole world. This, of course, is almost invariably what happens in real life." The distinction seems a shorthand way of differentiating the classic whodunit (as practiced par excellence by Agatha Christie) from the hard-boiled American novel or the contemporary police procedural. The hard-boiled novel, striving to give the illusion of "what happens in real life," renounces the "house-party" murder in favor of an urban criminal milieu. The classic whodunit, being by nature indifferent to "what happens in real life," is drawn to the artificial limitations of the closed murder as a defining trait.

We tend to associate the classic whodunit with hermetically sealed chambers, secret passages, and remote country mansions— apt metaphors for a wished-for condition of isolation and insularity. In Ross Macdonald's words, "neither wars nor the dissolution of governments and societies interrupt that long weekend in the country house which is often, with more or less unconscious symbolism, cut off by a failure in communications from the outside world."[2] The locked-room puzzle is only the most baroque form of this removal from the newspaper's version of reality; "the fateful chamber is a compartment doubly sealed," as the French critic Roger Caillois put it, since the detective novel itself can take place only in a world separate from our own.[3]

Tom Stoppard has a lot of fun with the theme of the isolated setting in *The Real Inspector Hound* (1968), his send-up of murder-mystery plays in general and Agatha Christie's *The Mousetrap* in particular. Mrs. Drudge, the charwoman in Stoppard's play who is always conveniently on the spot when one or another character utters a death threat, paints the picture for us. She answers the phone with "Hello, the drawing-room of Lady Muldoon's country residence one morning in early spring?" To a mysterious visitor, who looks an awful lot like the dangerous madman that the radio has just warned us to expect, Mrs. Drudge adds other useful details. Lady Muldoon's "strangely inaccessible" Queen Anne mansion is apparently surrounded by swamps and smugglers' trails. "Yes," says Mrs. Drudge, "many visitors have remarked on the topographical quirk in the local strata whereby there are no roads leading from the Manor, though there *are* ways of getting *to* it, weather allowing." The fog, she adds in a perfect parody of "literary" language, "rolls off the sea without warning, shrouding the cliffs in a deadly mantle of blind man's buff." When Lady Muldoon makes her entrance, formally coiffed and with tennis racket in hand, we half expect her to say, "Murder, anyone?" The corpse under the sofa, which has been there from the start of the action, occasions little surprise when it is finally discovered. It is one more entertaining diversion in a timeless evening of fun and games, bridge and gossip and amatory advances.

The remote country mansion, where a convention of eccentrics is in progress, is certainly a natural habitat for the classic whodunit—the ease with which it can be parodied argues no less. But the basic ingredients are easily adaptable to other settings. What's needed is a place that runs on its own clocks, able to keep the world at large from encroaching on its privileged boundaries. A tropical island would work fine; an even better venue would be a luxury ship on a Caribbean or Mediterranean cruise. A cruise automatically fulfills several of the genre's basic requirements—which is surely one reason for the recent vogue of murder-mystery cruise vacations.[4] Like the cast of suspects in a Christie mystery, the passengers on a cruise have, or give the appearance of having, lots of disposable income and endless amounts of leisure time. They're on holiday, in a mood for parlor games, looking for diversions and distractions—and what can better do the trick than the discovery of a putative corpse amid the black-tie patrons of the gaming room on the ship's quarterdeck? Who can concentrate on the vagaries of interest rates or junior's chances of getting into Harvard when there's a homicidal puzzle to be solved and the culprit and victim are doing their danse macabre at the foot of the horseshoe staircase in the grand salon?

To enter the fictional universe of the murder mystery is, during a luxury cruise, surprisingly plausible and quite compelling. For one thing, it isn't hard to find someone everyone else would like to eliminate, even among relative strangers. The passengers on a cruise inhabit a separate world, far removed from their usual spheres of action, beyond the jurisdiction of their usual authorities—and well out of earshot. The news of the week is effectively shut out; the Dow Jones Industrial Average might go down ninety-plus points in one day, but you wouldn't know it from the news digest slipped under the cabin doors, which tends to favor items like "Surrogate Mother is Grandmother": "South African grandmother Pat Anthony, 48, gave birth to triplets—becoming the world's first surrogate mother of her own grandchildren." The cruise director, meanwhile, is likely to be governed by the principle enunciated in Simon Nash's *Death Over Deep Water* (1963), where the murder takes place on a Mediterranean cruise: "People who have set out to enjoy themselves must always be made to do so." Another requisite of the detective novel fulfilled: The characters have all the time in the world on their hands, and a plain need for the sort of jolly amusement that a well-executed murder can be sure to provide.

A British luxury ship is an apt murder mystery vessel for one other reason: It has its natural upstairs-downstairs division of officers and mess crew—it's a floating island, a romanticized metaphor if not a microcosm of the mother island, England. Conspiracy theories, paranoid scenarios, and rumors of imposture and false identity—the plot mechanisms of the detective story—tend to flourish on a cruise as anonymous faces gradually become familiar masks and a closed society of suspects and suspicious persons rapidly establishes itself. As Nash puts it in *Death Over Deep Water,* "Here, where there was no sight of land but only the fluidity of endless motion, a little community was formed that might have had no contact with any other reality. Its loves and hates were turned in among themselves, and there was no escape."

This sense of an island remoteness from which there is "no es-cape" is what all the whodunit's classic settings have in common. It's as true of the exclusive prep school, the antique university town, the provincial vicarage, and the titled estate where the week-end guests try their hand at amateur theatricals. In each case, the setting is an implicit celebration of limits, order, and rules even though—or because—the plot involves a violation of that order and those rules. Therefore, any self-enclosed community with a firm social hierarchy and enough local color to make it an object of nostalgic desire will serve. The line between appearance and real-ity, never very strong for the participants of these dramas, blurs entirely. In the murder mystery in its purest forms, the assembled suspects inhabit a world out of time, measuring out their lives in cups of sherry and glasses of port. Everyone knows his place; each must be conscious of his assigned role in the local scheme of things and his irrelevance to the wide world outside. Nobody seems to work very hard, if at all, for a living; for all the bickering going on beneath the surface, life seems blissful and murder an incongruity, as in Paul McGuire's *A Funeral in Eden* (1938), which is set in a tropical but suitably anglicized Pacific isle. McGuire's title says it all.

The American version of the leisurely whodunit, with its "pseudo-gentility" that Raymond Chandler derided, can approach pure camp. "Fundamentally," wrote Chandler with considerable justice, though with an animus one needn't share, "it is the same careful grouping of suspects, the same utterly incomprehensible trick of how somebody stabbed Mrs. Pottington Postlethwaite III with the solid platinum poignard just as she flatted on the top note of the Bell Song from *Lakmé* in the presence of fifteen ill-assorted guests; the same ingenue in fur-trimmed pajamas screaming in the night to make the company pop in and out of doors and ball up the timetable; the same moody silence next day as they sit around sipping Singapore slings and sneering at each other, while the flat-feet crawl to and fro under the Persian rugs, with their derby hats on."[5] The English are better at this sort of masterpiece-theater murder, for the simple reason that English fiction can easily tap into a familiar past, a recognizable class structure, a code of manners, and a terrain of short distances and definite places, while the governing condition of most American fiction is a sense of continual transition, expanding frontiers, social fluidity and short-term trends. It was no accident that the hard-boiled crime novel with its quickened pace and its untidy surface was an American invention.

◆

If a detective novel in the Hammett-Chandler-Ross Macdonald manner appeals to our restless dissatisfaction with things as they are, the opposite is true of the British, or Anglophiliac, puzzler. Where the former encourages us to suspect the worst of our legally appointed guardians of the peace, the latter pokes mild fun at its policemen but stops well short of expressing contempt or indignation. The police inspector in a Hercule Poirot or Jane Marple mystery may be a hopeless incompetent, but more often he merely lacks imagination; and unlike the shady cops we meet in Hammett and Chandler, he rarely resists the sleuth's intrusion into his bailiwick. Moreover, wealth here is a very different thing from sleaze. Far from giving off a bad stench, the lucre in this fictional universe has been laundered the old-fashioned way, in legacies and landed estates. Where, in short, there's something implicitly subversive about the tough-guy genre, the classic whodunit has a relaxed and somewhat dreamily complacent worldview—and that is part of its charm.

E. C. Bentley's *Trent's Last Case* (1912), the archetypal "closed murder" whodunit, readily invokes a world of old Etonians, a world whose continuity with the past rests in the received hierarchy of the present. Trent instinctively knows that the suspect named Marlowe must be in the clear, for Marlowe's voice reflects "the influence of a special sort of training"—Marlowe is an Oxford man. (Perhaps Raymond Chandler meant to give Bentley's example a good shake when he gave his irreverent, down-at-the-heels sleuth the impeccably "English" name Philip Marlowe.) As Ross Macdonald put it, works like *Trent's Last Case* appeal to our "nostalgia for a privileged society."[6]

That's certainly true of Agatha Christie, who stands in the same relation to the classic whodunit as, say, Claude Monet stands in relation to impressionism. Consider *Death on the Nile* (1938)—either the novel or the excellent movie version (1978)—whose cast includes such murder-mystery stalwarts as the mustachioed British colonel (David Niven), the excitable romantic novelist (Angela Lansbury), the hardnosed greedy American attorney (George Kennedy), and the armchair revolutionary (Jon Finch). Theirs is a world of French maids and hired companions; when they aren't killing or getting killed, they visit pyramids and temples, play bridge, drink fancy drinks, and change into evening clothes for dinner. In the movie, the characters' clothes tell you it's the late 1930s, but you'd never guess that a depression was going on and a world war about to break out. Out of history they are, these well-heeled schemers and their accomplices. For them, murder almost seems a form— the supreme form—of entertainment. Christie, like a gracious hostess, has given each of them a motive for killing Linnet Ridgeway, which makes her the perfect victim. She obliges them all by getting shot—at a time when each had the opportunity to do it, and in circumstances decidedly picturesque: aboard a steamer going down the Nile, on a holiday cruise that has become a more intimate affair and, though none of the survivors will admit it, a quite festive one as well.

Christie worked an astonishing number of clever variations on the closed circle of suspects in the remote bastion of privilege. Her first Poirot, *The Mysterious Affair at Styles* (1920), offers the classic country-mansion setting. Let David Grossvogel list the attributes of the place:

> In a place like Styles, the plumbing is never erratic (unless for the limited purpose of serving the plot), personal sorrow is as evanescent and inconsequential as a summer shower, age and decay cannot inform the exemplary and unyielding mien of its people: the young know that they will be young forever, the professionals are admirably suited to their faces ("Mr. Wells was a pleasant man of middle-age, with keen eyes, and the typical lawyer's mouth") and the good-natured fool (the one character who is only seldom a suspect) will neither mature nor learn, however many of life's grimmer vicissitudes he is exposed to.

"In such a garden of delightfully fulfilled expectations," Grossvogel concludes, striking a suitably jolly tone, "there rarely occurs anything worse than murder."[7]

Several of Christie's most memorable performances involve a metamorphosis of the setting, as we move from a seemingly open to a definitely closed murder—and Styles, by any other name, reestablishes itself. The train in *Murder on the Orient Express* (1934), for example, would at first appear to be a completely anonymous locale, its passengers accidentally thrown together by an arbitrary coincidence of railway schedules and travel itineraries. Yet the setting here is pure camouflage. It turns out that everyone in the fateful coach is intimately acquainted, in league with one another though it suits their conspiratorial purpose to feign being strangers; and before we know it, the Orient Express has metamorphosed into one more example of Styles, replete with retainers and relatives. Styles itself is immune to change, outward appearances notwithstanding. In *Curtain* (1975), Poirot's final bow, we're told that decades have gone by since *The Mysterious Affair at Styles* and that the Styles mansion has, in keeping with the times, become "a guest house." Not for long, of course, or not for real. Poirot helps Captain Hastings, slow as ever, to see the light. "The people assembled under this roof are not a collection of strangers who have arrived here independently," Poirot explains. "This is not a hotel in the usual sense of the word." How could it be? They all have a murder to share. Or take *What Mrs. McGillicuddy Saw* (1957), which situates us, at the start, in the most prosaic, drab, and anonymous of locales. The unremarkable Mrs. McGillicuddy, her Christmas purchases in tow, is riding home on the 4:54 train from Paddington Station in London. Through her window she sees, or thinks she sees, a man strangling a woman in the compartment of a train going by on parallel tracks. Yet the body of the deceased turns up where we always knew it would—in the most outrageously remote place: inside "a huge sarcophagus of a decadent Greco-Roman period" in the little-used barn of Rutherford Hall, seat of the Crackenthorpe estate. The murderer had to have disposed of the body out the train window at just the spot where a steep embankment gives to the Crackenthorpe land. As usual, the artifice of murder far exceeds what efficiency requires; imperial means have been used to achieve a simple end. As Miss Marple explains, "He knew—he must have known—all about Rutherford Hall—its geographical position, I mean, its queer isolation: an island bounded by railway lines." No wonder the characters in classic whodunits are often heard to speculate about the exact relation of providence to chance.

Of course, in practiced hands, the classic whodunit could come to support a commercial orientation and a less genteel cast of suspects in a less fanciful choice of milieu. The preposterously exaggerated scenarios that Chandler lampooned were quickly superseded, on both sides of the ocean, by homicidal plots that were far more credible if seldom quite as ingenious. Dorothy Sayers set

Murder Must Advertise (1933), arguably her best Wimsey, in a London advertising firm. The task of writing advertising copy is rendered vividly and with a satirically affectionate wit; Sayers had her own experience at an advertising agency to help authenticate the details. Add the liveliness of those parts of the novel involving mayhem in Mayfair, the antics of the period's Bright Young Things—particularly the scenes in which Wimsey masquerades as Harlequin at a festive but somewhat sinister costume party—and the formal problem of who killed Victor Dean seems decidedly a subsidiary pleasure. Nicholas Blake, eschewing the weekend-in-the-mansion setting of his *Thou Shell of Death* (1936), went on to *Minute for Murder* (1947), which is set in Britain's "Ministry of Morale" during World War II, and *End of Chapter* (1957), set in a London publishing house no more byzantine than the real thing. Kenneth Fearing's *Dagger of the Mind* (1941) takes place in the closed confines of an artists' colony in New England, a suitably remote setting that has its correlative in actuality; the ways of the eccentric residents are satirically exaggerated but not by much. Even better, Fearing's *The Big Clock* (1946) gives us the closed murder within the wide open spaces of New York City by the simple expedient of setting the puzzle at the headquarters of a newsmagazine empire, whose identity may be inferred from the book's title. In sum, the gain for realism was considerable when whodunit writers began to capitalize on the perception that our working and social lives provide us with countless opportunities for closed murders. All one need do is grant the presence of a metaphoric corpse, and see how quickly a university department, a government office, or a sales conference springs into life, organizing itself into a closed murder, full of hidden relations and secret agendas.

More and more realism can be incorporated into the setting, and has been—in all these cases, a realistic milieu, captured with a fidelity to detail, gives the whodunit the veneer of the comedy of manners. However, whether we find ourselves in Christieland or in a place more closely resembling the places we know, an essential point remains the same. In this world of fixed limits and closely defined relationships, society is seen to consist of closed circles, some of which overlap; and it's a characteristic of the closed setting that it serves as a backdrop for motive. It is a far cry from the random violence of the modern metropolis. Murder in the classic whodunit is a matter of individual motive, be it greed or envy or revenge, lust thwarted, or intimacy betrayed. But if the crime is invariably comprehensible, it is anything but the norm; it must indeed come as a shock. It is an exceptional but finally temporary violation of the social order, not the mark of endemic rot within it. Solving the murder thus becomes an act of social criticism, if only in the limited sense that pertains to any comedy of manners. That's why the scene of revelation so often finds the suspects reassembling for a final group portrait, as though a cast party were about to take place; nabbing the culprit is a collective concern, calling for drinks all around. The detective, on his way to setting things right, has illuminated the intricate web of mores and prejudices that bind the community together and constitute a social order. It can now be re-constituted, the crisis over, the drama at an end, with the expulsion of the villain, the one who didn't fit and doesn't belong. Expulsion, prompting the image of a deviant schoolboy, conveys the right tone. We imagine the unmasked culprit looking forlorn at the gates of his Oxford college, carrying his duffel bag to the station. Or, to take a rival image that the genre calls to mind, we imagine him cast adrift on a rowboat while the luxury yacht sails peacefully into the sunset.

The unmasking of the villain completes the symmetry of the classic whodunit. We end as we began, with the elimination of a socially undesirable figure—first the victim, now his executioner. A social code has been enforced, and rather strictly. The restoration of order affirms the rightness of that order; the violation of decorum—for such, in this context, is what a murder amounts to—has been isolated, and now the little community can pick up where it left off; the homicidal interruption has been contained as between the marks of a parenthesis. Crime is to chaos as detection is to order, and the latter is fated to prevail. And since the logical conundrums we've encountered along the way—the footprints in the snow where no one walked, the absence of a murder weapon, the disappearance of a corpse—admit of solution, the affirmation of the social structure doubles as an affirmation of the rational intellect. The classical detective story is thus a striking throwback to the Platonic equation of the true and the good and to the Platonic confidence in the mind. For the exonerated suspects, the feeling is one of relief; and the confident expectation of that relief—the certainty of a happy ending—is what makes the earlier tension not only bearable but desirable. For the reader, however, the relief is almost always tinged with disappointment, for the reader is necessarily excluded from the seat of Eden restored, which awaits the novel's protagonists. For the reader, the solution when it comes eliminates all other possible scenarios and signifies the end of the guessing game. Our revels now are ended. "And so," as David Grossvogel puts it, "the trivial unpleasantness that was contrived for the purpose of ending it is brought to a close."[8] What has occurred within the closed circle has been a version of pastoral draped around a puzzle—a kind of paranoid pastoral.

Where the puzzle is a supernal value, as in Agatha Christie, the ingenuity of the plot varies inversely with the credibility of the characters. The suspects in *The Body in the Library* (1941), the quintessential Miss Marple murder mystery, correspond exactly to villagers in her native St. Mary Mead, though the book is set in another locale entirely. Each suspect wears his tag on his lapel like an identity card. Basil Blake brings to mind a schoolboy prankster with an inferiority complex; Mark Gaskell reminds Miss Marple of "Mr. Cargill, the builder," who "bluffed a lot of people into having things done to their houses they never meant to do"; Josie Turner resembles the baker's daughter, who married above her station; Conway Jefferson is an elderly gentleman on the model of "Mr. Badger, who had the chemist's shop," and is easy prey for an enterprising golddigger. Yet to say that Christie's characters are one-dimensional, her setting predictable, and her prose never better than pedestrian, is scarcely as damning as it sounds. The simplicity of her syntax and vocabulary (which makes her greatly popular among foreign-language instructors of English) simply underscores the extent to which her puzzles resemble the fairy tales of our age. And surely, they should be read and judged as such. Approach fiction with a child's bottomless appetite for narrative inventions, and Christie will not disappoint you.

In the ingenuity of Christie's puzzles, and in her simplicity, rests her originality. If everyone had the motive to do it, why not make everyone the culprit? Thus the plot of *Murder on the Orient Express.* If all the suspects are equally guilty in some sense, why not a novel in which all the suspects (including the actual culprit) are turned into victims? Thus the plot of *And Then There Were None* (1940). If mystery readers, conditioned to discount appearances, are apt to overlook the character standing over the just-discovered corpse, gun in hand, why not a novel in which the least likely suspect and the most obvious culprit turn out to be the same person? Thus the subterfuge Christie weaves in *The Hollow* (1946). Indeed, if Christie's characters had more character they'd be less interesting as suspects, less useful as pieces to be moved on a chessboard; an inner life is the one thing we can't imagine them having. And somehow a nondescript writing style seems perfectly in keeping with their world.

———◆———

Christie specialized in the least likely suspect—another way of saying that her culprits are at their cleverest in deflecting attention from themselves. Arguably the most creative of these schemes is the enigmatic series of crimes that confronts Poirot and Hastings in *The ABC Murders* (1936). The murders seem to have rhyme but no reason; they form a pattern that lacks a probable cause. First a Mrs. Ascher, an elderly shopkeeper, falls victim to a blunt instrument in Andover. A month later, a young waitress named Betty Barnard is strangled in Bexhill. A month after that, Sir Carmichael Clarke meets his end in Churston. Each murder is announced in advance in letters to Poirot signed "A.B.C."; an A.B.C. railway guide is found on or near each of the corpses. Clearly, an alphabetical series has been established—but for what discernible end? Who could have wanted to kill three persons, in three separate locales, none of whom had ever come into contact with either of the others? Since none of the likely suspects would stand to benefit from more than one of the murders, they must be the handiwork of a homicidal maniac, right? Wrong. That's just what the culprit wants us to think. In fact, A and B have been killed merely to make the death of C seem part of a series and thus to deflect attention from anyone with a motive for killing C alone. The culprit has come up with the ultimate in red herrings: a pair of corpses. As Poirot explains: "When do you notice an individual murder least? When it is one of *a series of related murders.*" The result is a kind of paranoid paradox. The deaths of A and B are no less random for being made to fit into a pattern. But to say that the pattern is arbitrary doesn't deny that the pattern exists.

As a rule, mystery writers are drawn to serial murders in which the pattern isn't mere camouflage. This is one of Ed McBain's favorite plot devices. In many of the 87th Precinct books, the cops' task is to figure out the true linkage between apparently unrelated homicides. Still, homage is regularly paid to Christie's formula of the arbitrary or trumped-up pattern. McBain makes use of the ploy in *Long Time No See* (1977), one of his best novels; filmmaker

Brian De Palma does likewise in *Blowout* (1981), not one of his best movies. Leave it to the late Jorge Luis Borges, who made no secret of his fondness for detective stories, to elevate Christie's ABC puzzle to the status of a metaphysical riddle. The masterly story "Death and the Compass" (1942) should teach us once and for all not to disparage the puzzle element in a detective novel.

Borges introduces us to a detective, Erik Lönnrot, whose last name contains the German word for red. In the next breath we meet Lönnrot's antagonist, Red Scharlach, alias "Scharlach the Dandy," alias Lönnrot's double; Scharlach, which means scarlet in German, also sounds a pun on Sherlock. The murderous game is afoot when a *kabbalah* scholar is killed on the night of December 3, in the Hotel du Nord; the note left in the typewriter declares: "The first letter of the Name has been spoken." Exactly one month later, a second body turns up, this time "in the most deserted and empty corner of the capital's western suburbs"; again the victim is Jewish, and again a message has been left: "The second letter of the Name has been spoken." There follows, on the night of February 3, a mysterious disappearance at an eastern point of the compass; this time: "The last of the letters of the Name has been spoken." Taking the final note at face value, the police commissioner assumes that the series has now ended. But Lönnrot is not so easily convinced. He has learned enough about cabalistic mysteries to know that the tetragrammaton—the symbol for the ineffable name of God—contains four letters, not three. He knows, too, that a Hebrew day begins at sundown; thus the crimes may be reckoned to have taken place on the fourth day of each month. Finally, there is the evidence of the compass; it tells him not only to anticipate a fourth murder but where it will occur: to the south of Buenos Aires, the direction of danger in Borges's stories.

South goes the detective, on the night of the 3rd of March, to the villa of Triste-le-Roy, as if his collection of clues constituted a personal invitation. And it does. A fourth murder has indeed been planned for the occasion—the murder of the detective himself. "To [the police] I sent the equilateral triangle," Scharlach explains to Lönnrot. "I sensed that you would supply the missing point." What had been a false pattern becomes a true one with Lönnrot's arrival; he completes the design with his destruction. The design existed in two minds only, his and his foe's. Scharlach's motive is revenge: "I swore," he says, "to weave a labyrinth around the man who had imprisoned my brother. I have woven it, and it holds: the materials are a dead writer on heresies, a compass, an eighteenth-century sect, a Greek word, a dagger, the rhombs of a paint shop." Lönnrot has been lured to his death, a victim of his own ingenuity—and his determination to apprehend patterns where others see only random signs. He has successfully solved the riddle, and his reward is death, his own death, at the hands of his double and rival and foil. Thus does Borges explode the very conventions he has lovingly adopted: this is what happens to the detective story when the mirror cracks and we enter a world of labyrinthine puzzles and arbitrary sign systems.[9]

It's bad luck all day, Dorothy Parker once quipped, if you don't mention Edith Wharton in the next breath after Henry James. The same might be true of Borges and Nabokov. Like Borges, Vladimir Nabokov takes a special delight in manipulating the conventions of the classic whodunit for his own radical purposes. He is similarly fascinated with dreams and mirrors, doubles and labyrinths, puzzles that exist at the vanishing point of detection; and similarly interested in seeing what happens when the plot of a detective story is presented minus the detective story's cheerful faith that God's in his heaven and all shall be well. In a brilliant metaphor, he shows us, along the left side of a lane, "a long wall with crossword puzzles of brick showing here and there through its rough greyness." There are messages to be deciphered in Nabokov's world, but they are like crossword puzzles without clues—or like incomplete manuscripts, as this characteristic simile suggests: "Then nothing but a lone star remained in the sky, like an asterisk leading to an undiscoverable footnote."[10]

In such novels as *Despair, Lolita,* and *Pale Fire,* Nabokov takes the universe of the detective novel and strips it of its epistemological bearings. In each case we are offered a coherent criminal design that turns out to be the product of pure paranoia. Reality, for the protagonists of these novels, is a system of delusions. And if this is so, then detection itself becomes an exercise in paranoia. The detective—and the literary artist, for that matter—is in the position of the insane lad in the story "Signs and Symbols": "Everything is a cipher and of everything he is the theme. Some of the spies are detached observers, such as glass surfaces and still pools; others, such as coats in store windows, are prejudiced witnesses, lynchers at heart; others again (running water, storms) are hysterical to the point of insanity, have a distorted opinion of him and grotesquely misinterpret his actions. He must be always on his guard and devote every minute and module of life to the decoding of the undulation of things.'' Where else but in detective stories do we find "coats in store windows" invested with such importance—as real clues or red herrings, as the case may be?

Among the supposed novels written by the eponymous but very shadowy protagonist of Nabokov's *The Real Life of Sebastian Knight* (1941), one—beguilingly titled *The Prismatic Bezel*—is like a parody of Christie that transcends both its source and its own mocking intentions. Nabokov presents *The Prismatic Bezel* in the form of a three-page plot summary, as though that allowed for the perfect exposition of a Christie whodunit, as though a full-length text would be a needless extravagance. The imaginary book begins with the discovery of a corpse at the paradigmatic boarding house. The twelve lodgers staying there appear at first to be as randomly assembled as, say, the twelve jurors at a murder trial. But then the first of several metamorphoses occurs.

> It gradually transpires that all the lodgers are in various ways connected with one another. The old lady in No. 3 turns out to be the mother of the violinist in No. 11. The novelist occupying the front bedroom is really the husband of the young lady in the third floor back. The fishy art-student is no less than this lady's brother. The solemn moonfaced person who is so very polite to everyone, happens to be butler to the crusty old colonel who, it appears, is the violinist's father. The gradual melting process continues through the art-student's being engaged to the fat little woman in No. 5, and she is the old lady's daughter by a previous marriage. And when the amateur lawn-tennis champion in No. 6 turns out to be the violinist's brother and the novelist their uncle and the old lady in No. 3 the crusty old colonel's wife, then the numbers on the doors are quietly wiped out and the boarding-house motif is painlessly and smoothly replaced by that of a country-house, with all its natural implications.[11]

At this point, the original premise of the story is quite forgotten, and "a new plot . . . seems to struggle for existence and break into light." But with the sudden arrival of the London detective, the metamorphosis is advanced another stage—the butterfly becomes a caterpillar again—as we return to the genre conventions from which we thought we had escaped. The detective "drops his h's," we're told, for this "is not a parody of the Sherlock Holmes vogue but a parody of the modern reaction from it." The comedy is complete when the corpse, which has disappeared, returns in the guise of that staunch Christie standby, the ambiguous character whom no one suspected. "You see," he says, removing his false whiskers and wig and glasses, "one dislikes being murdered."

The Prismatic Bezel invokes detective novel conventions only to deviate from them and then surprises us a second time by complying with them in the end. (The pattern is the same in Jean-Luc Godard's film *Breathless,* where the conventions played with are those of a Humphrey Bogart gangster picture.) By putting the spotlight on these conventions, Nabokov exposes not only their artificiality but their power as artifice. The hotel in *The Prismatic Bezel* performs on the random lives congregated therein a metamorphosis like that conferred by any novel upon its subjects. The mysterious corpse is a convenient pretext for transforming a boarding house into a country mansion, an anonymous way station into a charmed circle of suspects. It's like a paranoiac's dream come true; no one is what he seems, everyone is in cahoots, and random signs vibrate with the symbolic significance of clues before the sham is exposed, order is restored, and ordinary logic puts an end to the fairy-tale metamorphoses of art. The magic of *The Prismatic Bezel,* though it exists only as a plot summary, is like that of some similarly unwritten books that Borges attributes to his made-up writers: Nabokov sketches out, in a few pages, the paranoid pastoral that is the essence of the classic whodunit.

11

———◆———

From Paradise to Poisonville

*H*ere, above all, there were broad roads and vast crossings
and tramway lines and hospitals and all the real marks of
civilisation. But though one never knew, in one sense, what one
would see next, there was one thing we knew we should not see—
anything really great, central, of the first class, anything that
humanity had adored. And with revulsion indescribable our
emotions returned, I think, to those really close and crooked
entries, to those really mean streets, to those genuine slums which
lie round the Thames and the City, in which nevertheless a real
possibility remains that at any chance corner the great cross of
the great cathedral of Wren may strike down the street like a
thunderbolt.

G. K. CHESTERTON, *The Club of Queer Trades*

The classic whodunit's marriage to the "closed murder" and the
isolated setting dates to its so-called golden age between world
wars. Go back to the detective story's origins, however, and you'll
find that its characteristic landscape is the big city with its crowded
thoroughfares, its factories, and its slums. It could be argued, in
fact, that when the history of the detective story forked into two
paths—when golden-age sleuths abandoned the city's mean streets
to the hard-boiled shamus and the plainclothes cop—the road of
baroque extravagance marked the real detour. The road to the iso-

lated country mansion has certainly turned out to be the road less traveled by. And this simply reflects a condition that was there from the start: the sense that the city is the natural habitat for what Poe calls "deep crime."

For Poe the city is the capital of "deep crime" because its crowds guarantee anonymity to each and an adequate homicidal motive to many. The city is Leviathan, Hobbes's monstrous image of a society based on the principle of open warfare. It is where a crowd can act with the singlemindedness of one person, but it is also where the anonymous stranger can repair to hide, preserve his anonymity, and feel more truly alone. While the city forces a close proximity of body to body, it makes real intimacy as hard to achieve as privacy. The smell of corruption is everywhere. Signs of desperation are as near as the drunk sprawled out on the sidewalk under the awning of the local bar. The threat of danger is constant, the sense of menace palpable.

A visit to the city of crime fiction tends to be either a tour of hell or a trip to some enchanted Circe's lair, where men, led by their lusts, turn into swine. There are exceptions, of course. In the London of Conan Doyle and Chesterton—and in Rex Stout's New York—the city remains charged with the potential for crime, but the prevailing atmosphere is one of benign enchantment, not menace. For the most part, however, it is Poe's vision of the city that later crime novelists would make their own. A vast metaphor for moral turbulence and social disorder, the modern city is conceived to be a barren place populated by phantoms, shadows, rootless hordes, and sundry agents of destruction: the city as envisioned in the most famous of all modern poetic nightmares, the city as "The Waste Land."

Against such a backdrop, the motive for metaphor is very different from what it was when a raffish impostor dispatched a detestable old miser on a Mediterranean cruise. In the metropolis, logic has its uses but its limits, too; no calculation can be exact, since there is always the possibility that a psychopath, obeying an incomprehensible logic of his own, did the foul deed. The rules are different in the city. Since crime is the norm and not the anomalous and exciting exception, detection becomes a habit of self-defense rather than an instrument for enforcing a social code. Sometimes the best the hero can hope for is not the truth but his own survival. Solving a crime depends less on fancy mental footwork than on a skeptical gaze, a stubborn streak, and a rebellious spirit. If these things add up to a criticism of life, it would seem to be one that is based on despair.

Ross Macdonald argues that the evolution of the detective story from Holmes to the present owes as much to Baudelaire's "vision of the city as inferno" as to his "dandyism." That vision stemmed directly from Poe. Turn to "The Man of the Crowd" (1840), a pre-Dupin story that historians, seeking an infinite regress in the origin of the genre, may reasonably cite. The city in "The Man of the Crowd" is London. Its definitive trait is an exploding population living at close quarters and often at cross-purposes. In the story the nameless narrator feels impelled to shadow an equally nameless man seen fleetingly on the mobbed streets of the city. The narrative resembles the skeleton of a plot lacking the flesh and blood of incident; it invites a sequel or, rather, it seems like the prolegomenon to "The Murders in the Rue Morgue." What happens is easy to summarize. The narrator—who "wore a pair of caoutchouc overshoes, and could move about in perfect silence," thus serving as the model for all future gumshoes—follows the stranger on an errant and seemingly directionless journey around London; tails him all through the night and on until "the shades of the second evening came on"; and finally concludes, though nothing has happened, that the object of his search is "the type and the genius of deep crime. He refuses to be alone. *He is the man of the crowd.*" This epiphany is the story's climax.

The narrator of "The Man of the Crowd" is a detective by nature if not by trade. He has trained himself as a critical observer and likes nothing better than to examine selected faces from the crowd. "In my then peculiar mental state," he tells us, "I could frequently read, even in that brief interval of a glance, the history of long years." Types are easy to pick out. Gamblers, for instance, are readily identifiable as such by "a certain sodden swarthiness of complexion, a filmy dimness of eye, and pallor and compression of lip," among other details. Far more rewarding to watch are the movements of a singular individual, like the story's mysterious stranger, for in him the crowd as a faceless entity has given way to a quintessential image of humanity: a conglomeration "of vast mental power, of caution, of penuriousness, of avarice, of coolness, of malice, of blood-thirstiness, of triumph, of merriment, of excessive terror, of intense—of supreme despair." It's as though the man of the crowd—the man on the street, we would say—is necessarily a criminal, at least potentially, for he has the force of the mob behind him, in all its anonymity and uniformity. When he cannot lose himself in an exultant display of public adulation for a popular tyrant, he will skulk off warily, all that energy waiting to be released. Watch him carefully; he has something to hide, and the city has provided him with countless dark corners to infect. Detection becomes, in these urban circumstances, a logical and desperate counteroffensive, the mind training itself in the ways of survival: *Trust no one! Confide in no one! Sleep with your revolver under your pillow, and don't be surprised if the phone rings at three in the morning!*

The chase in "The Man of the Crowd" begins at night, when the mob is afoot, and "The Murders in the Rue Morgue" picks up where the other left off. Dupin and his friend keep their shutters closed by day, spending their time in quiet reverie "until warned by the clock of the advent of the true Darkness. Then we sallied forth into the streets, arm in arm, continuing the topics of the day, or roaming far and wide until a late hour, seeking, amid the wild lights and shadows of the populous city, that infinity of mental excitement which quiet observation can afford." For the peripatetic detective-critic, striving to see things clearly and whole, the city as it really is comes to life "with the advent of the true Darkness." The city's nightmare version is its true one; what it looks like in the light of day is a false facade. To put it in Freudian terms, the city sublimates its instinctual desires during the day—but out they come at night, the more furious for the force with which they've been repressed. The busy boulevards and congested slums of the nineteenth century have made a new sort of crime possible: anonymous murders that take place in the dead of night, on the aptly named *rue morgue*: the street of death.

Put in these terms, the detective's mission is understood to have a moral dimension very different from that of the foppish fellow who solves the "unpleasantness" at the posh club or country estate. The literature's first master sleuths—Dupin, Sherlock Holmes, and Chesterton's Father Brown—operate in the open city, where they stand for a principle of order, reason, and truth. Each subordinates his artistic temperament to the governance of his critical intellect. Each is therefore able to give anonymity a name and make the urban darkness yield to his flashlight. Subtract him from the picture, and all hell would break loose.

> No one can have failed to notice that in these stories the hero or the investigator crosses London with something of the loneliness and liberty of a prince in a tale of elfland.
>
> G. K. CHESTERTON, "A Defence of Detective Stories"

Just as Poe introduced and Doyle perfected the formula of the sleuth as mastermind and his companion as a mix of Sancho Panza and Boswell, so with their renderings of the nineteenth-century city. Poe introduced the city setting; Doyle made his a universally recognized landmark. Where the purely imaginary Paris of Poe's detective stories lacks any specific authority of detail, Doyle's London smacks so vividly of its historic era that countless readers have made the pilgrimage to Baker Street, expecting to find there the model of Holmes's digs.

Poe's Paris has a quality of anonymity entirely in keeping with a vision of inferno. Doyle's London, in contrast, seems bathed in a glow of infinite nostalgia—its predominant trait is charm, not menace. (Doyle achieves real menace only when he yanks his hero out of London and onto the primordial Devonshire moors of *The Hound of the Baskervilles*.) Any attempt to explain the magic of Sherlock Holmes must surely rank the atmosphere of London as second in importance only to the immortality of the two leading characters. We forget the nefarious plot of "The Red-Headed League" and remember instead the hansom cabs, the crowded thoroughfares, the cobblestone streets, the gaslight, the fog. A romantic aura surrounds the place: The city here had an exotic flavor even for its first readers. *New Arabian Nights,* the title of Robert Louis Stevenson's wonderful collection of stories, would work for the Holmes tales as well. "For it is not intricacy or bafflement that causes the tales to be read and re-read with a never diminishing thrill," Howard Haycraft wrote in *Murder for Pleasure.*

> It is the "romantic reality" of their comfortable, nostalgic British heartiness. It is the small boy in all of us, sitting before an open fire, with the winter wind howling around the windows, a-wriggle with

sheer pleasure. It is the "snug peril" of fin de siècle Baker Street, with hansom cabs rumbling distantly on wet cobblestones, and Moriarty and his minions lurking in the fog. It is the warmth behind drawn curtains, the reek of strong tobacco, the patriotic "V" done in bullet-pocks on the wall, the gasogene, the spirit lamp, the dressing-gown, the violin—and the "needle." It is the inevitable bell, the summons to duty and high adventure.[1]

Rex Stout was by far the most successful of Conan Doyle's numerous imitators. The secret of Stout's great appeal was simple: He retained what we might call the deep structure of the Holmes adventures but changed all the particulars, brought them up to date, and adapted them to the sights and sounds of twentieth-century New York. The city in Stout's Nero Wolfe novels has a cosmopolitan rather than an exotic flavor, but otherwise it remains what it was for Watson and Holmes: a matter of bright boulevards rather than an assemblage of mean streets and dark alleys. Stout complicates the formula rather ingeniously, however. By making a West Thirty-fifth Street brownstone the headquarters for Nero Wolfe and Archie Goodwin, he manages a tricky balancing act. On the one hand, Wolfe is the closest thing to a pure armchair detective this side of Sherlock Holmes's older brother Mycroft, and his lair carries a suggestion of the self-contained, self-enclosed-island setting of the classic whodunit. Wolfe's evident disgust for humanity links him to the aristocratic disdain of Poe's Dupin in his shuttered Paris apartment. Curmudgeonly and reclusive, he keeps the city at arm's length at all times, as if an island retreat were available in the very confines of his house, in the very center of the metropolis. In the person of Archie Goodwin, on the other hand, Stout gives us a vigorously active man-about-town, the better to open up the closed murder—bringing to the surface the radio hum and buzz of a city of seven million souls, at a time when administrative assistants were still called secretaries, men wore hats, the subway was safe, and catching a taxi meant (as it still does) grabbing it "from under the chins of two other prospective customers."[2]

G. K. Chesterton was the great champion of the view that the detective story was the folktale of the modern metropolis. He put the case in his "A Defence of Detective Stories," composed in 1901 and still among the best things ever written on the subject. The detective story, Chesterton wrote, is "the earliest and only form of popular literature in which is expressed some sense of the poetry of modern life." As befits his theme, Chesterton waxes poetic:

> Of this realization of a great city itself as something wild and obvious the detective story is certainly the "Iliad." No one can have failed to notice that in these stories the hero or the investigator crosses London with something of the loneliness and liberty of a prince in a tale of elfland, that in the course of that incalculable journey the casual omnibus assumes the primal colours of a fairy ship. The lights of the city begin to glow like innumerable goblin eyes, since they are the guardians of some secret, however crude, which the writer knows and the reader does not. Every twist of the road is like a finger pointing to it; every fantastic skyline of chimney-pots seems wildly and derisively signalling the meaning of the mystery.[3]

The city, in short, is a version of fairyland.

Chesterton's Father Brown, roaming as he does from parish to parish in the ad hoc performance of his ecclesiastical chores, frequently leaves London for out-of-the-way places but always takes with him this sense of an enchanted landscape. In "The Honour of Israel Gow," he finds himself at the castle of Glengyle in Scotland, the sight of which prompts an explosion of similes: "It stopped one end of the glen or hollow like a blind alley; and it looked like the end of the world. Rising in steep roofs and spires of seagreen slate in the manner of the old French-Scottish châteaux, it reminded an Englishman of the sinister steeple-hats of witches in fairy tales; and the pine woods that rocked round the green turrets looked, by comparison, as black as numberless flocks of ravens." The similes make the linkages for us—between detective stories ("like a blind alley") and apocalyptic fables ("like the end of the world"), fairy tales ("of the sinister steeple-hats of witches in fairy tales"), and gothic fantasy ("as black as numberless flocks of ravens"). The landscape itself announces Chesterton's dominant tone: the "note of a dreamy, almost a sleepy devilry."

"It isn't only nice things that happen in fairyland," Father Brown warns in "The Sins of Prince Saradine," but Chesterton, in his upbeat way, minimized the dark side of the fairy tale. As he saw it, the detective story "declines to regard the present as prosaic or the common as commonplace"; what it offers are healthy enchantment and white magic. Chesterton's imagination transmutes the evil into the healthily sinister. Moreover, the form affirms the triumph of order over chaos. Chesterton characteristically casts his allegory in the form of a paradox: "It is the agent of social justice who is the original and poetic figure, while the burglars and footpads are merely placid old cosmic conservatives, happy in the immemorial respectability of apes and wolves."[4]

Chesterton's own Father Brown stories are cheerfully didactic in just this way. They are comic nightmares, fairy tales that end happily for all, affirmations of a religious universe in which sins are forgiven and bodies can rise from the dead. This seems as much a measure of Chesterton's temperament as of his Christian religiosity. Instinctively, he renders evil as something picturesque but not threatening. An aura of comedy hangs over all the crimes committed in this Edwardian elfland. The "crimes" described in *The Club of Queer Trades* (1905) are crimes in appearance only; each turns out to be a perfectly legitimate, innocuous or even beneficial, and hugely entertaining activity. The solution to the mystery is thus also an absolution from guilt. The arrangement of pansies that spells out "Death to Major Brown" on a public lawn is, for example, pretty threatening if you aren't expecting to see it, as the story's Major Brown isn't. But postulate the existence of "the Adventure and Romance Agency," which for an annual fee promises to surround a man "with startling and weird events," and not only is the mystery cleared up but no stains are left and no one needs to be punished in order for justice to take place; the explanation unmasks the apparent "villain" as one whose villainy was in jest.

That same aura of comedy surrounds the flamboyantly impish crimes committed by the master thief Flambeau, "an artist and a sportsman," who is introduced to us in "The Blue Cross" and who makes several lively return appearances in *The Innocence of Father Brown* (1911), the first and best of the Father Brown collections. "It is said he once repainted all the numbers in a street in the dead of night merely to divert one traveller into a trap," Chesterton tells us. "It is quite certain that he invented a portable pillar-box, which he put up at corners in quiet suburbs on the chance of strangers dropping postal orders into it." Flambeau, though a veteran lawbreaker, turns out to be Father Brown's sidekick in some of the subsequent stories. It's the same pattern all over again: Apparent evil is really good done up to look sinister. "The Queer Feet" details a stage in the conversion of the flamboyant thief into the law-abiding sportsman; it's the story of how Father Brown "averted a crime" and thus "perhaps, saved a soul." Flambeau is about to escape with the valuable silver he'd stolen by impersonating a waiter in a select club. Father Brown deduces the exact details of the crime "merely by listening to a few footsteps in a passage." It is the oddness of the footsteps—their abrupt changes of pace—that gives the impostor away; they're the footsteps of a "gentleman" in a waiter's attire. Once he extracts a confession from Flambeau and recovers the stolen silver, Father Brown blithely lets him go, confident that reason and goodness have triumphed again in the eternal comedy of crime. As Chesterton's surrogate, he is less interested in legal justice than in the rule of reason at the service of Christian theology; redemption, not punishment, is the desired end.

The frankly admiring Jorge Luis Borges, identifying the "precarious subjection of a demoniacal will" as Chesterton's central theme, finds its emblematic expression in these stories, "each of which undertakes to explain an inexplicable event by reason alone." A qualification is necessary, however, and Borges provides it: "the 'reason' to which Chesterton subjected his imaginings was not precisely reason but the Catholic faith or rather a collection of Hebrew imaginings that had been subjected to Plato and Aristotle."[5] Chesterton's faith in reason is really a faith in faith itself; his is the sort of criticism of life that affirms even as it delivers a rebuke. Chesterton rebukes us for our willingness to be taken in by one or another plausible heresy, and at the same time he obliges us to suspend our disbelief and credit "an element of elfin coincidence" in our lives. He affirms that a touch of the sinister is healthy and that life is not the drab prosaic repetitive affair it may seem to be to office workers who punch in at nine and out again at five every day. If sins can be forgiven and sinners redeemed, the wicked city on the plain is headed not for anarchy or destruction but for new revelations, signs, and wonders. "A tree does stand up in the landscape of a doubtful journey in the exact and elaborate shape of a note of interrogation," Chesterton insists in "The Blue Cross." "Nelson does die in the instant of victory; and a man named Williams does quite accidentally murder a man named Williamson; it sounds like a sort of infanticide. In short, there is in life an element of elfin coincidence which people reckoning on the prosaic may perpetually miss." It's precisely as an affirmation of the poetic that Chesterton prepared the enchanted landscapes that beckon Father Brown.

> This damned burg's getting to me. If I don't get away soon I'll be going blood-simple like the natives.
>
> DASHIELL HAMMETT, *Red Harvest*

In *The Great Gatsby,* we're told about "some wild wag of an oculist" who advertised his practice with a pair of "blue and gigantic" eyes behind "enormous yellow spectacles." In its grotesqueness— and its proximity to a dumping ground that the book's narrator calls "the valley of ashes"—the image of doctor T. J. Eckleburg's unseeing eyes mocks the moral blindness of Scott Fitzgerald's characters. There's a roadside billboard in Jim Thompson's *The Killer Inside Me* that performs a similar function—it makes a point not only about this extraordinary novel but about the entire hard-boiled genre, which Thompson illustrates in some ways and subverts in others. The sign in *The Killer Inside Me* is a monument to small-town boosterism. The words on the sign are meant to signal the virtues of "Central City, Texas," the obscure town with the generic name where the action takes place. But the effect of the sign—which has been put up by the local chamber of commerce— is to ridicule the town's aspirations toward growth and prosperity. The billboard is "almost unique," says one character. "I don't suppose you'll find more than forty or fifty thousand billboards like that one in the United States." This is what the billboard says:

You Are Now Nearing
CENTRAL CITY, TEX.
"Where the hand clasp's a little stronger."
Pop. (1932) 4,800   Pop. (1952) 48,000
WATCH US GROW!!

The population of Central City has multiplied tenfold in the two decades chronicled, the billboard reminds us. It is good to be reminded. There is little evidence in the narrative itself of any collective wish on the part of humanity to survive. *The Killer Inside Me* situates us in the vicious and paranoid mind of the book's narrator and protagonist, a deputy sheriff named Lou Ford. Ford is responsible for the corpses that pile up in *The Killer Inside Me.* There are six of them, leaving out the casualties of the cataclysm on the novel's last page. It is no exaggeration to say that a violent death is in store for every character who comes into any kind of contact with Lou Ford—who is, please remember, a duly appointed, generally respected officer of the law in that burgeoning Texas city. No wonder Lou Ford says he "grin[s] in spite of myself" when he drives past the "watch it grow" billboard. "That's quite a sign, all right," he says.

That billboard welcomes us to the paradigmatic city of modern crime fiction. The signs all say it is a booming, growing, confident place, but the signs can't be seen at night, in the shadows, where we live. The city in the hard-boiled tradition of Dashiell Hammett and Raymond Chandler isn't quite the nihilist's nightmare of Thompson's novel, but it isn't a pretty place. (An exception in the Hammett oeuvre is *The Thin Man,* that vehicle for the elegant murder mysteries of William Powell and Myrna Loy, in which New York City means black-tie urbanity, charm, and "liquor to cut the phlegm" on hung over mornings.) For all the effort at exact description that Hammett and Chandler put into their work, their cities tend to be generalized, almost allegorical landscapes. Hammett's "Personville" (pronounced "Poisonville," as if in an exaggerated Brooklyn accent) is the perfect name for the gangster burg of *Red Harvest,* "an ugly city of forty thousand people, set in an ugly notch between two ugly mountains that has been all dirtied up by mining." This isn't a case of gratuitous wordplay, as the novel's opening paragraph makes plain:

> I first heard Personville called Poisonville by a red-haired mucker named Hickey Dewey in the Big Ship in Butte. He also called his shirt a shoit. I didn't think anything of what he had done to the city's name. Later I heard men who could manage their r's give it the same pronunciation. I still didn't see anything in it but the meaningless sort of humor that used to make richardsnary the thieves' word for dictionary. A few years later I went to Personville and learned better.

If "person" equals "poison," man is unredeemable. The bloodbath designated by the book's title is, we're meant to see, inevitable, the result of the seemingly pointless criminal violence that reflects, on a human scale, the violent irrationality of the cosmos.

Hammett's cities are the breeding grounds of political corruption and the killing grounds of gang warfare, and his heroes are no angels—they go about their business for complicated reasons, on the list of which a sense of abstract justice ranks fairly low; it's likely that neither Sam Spade in *The Maltese Falcon* nor Ned Beaumont in *The Glass Key* could tell you just what he expects to prove, and for what purpose, though the former might mention money while the latter would speak of his friendship with the falsely accused Paul Madvig. Spade and Beaumont are men of the city, which means they are tough enough to take chances and survive. It also means that they turn a skeptical gaze on the world—and on themselves. They do not fancy themselves to be the instruments of social justice, and if they did, they would never admit it.

In both *The Maltese Falcon* and *The Glass Key*, the tale's ending is happy only in the limited sense that the detective has survived and that he has accomplished his mission. And in both books, the nature of that mission is itself shrouded in ambiguity. Only in retrospect is it clear, for example, that Sam Spade's mission is to avenge his late partner's death by capturing his murderer. It had seemed all along that Spade was in cahoots with the criminals, at least with some of them. There is something of the con man about him, and this is part of his appeal. In any event, the ending of *The Maltese Falcon* is scarcely happy in any conventional sense—not if a property of comedy is that it ends with a marriage where a tragedy ends with a death. For that affirmative brand of comedy, *The Maltese Falcon* substitutes a quality of humor that is both black and bleak, never more malevolent than when Spade rejects Brigid O'Shaughnessy and turns her over to the police in a gesture as stylized and flamboyant in its way as its exact opposite, the king of England's rejection of his throne in favor of the woman he loved.

It's impossible to imagine *The Maltese Falcon* taking place anywhere but a modern coastal city—with a large terminal that has public lockers that may be rented for the hour or the day, with a daily newspaper that announces expected times of arrival for incoming ships, and with a harbor where those ships may dock. Hammett presents the San Francisco of *The Maltese Falcon* in a studiously neutral way. By contrast, Raymond Chandler cannot paint an urban picture without commenting on it. His Los Angeles resembles Chesterton's fairyland minus the enchantment, into which the detective as knight-errant must nonetheless sally forth, though he knows that his native chivalry (which he keeps carefully concealed beneath his hard-boiled demeanor) is as hopeless as it is incongruous. The gambling casinos and clubs that Philip Marlowe must enter are like the bowers of bliss (all ersatz glitter, no substance) that test the epic hero embarked on a quest romance. The city as a whole resembles nothing so much as the Idle Valley country club in *The High Window,* a place of decadence and decay faintly camouflaged in kitsch decor. Chandler sums it up with a pair of his patented similes: "The lobby looked like a high-budget musical. A lot of light and glitter, a lot of scenery, a lot of clothes, a lot of sound, an all-star cast, and a plot with all the originality and drive of a split fingernail."

Setting supplied motive in the classic whodunit; setting, in Hammett and Chandler, supplies the backdrop for corpses dispatched casually, often by error or miscalculation, sometimes for the sake of political expediency, more often because of greed. There is, when we "get" the plot of *The Big Sleep,* a quality of randomness that remains; just who killed whom, and why? And couldn't it have happened some other way? Not so much the murders themselves but their apparent randomness—the lack of a motive equal to the enormity of the deed—signifies or confirms a permanent rupture in the moral order.

In *The Maltese Falcon,* Hammett's Sam Spade responds to his environment with something resembling an existential shrug. Spade, whom the Fat Man rightly calls "unpredictable," means to keep in step with an unpredictable universe by constantly breaking his stride. So ambiguous is his behavior that his moral intentions seem murky even after he announces them at the end of *The Maltese Falcon.* Chandler, by far the more romantic of the two writers, transforms Spade into Philip Marlowe, "the shop-soiled Galahad" whose knightly mission is doomed to fail though he arrives at the solution of a murder. The swift tempo of Chandler's prose—Marlowe employs wisecracks as both a weapon and a shield—is eminently suited to a setting that seems to be in constant motion, as Los Angeles keeps dissolving and rematerializing in Philip Marlowe's windshield. And the city's urban sprawl is a fit vehicle for a moral vision as severe and as earnest as a turn-of-the-century muckraker's. Chandler's novels, wrote Ross Macdonald, "could almost be described as novels of sensibility. Their constant theme is big-city loneliness, and the wry pain of a sensitive man coping with the roughest elements of a corrupt society."[6]

Chandler's Los Angeles runs to extremes of poverty and wealth.

From the exclusive country club to the fleabag hotel, from the ersatz rare book shop to the deserted office building, from the swanky Sternwood mansion with its butlers and chauffeurs to the ugly oil sump from which the Sternwood money came—all in a day's work—is an easy drive in Marlowe's Chrysler. The didactic point is plain: These places are in moral as well as geographical proximity. Crime crosses class lines, crosses them back and forth, if "organized crime is just the dirty side of the sharp dollar," as Marlowe puts it in *The Long Goodbye.* (Asked what the clean side was, he says, "I never saw it.") In a city dominated by the motorcar, as Marlowe's Los Angeles is, the concept of the closed murder is incongruous. Crime in these precincts is the accepted norm, not the exceptional circumstance, and the multiple effects of a crime spread with the speed of a getaway car from one point of the city to the next.

Yet Marlowe refuses to leave the city, refuses to renounce a habitat that would appear to repel him. He explains why in *The Long Goodbye,* at that point in the action when the detective's weariness forces a moment of crisis. Part of him wants to follow through on his investigations, though he knows all too well that more corpses are likely in the near future—that, before he can solve a murder, another will happen. "The other part of me wanted to get out and stay out," Marlowe says, "but this was the part I never listened to. Because if I ever had I would have stayed in the town where I was born and worked in the hardware store and married the boss's daughter and had five kids and read them the funny paper on Sunday morning and smacked their heads when they got out of line and squabbled with the wife about how much spending money they were to get and what programs they could have on the radio or TV set. I might even have got rich—small-town rich, an eight-room house, two cars in the garage, chicken every Sunday and the *Reader's Digest* on the living room table, the wife with a cast-iron permanent and me with a brain like a sack of Portland cement. You take it, friend. I'll take the big sordid dirty crooked city." Marlowe's urban existence is unsponsored (he is rarely ruled by his client's wishes), free, without the usual comforts of companionship or the responsibilities of a family, led according to a private code of honor, with a hardened indifference to material pleasure. He remains defiantly an outsider—that's the specific form his sense of rebellion takes. It's as though *realism*—a term Chandler used insistently, if not quite accurately, to extol the hard-boiled novel over the classic tale—were a big city affair; as though the scenario for small-town success so pitilessly evoked in *The Long Goodbye* could be only hollow artifice; as though, in order to have an experience of the real, one must submit oneself to the life of lawless cities.

> The bitch city is something different on Saturday night, sophisticated in black, scented and powdered, but somehow not as unassailable, shiveringly beautiful in a dazzle of blinking lights. Reds and oranges, electric blues and vibrant greens assault the eye incessantly, and the resultant turn-on is as sweet as a quick sharp fix in a penthouse pad, a liquid cool that conjures dreams of towering glass spires and enameled minarets. There is excitement in this city on Saturday night, but it is tempered by romantic expectancy. She is not a bitch, this city. Not on Saturday night.
>
> ED MCBAIN, *Fuzz*

The city remains the omnipresent scene of the crime in Ed Mc-Bain's police procedurals, but McBain crucially revises the vision of chaos—a moral chaos that remains after the case is wrapped up—that we get in Hammett and Chandler. In McBain's 87th Precinct series, now more than three dozen novels strong, the sordid and brutal aspects of murder are emphasized as they are in hard-boiled fiction—with, if anything, a surer sense of the varieties of criminal experience. But McBain's conglomerate hero is a platoon of policemen, the cops of the 87th Precinct, and the effect is to affirm what Hammett and Chandler denied: that, as McBain once told an interviewer, "a society of laws can work." While he lodges his faith in the police rather than in Christian theology, McBain has in common with Chesterton not only an optimism at odds with the hard-boiled tradition but a strong sense of the poetry of the metropolis. McBain's plots are often quite symmetrical: serial murders, with various recurring features. They deserve to be called urban nightmares not because they are especially gruesome (though some are) but because they exhibit the macabre logic of dreams.

To safeguard his poetic license, McBain calls his city Isola, and the name itself suggests the sense of isolation within a thronged metropolis that Poe saw as the necessary condition for "deep crime." By whatever name you call it, however, the city is recognizably New York, and the narrator speaks with the melancholic tone of a man who has monitored a lifelong lover's quarrel with the place. "It was some city, this city," we're told in *Long Time No See* prior to a visit to the ghetto. "If you're a boy you're anybody's to beat up on, anybody's to rob, anybody's to cut or burn or snuff. If you're a girl, you're anybody's to hurt, anybody's to fuck, anybody's to do with what they want. This is the city. You need insurance here."

Isola offers a field day for thieves and dope peddlers, pornographers and pimps, as well as assorted psychopaths. The repeat rapist in *Lightning* has a fetish for teenage female track stars; the rooftop sniper in *Ten Plus One* derives his logic from a theater playbill for a high school production that took place in the distant past; the killer in *Long Time No See* favors blind victims exclusively. Hanging over all such cases is "the possibility that the murders were motiveless" and that the detective novel's "good old days" of cause and effect are over for good. As McBain puts it in *Long Time No See*:

> In the good old days you wrapped a thing up in three, four hours sometimes—between lunch and cocktails, so to speak. And usually it wasn't the butler who did it, nor even the foul fiend Flibbertigibbet, but instead your own brother or your brother's wife or your Uncle Tim from Nome, Alaska. Nowadays it was different. One-third of all the homicides committed in this city involved a victim and a murderer who didn't even *know* each other when the crime was committed. Perfect strangers, total and utter, locked in the ultimate intimate obscenity for the mere seconds it took to squeeze a trigger or plunge a blade.

Yet McBain's city is not the dismal wasteland that a fatigued Marlowe can never redeem. For all the crime within its precincts, for all the randomness of behavior within the city limits, Isola is never quite lawless—the forces of law and order start out at a disadvantage but have formidable resources at their disposal, and they do win out in the end. McBain's attitude toward his city differs drastically from Marlowe's wisecracking skepticism. Scene-setting paragraphs throughout McBain's novels resemble odes to the modern metropolis—odes of joy and melancholy and something like reverence.

McBain has always operated on the assumption that "the only valid people to deal with crime are policemen: you don't have to suspend your disbelief."[7] *Long Time No See* ridicules alike the classic whodunit in the manner of Agatha Christie ("written by ladies who lived in Sussex. Thrillers. About as thrilling as Aunt Lucy's tattered nightcap") and the psychoanalytic detective novel in the manner of Ross Macdonald (and other "California mystery writers who seemed to believe that murder was something brewed in a pot for half a century, coming to a boil only when a private detective needed a job. The last time Carella had met a private detective investigating a homicide was never.") The simulation of police procedure in the 87th Precinct novels is what authenticates them, what makes readers agree to suspend their disbelief. But it is more than that. It is also a statement of belief, the author's affirmation of an American democratic ideal, which links justice with truth and progress. The police here are uncorrupted, good citizens, married with children. Their routine procedures—which include ballistics tests and microscopic examinations—demonstrate that they have science on their side. Their heroism is the quiet, practical, everyday kind: Call it line-of-duty heroism.

Against the perversity of the city in the raw stands this squad that resembles a family. The family comes replete with black sheep, dutiful sons and, of late, gutsy daughters, like Eileen Burke in *Ice,* who foils the "Dirty Panties Bandit," so called because he robs "hapless laundromat ladies" of their money and jewelry and has them remove their panties into the bargain. The four officers in charge of the case in *Ice*—the "Dirty Panties Bandit" being but a mere diversion on the way—are Carella, Meyer, Kling, and Brown, whose ethnic identities correspond to the sandwiches they eat for lunch: sausage and peppers on a roll, hot pastrami on rye, tuna on white, and ham on toasted whole wheat, respectively. Here, then, is a cross-section of ethnic New York at its most resilient, "beyond the melting pot" New York, fictive proof that nothing brings out the soul in New Yorkers better than a sudden crisis.

At his best, McBain invests his crimes with an ingenuity we do not expect in the police procedural—and indeed it is McBain's special achievement to have taken this subgenre and advanced it so far from the days when pipe-smoking Scotland Yard inspectors plodded their way to the truth by cracking alibis and tracing fingerprints. The solution of *Long Time No See,* a brilliant example, depends on the proper interpretation of a Vietnam veteran's nightmare—which requires analyzing it twice over, since the dream is at once a symbolic translation of a mutinous incident in combat years ago and an anticipation of something happening in the "now" of Isola, years later.

Perhaps nowhere does McBain trace the logic of an urban nightmare with surer strokes than in *Ice*. The title works overtime, multiplying its meanings until the word's ramifications have branched out to touch every sector of the city, from its theater district to its major university and from its high-rent high-rises to its burnt-out tenements. As often in a McBain novel, the cops are up against a serial murderer; they have to break the hidden code that links apparently unrelated homicides. A dancer in a hit musical, a cocaine-pushing punk, and a middle-aged diamond dealer have all been "iced" by bullets fired directly at their faces. The action takes place, of course, in the dead of winter; the city's windows are "rimed with ice," and the rhymes continue. Before she herself is "iced," one character stanches a wound with an ice pack. Another wittily hides his "ice," or ill-gotten jewelry, in a tray of ice cubes. Some of the theater performers are "doing ice," a particularly profitable form of ticket scalping. ("A hot show *always* generates ice," a producer explains.) With the proceeds, they indulge an appetite for "snow," also known as "sleigh ride," "flake," "star dust" and cocaine. In the precinct of McBain's imagination, winter kills. Where there's ice, there's likely to be gunfire as well.

Yet Isola's population shows no signs of falling off. It remains an inexhaustible source of stories and of characters as uniquely of their time and place as the surly man in the subway token booth in *Ten Plus One*. His name, he says, is "Stan Quentin," but he doesn't quite grasp the jokes made at his expense: "What do you mean, Alcatraz? How's that named after me?" Better yet, in the same book, is David Arthur Cohen, "a sad little man who made his living being funny." Cohen writes gags for cartoonists to put in pictorial form—and treats his trade with a professionalism that suggests the way a lyricist treats a song. An example of his work, no caption needed: "A barroom. Two men are having a violent fist fight. In the background are the usual men standing at the bar. They are all watching a fight on the television set." "Either you get them or you don't," Cohen mutters. Officers Carella and Meyer are intrigued. "For a moment the three men had forgotten why they were in that office. They were in that office to discuss six murders, but for the moment Cohen was a professional explaining his craft, and Meyer and Carella were two quite different professionals who were fascinated by the details of another man's work." *Professional* is the operative word here. The city is no place for amateurs.

12

———◆———

The Hard-boiled Romance

*T*he realist in murder writes of a world in which gangsters
can rule nations and almost rule cities, in which hotels and
apartment houses and celebrated restaurants are owned by men
who made their money out of brothels, in which a screen star can
be the finger man for a mob, and the nice man down the hall is a
boss of the numbers racket; a world where a judge with a cellar
full of bootleg liquor can send a man to jail for having a pint in
his pocket, where the mayor of your town may have condoned
murder as an instrument of money-making, where no man can
walk down a dark street in safety because law and order are
things we talk about but refrain from practicing; a world where
you may witness a hold-up in broad daylight and see who did it,
but you will fade quickly back into the crowd rather than tell
anyone, because the hold-up men may have friends with long
guns, or the police may not like your testimony, and in any case
the shyster for the defence will be allowed to abuse and vilify you
in open court, before a jury of selected morons, without any but
the most perfunctory interference from a political judge.

—RAYMOND CHANDLER, "The Simple Art of Murder"

A pure product of the American century, the hard-boiled detective
novel was born against a backdrop of prohibition and gangster-
ism—and came of age around the time the bubble of American

bliss burst and the nation headed into its age of jitters. From the modern metropolis the new genre derived its sense of gutter glamour as well as its distinctive idiom: hard-edged, frank, streetwise, sarcastic. Jazz is its background music, sharp dialogue its stock-in-trade. As a form of fiction, the hard-boiled novel supplied marvelous raw material for Hollywood dream-makers. It was "the stuff dreams are made of," as Humphrey Bogart playing Sam Spade says of the spurious statuette—a line that doesn't appear in the book—at the end of John Huston's 1941 movie of *The Maltese Falcon.*

In forties *films noirs* the hard-boiled novel found its perfect pictorial complement: a chiaroscuro world of dark angles and elongated shadows, rained-on streets on which a solitary walker pauses to light his cigarette and a flickering neon sign punctuates the night. A shot rings out: there is the sound of footsteps hurrying down stairs, and then all is silence again: in the fleabag hotel room where the dead man lies, a gauze curtain rustles lazily in its half-open window. Silence; and then a scream. Hollywood provided the shadows and the stars; Dashiell Hammett and Raymond Chandler contributed the texts and the inspiration.

Hard-boiled fiction didn't, at first, declare itself to be literature. On the contrary, it found its seeding ground in pulp magazines— so called because they were printed on wood pulp. The magazines had names like *Black Mask* and *Spicy Detective* and paid writers at the going rate of a penny a word.[1] Chandler was proud of these lowly origins, as if they confirmed the democratic, street-level authenticity of the genre at its best. "Pulp paper never dreamed of posterity and most of it must be a dirty brown color by now," he wrote in a 1950 introduction to his short stories. "And it takes a very open mind indeed to look beyond the unnecessarily gaudy covers, trashy titles, and the barely acceptable advertisements and recognize the authentic power of a kind of writing that even at its most mannered and artificial made most of the fiction of the time taste like a cup of lukewarm consommé at a spinsterish tearoom."[2] The simile that ends that sentence is entirely characteristic. Chandler turned wisecracks into similes and then made similes his chief rhetorical stratagem, which he employed to devastating effect: "like a cup of lukewarm consommé at a spinsterish tearoom."

Among hard-boiled novelists, Chandler is the paradigmatic figure—his influence exceeds even that of Dashiell Hammett, his own acknowledged master. Certainly Chandler polemicized effectively for the hard-boiled cause; his essay "The Simple Art of Murder" is a brilliant, pungent manifesto for his own novels and for Hammett's. Educated in England, Chandler remained a lifelong Anglophile and chose to live in London late in life, enjoying his greatest critical success there. Yet his contribution to modern literature followed precisely from his rejection of the English "crossword puzzle" type of detective story and his advocacy of an American alternative. In Ross Macdonald's words, Chandler's English upbringing and education "put a special edge on his passion for our new language, and a special edge on his feelings against privilege. Socially mobile and essentially classless (he went to college but has a working-class bias), Marlowe liberated his author's imagination into an overheard democratic prose."[3]

For Chandler, the classic whodunit was too stuffy, too genteel, and too suffused with nostalgia for a privileged society. "What I don't seem to cotton to is the affectation of gentility which does not belong to the job and which is in effect a subconscious expression of snobbery, the kind of thing that reached its high-water mark in Dorothy Sayers," Chandler wrote. "Perhaps the trouble is that I'm an English Public School man myself and know these birds inside out. And the only kind of Public School man who could make a real detective would be the Public School man in revolt, like George Orwell."[4] Chandler's novels begin in this feeling of revolt. The defiantly American genre he championed retained the essential detective-story elements but cut against their grain—it defined itself in reaction against the elegance and aestheticism of the older tradition. The urban world had changed its look since the gaslight days of Victorian London—so the detective story had to change its look and tone as well. It had to produce a verbal texture more in keeping with the skyscraper heights and subway depths of the twentieth-century city. Different props would be required, brandy rather than lukewarm consommé, in a gin joint rather than a spinsterish tearoom. But it wasn't only a matter of different props. The "realist in murder," in Chandler's misleading phrase, needed a different method and manner and mood, a change in idiom to go with the change of scene. The stuff of Sherlock Holmes would henceforth be filtered to us through the accents and attitude of Ernest Hemingway. The detective himself would undergo a complete transformation. He could scarcely be a fop in populist America; he needed to be a working stiff, capable of using his fists or his gun, who doesn't so much outsmart his opponents as outlast them. Yet he would remain an idealized and romantic figure. Scratch him, and he would bleed for the millions.

Thus was born a new hero. The hard-drinking, down-at-the-heels shamus in Chandler's hard-boiled scenario is your basic cynic as frustrated romantic—or "ferocious romantic," in Chandler's self-description.[5] He is somewhat quixotic in his mission, but his shrewdness and his caustic tongue keep him from looking ridiculous as he tilts at windmills. He doesn't need a Sancho Panza side-kick to tell his tale and stand as an intermediary between him and us, for he is neither a genius nor an inspired lunatic. He was once, no doubt, more respectable than he is now. He may have been an assistant D.A. before events conspired to sour him on the criminal justice system. Perhaps he was fired for insubordination, which was the experience of Philip Marlowe, the detective and narrator of Chandler's novels. Or perhaps, like Jacob Asch in Arthur Lyons's *Hard Trade* (1981), he was an investigative reporter who started his private-eye shop after he went to jail for refusing to reveal a source. The hard-boiled hero has his stubborn integrity, then, but he's also an inveterate snoop and not a forgiving man. To him, human society is criminally contaminated beyond the possibility of correction, though neither that nor the lack of pecuniary enticements deters him from his quest. His exploits require us to suspend our disbelief, which we willingly, gratefully do. He is, after all, Emersonian in his self-reliance: the last just and incorruptible man, with an almost perverse sense of honor.

Draw up a one-size-fits-all example, a kind of logarithm of the hard-boiled novel, and the one irreducible element is the character of the sleuth. We meet him right away, on the opening page. In general he is in the act of visiting a prospective client (as Marlowe does in *The Big Sleep*) or waiting for one to call on him (Sam Spade's situation in Hammett's *The Maltese Falcon*). Two types of client seem to recur with the greatest frequency. One is Sex, the other Money. On one side is the possible love interest: the damsel in distress, who often turns out to be a femme fatale, looking for a man to "play the sap" for her, as Spade puts it. On the other side is the wealthy and sometimes imperious character of either sex, generally older than our hero and often as eccentric as the sleuths in the other main branch of the literature. In Chandler's *The Big Sleep*, the client is a dissipated retired general who whiles away his days in a hothouse; in James Crumley's *Dancing Bear*, (1985) it's an old lady in a wheelchair who smokes joints for relaxation. The eccentricity in both cases is a sign of dissipation, but it is also a badge of wealth. And *chercher l'argent* and *chercher la femme* are the two principles of the sleuth's *modus operandi*. It's as though, as an article of faith, Money and Sex in the world of mean streets are, both of them, always and ever dirty, and all the more so when they coincide in one person. The hard-boiled sleuth will be tested by one or both of these temptations—tested in the sense that the medieval romance as a genre called for a test, a quest, and an adventure.

With a Holmes or a Nero Wolfe, we always think it's just a matter of time before the apparently impossible problem yields its secret to his superior intelligence. But for the hard-boiled sleuth, especially the Marlowe model, the course of true detection never does run smooth. Whether by accident or by somebody's nefarious design, our hero goes off to perform the relatively routine task he was hired for—tailing somebody, let's say—but finds himself on a wild-goose chase involving petty blackmail schemes, or a jewel swindle, or a mysteriously missing mistress. He happens upon a dead body or two, gets coshed or beaten unconscious, is drugged, has a tiff with the cops, employs what ruses he deems necessary to trick the truth out of people. He can't be a slouch at the interpretation of clues; just as Sam Spade understands the meaning of the clipped newspaper in the hotel room's waste paper basket, so any self-respecting sleuth today knows how to take advantage of a telephone's "memory," which tells him who spoke to the murder victim just before he was killed.[6] His is a technical rather than a conceptual intelligence. It is self-consciously, defiantly American in its pragmatism, its populism, and its disdain of airy pretension.

Merely to survive, let alone prevail, the hard-boiled hero must be relentless, seemingly in constant motion, able to get by on little sleep and to cover vast amounts of ground, and masochistic enough to walk straight into the room where assorted torturers and hired guns prepare to administer the mandatory beating the sleuth must endure before he can get to the bottom of the case. The beating scarcely slows our man down; he doesn't know how to stop. No desk work for him; from one chapter to the next, he travels from the slums to the suburbs and then to the gold coast, to executive suites and sleazy lawyers' offices, with side-trips to fancy art deco shops and singles' bars. The smell of cheap hooch from the previous chapter is still in the air when we find ourselves in a manor with even "a special brand of sunshine, very quiet, put up in noiseproof containers just for the upper classes.''[7] Perhaps, if the author sees things at a particularly psychological slant, the trail will lead to somebody's long-since abandoned home town. More often, the minotaur at the heart of the maze will turn out to occupy city hall or the police commissioner's desk: confirmation that the authority of the law can be bought and sold, that justice and money are related in curious, sometimes casual ways. We suspected it all along—ever since our sleuth laid eyes on his client.

By temperament and necessity, the hard-boiled hero is—as he keeps reminding us—the stranger, the outsider, the unconnected man. He is almost always unmarried ("because I don't like policemen's wives," says Marlowe in *The Big Sleep*) or divorced (because his wife "wanted a settled life, and a husband she could count on to be there," says Lew Archer in Ross Macdonald's *The Goodbye Look* [1969]). Marlowe elaborates the theme in *The Long Goodbye* (1954). He declares himself to be "a lone wolf, unmarried, getting middle-aged, and not rich. I've been in jail more than once, and I don't do divorce business. I like liquor and women and chess and a few other things. The cops don't like me too well, but I know a couple I get along with. I'm a native son, born in Santa Rosa, both parents dead, no brothers or sisters, and when I get knocked off in a dark alley sometime, if it happens, as it could to anyone in my business, and to plenty of people in any business or no business at all these days, nobody will feel that the bottom has dropped out of his or her life."

In his aloof self-reliance, the hard-boiled sleuth in the gray fedora and double-breasted blue serge suit resembles the lone, nononsense lawman—as played by Gary Cooper or James Stewart—outnumbered by desperadoes in the frontier town. He is proof that violence is needed to contain violence, that the individual is preeminent over the corrupt multitude, that the one just man will prevail. Probably the most fundamental truth about him is that he is solitary and self-sufficient and "tests very high on insubordination," as Marlowe says. He knows that insubordination becomes an admirable trait in an age when the torturer's first line of defense is that he was merely obeying orders. He is too bullheaded to be a team player and too wise to trust a politician—or just about anyone else. His alliances are temporary and grounded in mutual suspicion; he can count on no one, least of all the client who's footing the bill or the policeman at his own door. If he nevertheless sticks his neck out for people whose credibility he has reason to doubt—and will keep a client's confidence at the risk of antagonizing the police— that's bacause of the strict code of his trade. He sets store by his loyalty—to friends, to clients—and doesn't find that virtue incompatible with his vaunted flair for insubordination. In any case he seems to relish being fired; he invariably replies by saying, as Lew Archer does in Ross Macdonald's *The Zebra-Striped Hearse* (1962): "You can't pull me off the case—I guess you know that. It's my case and I'll finish it on my own time if I have to." With his pluck and determination, he will always see a case through to its finish. He is committed to the truth—to plucking out the heart of the mystery. But he doesn't expect a redemptive denouement; he doesn't expect his solution to confer general absolution. Maybe a character under suspicion will be vindicated, maybe not. In the meanwhile, the Sam Spades of the world can afford to take no chances. As Spade's lawyer puts it in *The Maltese Falcon,* "You don't cash many checks for strangers, do you, Sammy?"

The death of Miles Archer, Spade's partner, at the beginning of *The Maltese Falcon* establishes a precondition of the whole hardboiled genre. The sleuth's partner—his friend, his companion, his (potential) Watson—is dead from the start in this friendless universe. It is true that Spade will, by the end of the book, invoke the memory of his partner. "When a man's partner is killed he's supposed to do something about it," Spade says to Brigid O'Shaughnessy, the guilty party, who is also as it were Spade's partner in romance. But except for this belated nod in Miles Archer's direction, the man is conveniently and completely forgotten—though who killed Miles Archer is the one formal puzzle in the book. (In a classic whodunit, we'd be constantly occupied with the problem.) Notice that after Archer's death Spade wastes no time in having his partner's name removed from the office's door and windows. (John Huston makes a point of showing this in the movie.) Spade also has Archer's desk removed—not something you'd do if you contemplated replacing your fallen partner. And that's just it: Spade means to go it alone as he was fated to do from the start. Miles Archer's importance in *The Maltese Falcon* is to seal that sense of definitive aloneness. It was witty of Ross Macdonald to name his sleuth—Lew Archer—after Spade's forgotten partner, whose most important function was to disappear. Very simply, the corpse of Miles Archer is the hard-boiled romance's corpse on page one; it is necessary that he be eliminated, with as little ceremony as possible, for Sam Spade to become the hero of his universe.

———◆———

To see the hard-boiled novel as a reflection of prohibition era jitters by no means explains everything, but it's a start. The violent excesses of prohibition—and the deprivations and desperation of the era that followed its repeal—made elegant amateurs like Lord Peter Wimsey seem obsolete. The real gang war on the streets outside mocked the reader's interest in the fancy-dress murder between hard covers. The word *prohibition* itself offered an object lesson in the treacheries of language—and in the wisecracking irony the hard-boiled sleuth adopts in self-defense—for *prohibition* seemed to signify its opposite, a time of licensed lawlessness. A public display of bluestocking morality, it made violations of that morality look sexy. The gangster was one kind of hero produced in this climate: the James Cagney or Edward G. Robinson character who talks dirty, treats his women badly, and dies a beautiful death. But hard-boiled fiction depicted a subtler form of moral chaos than did the gangster movie. The ambiguous person of the detective is interposed between the criminal and the police, those old antagonists, and suddenly there appears to be a detached, independent point of view with which we can identify ourselves—beyond cop and robber, beyond good and evil. Not the loser but the outsider. Not the winner but the stranger. The exception, the loner.

Crime in the hard-boiled novel is not an extraordinary circumstance but something like a banal evil. Behind every Agatha Christie puzzle lies a puzzlemaker's universe, where every piece of the puzzle has its place. Behind Raymond Chandler's novels—whose plots are so difficult to follow—there is chaos. You begin not with a case of order, Edenic or otherwise, that's about to be violated. Rather you begin with systems running amok, patterns of confusion. You begin with organized criminality, a society in which disrespect for the law is general. The novel that grows out of such circumstances will necessarily critique rather than affirm the prevailing social order.

Prohibition was the law of the land from the time the Senate failed to ratify Woodrow Wilson's peace until the first 100 days of Franklin Roosevelt's first administration—a period encompassing the "lost generation," the "jazz age," the stock market crash, and the first three years of the Great Depression. During this period—the period of *Black Mask* and all of Dashiell Hammett's novels—crime inevitably took on a more ambiguous and complicated character. Was it still a crime if everyone did it? It was easy to break the law—all you had to do was have a drink. But the implications were more serious than a drink. That inch of Scotch at the speakeasy was the last link on a chain of criminal actions. By drinking you had become an accessory after the fact, dependent on people who were willing to break the law in violent and dramatic ways, and you couldn't condemn them unequivocally without risk of hypocrisy. It was a time, wrote Chandler indignantly, in which "a judge with a cellar full of bootleg liquor can send a man to jail for having a pint in his pocket."[8]

During prohibition, criminals began to organize themselves in the manner of industrial corporations—a process depicted and romanticized in *The Godfather*. The process had the effect of either endowing the criminals with a spurious legitimacy or seeming to throw suspicion on the corporations. Fortunes were made and quickly laundered. Crime was simply business by other means—or could be so portrayed. Keep this picture of depression-era America in mind, and Chandler's animus toward big money and big power becomes entirely understandable. He is not at his most charming when he mounts the soapbox, but a kind of moral anger—of the old-fashioned "avarice is the root of evil" school—is a key ingredient in his best novels. By any standard, the passion and conviction of the anti-money tirades in *The Long Goodbye* are unusual. Bernie Ohls, Chandler's concession to the supposition that good cops do exist, states the theme:

> There ain't no clean way to make a hundred million bucks. . . .
> Maybe the head man thinks his hands are clean but somewhere
> along the line guys got pushed to the wall, nice little businesses got
> the ground cut out from under them and had to sell out for nickels,
> decent people lost their jobs, stocks got rigged on the market,
> proxies got bought up like a pennyweight of old gold, and the five
> percenters and big law firms got paid hundred-grand fees for beating
> some law the people wanted but the rich guys didn't, on account of
> it cut into their profits. Big money is big power and big power gets
> used wrong. It's the system. Maybe it's the best we can get, but it
> still ain't any Ivory Soap deal.

"We're a big rough rich wild people and crime is the price we pay for it, and organized crime is the price we pay for organization," Marlowe says a little further along. "Organized crime is just the dirty side of the sharp dollar." The most anomalous thing about Marlowe is that he is one of the few characters in the universe of his novels—all seven of them—who is motivated by something other than greed.

The contract between the reader and writer of a Chandler novel calls for a shared view of our social world as universally corrupt. To fulfill our expectations, the plot must leave no sector of society untouched, untainted by a criminal environment whose circumference keeps widening and whose center lies at the heart of the city's intricate maze. No murder occurs in isolation. Each sets off a chain reaction of subsequent crimes and cover-ups, conspiracies, and corpses. Everyone is implicated; no one is safe. Which is also why Marlowe tends to stumble on more than one crime that's seemingly irrelevant to the case at hand. These may be false scents—and how *The Big Sleep* reeks of them—but they double as true indicators of how much we all have to hide, how incriminating our associations would appear if someone took a magnifying glass to our lives.

Chandler once wrote that "the fictional detective is a catalyst not a Casanova," and this is certainly true of Marlowe, who so resolutely resists the advances of the amorous Sternwood sisters in *The Big Sleep*. Between fending off femmes fatales, Marlowe favors the method of the Continental Op, Hammett's detective in *Red Harvest* (1929), who says he likes "to stir things up." Marlowe acts upon the rest of the cast as a catalyst, himself unchanged in the various violent transactions that ensue. "The whole point," Chandler wrote in a letter, "is that the detective exists complete and entire and unchanged by anything that happens, that he is, as detective, outside the story and above it, and always will be. That is why he never gets the girl, never marries, never really has any private life, except insofar as he must eat and sleep and have a place to keep his clothes."[9] In Murray Kempton's words, Hammett's Continental Op is "just a shady fellow who set Thesis to combat Antithesis and then collected his fee by producing Synthesis from the wreckage."[10] Marlowe's method, similarly, is to make things happen; his presence alone suffices to bring the real Los Angeles up to the surface, just as the police's barge crew yanks the big Buick with the chauffeur's corpse in it up from the depths off the Lido fish pier.

A word is in order about the differences between *The Big Sleep*, the novel (1939), and *The Big Sleep*, the movie (1946). The latter departs radically from the former—in part because Chandler's plotting was so loose (it's the one area in which his writing is clearly inferior to both Hammett's and Macdonald's). It had become apparent to director Howard Hawks and his scriptwriters (among them William Faulkner) that the chauffeur's death remains an unexplained mystery in the book. Hawks wired Chandler to ask who killed Owen Taylor. Chandler cabled back that he didn't know. You could argue that it doesn't much matter, since the essential question in Chandler country is whodun*what*—and besides, there's an element of poetic justice in the idea of an extra corpse, a crime that doesn't add up. A pragmatic excuse for the plot confusion is that Chandler cannibalized his early short stories in writing his novels. Ten chapters of *The Big Sleep* were adapted from "The Curtain" (revised and enlarged, naturally) and eleven from "Killer in the Rain"; unity of action is a likely casualty of such a procedure. For Hawks, however, the fuzziness of Chandler's plot was a blessing in disguise—it meant that all liberties were licensed.

The movie's great charm is a consequence of such liberties; the film constantly subverts the hard-boiled conventions it invokes. The transformation of Mrs. Vivian Regan, née Sternwood, into Lauren Bacall ("Mrs. Rutledge") makes sense in cinematic terms but plays havoc with the book's strict morality. It's as if the Bogart-Bacall relationship in *To Have and Have Not,* two years earlier, had smuggled itself into the picture. Where the plot seems to require the Bacall character to be antagonistic to Bogart, she joins him instead in comedy routines and sexy banter. One such confrontation takes place in Bogart's office. Bacall angrily calls the police but—as soon as the call goes through—the hostility between them dissolves and they team up to double-talk the policeman on the other end of the line; they play the telephone scene as if they were Cary Grant and Rosalind Russell in *His Girl Friday,* Hawks's screwball comedy. This is an example of what Hawks had in mind when he told a group of film critics, before *The Big Sleep* was released, "You're not going to know what to make of this damned picture; it holds out its hand for a right-turn signal, then takes a left."[11]

Consider the distance between the end of the book and the end of the movie. The book ends on the funereal theme announced in the title: "You just slept the big sleep, not caring about the nastiness of how you died or where you fell." The movie ends with movie logic, Bogart and Bacall in a clinch:

Marlowe: "What's wrong with you?"
Vivian: "Nothing you can't fix."

There's something subversive about the hard-boiled genre to begin with, which makes Hawks's movie subversive twice over. It knows that we know it's a movie. "You want me to count to three like they do in the movies?" says the gunman to his victim. And Marlowe repeats the line when he finally corners his antagonist in the film, Eddie Mars: "What do you want me to do, count three like they do in the movies?"

In both book and movie, Marlowe is forever penetrating behind the city's closed doors and forever stumbling on fresh corpses. It's as though he, the witness of social disorder, were also, paradoxically, its agent. How else to explain the number of casualties that attend his presence? He is conveniently parked outside the Arthur Geiger residence when the shots ring out that end Geiger's life. He drops in on Joe Brody, another petty blackmailer, and sets off a whole chain of catalytic reactions. First Brody pulls a black police .39 on him. ("Such a lot of guns around town and so few brains," is Marlowe's comment.) The doorbell rings and in steps Carmen Sternwood, gun in hand. No sooner has this crisis been resolved, all parties disarmed by Marlowe, than the doorbell rings again. "When in doubt, have a man come through a door with a gun in his hand," Chandler once wrote in a kidding spirit, but that's exactly what happens here: The gunsel at the door dispatches Joe Brody to his maker. ("You shot the wrong guy," Marlowe informs the killer—a mistake that could never happen in Christieland). Or again, when Marlowe heads for an appointment with small-time hood Harry Jones—a character made to order for Elisha Cook, Jr.—he gets there just in time to witness, himself unseen, the man's fatal encounter with Eddie Mars's top gunman, Lash Canino.

In its simplest and least interesting form, Chandler's brand of social criticism is an undisguised expression of class resentment. "To hell with the rich," Marlowe says in *The Big Sleep*. "They made me sick." The book's unity of purpose is clear from the placement of chapter one in the Sternwood mansion and the placement of the denouement in the oil sump, where Rusty Regan's putrified body lies. All the corpses in the book relate, as from effect to cause, to the vices of Carmen Sternwood; the progress of wealth, like its source, is dirty. The plot illustrates perfectly Balzac's oft-quoted statement that a crime stands at the source of every fortune, little or great. But this theme affects us less profoundly than does

Chandler's evocation of Los Angeles as a city of menace—just as, in *film noir,* the atmosphere of threat is more real and more vivid than the substance of that threat.

Probably the most threatening scene in both the book and movie versions of *The Big Sleep* is the one in which Canino forces Harry Jones to drink the cup of whiskey spiked with cyanide. Canino and Jones, villain and victim, play out their melodrama in a *mise-en-scene* that could define *film noir.* It happens in an office building whose directory lists "numbers with names and numbers without names. Plenty of vacancies or plenty of tenants who wished to remain anonymous." It has rained and will continue to rain later; there are probably as many rain outs in *The Big Sleep* as in the entire history of the Los Angeles Dodgers. It is nighttime, of course, and the single droplight in the lobby merely confirms the darkness. Up the unswept fire stairs goes Marlowe, emerging onto a fourth floor of frayed mats and dirty spittoons. Noiselessly he enters the darkened office adjacent to the one in which Canino and Jones do their dance of death, a pair of silhouettes on the shaded glass wall. Like a moviegoer, like us, Marlowe can only watch; he peers into the shadows, listening to the disembodied voices of a murderer and his victim, helpless to change the script. Marlowe has, alas, failed to bring his gun along; the only thing he shoots here is a mental photograph. The heavy rain outside, resuming after a brief "breathing spell," provides the appropriate sound effect. The storm has now finished brewing. But the streets of the city remain uncleansed.

———◆———

The ire in Chandler's novels is focused more or less narrowly on social, political, or religious institutions that are presumed to be corrupt. But enough anger or resentment is left over to fuel a literary vendetta, a continued protest against the classic murder mystery. "The Simple Art of Murder," Chandler's hard-boiled manifesto, is full of splendidly splenetic barbs hurled at golden-age whodunits. Agatha Christie's *Murder on the Orient Express,* he writes, "is guaranteed to knock the keenest mind for a loop. Only a halfwit could guess it." Of an elaborate plot contrivance in a story by Dorothy Sayers he comments, "This is what is vulgarly known as having God sit in your lap; a murderer who needs that much help from Providence must be in the wrong business."[12] What Chandler objected to most in classic detective stories was their air of unreality, of propriety and decorum. "Nobody grieves, nobody bleeds," in Jessica Mann's happy phrase.[13]

Murder, in golden-age whodunits, had become the literary equivalent of a sophisticated parlor game. And where the puzzle's the chief thing, the dead body in the library is just the convenient first premise in a brain-teasing problem in logic. Though Chandler broke with this whodunit tradition, he necessarily absorbed whole parts of it: the fact of homicide, the corpse on page one (or in chapter one), the retrospective nature of the plot, the detective's superiority over the police, and so forth. It's as a sort of vestigial reminder of the older tradition that Chandler shows us Marlowe trying—vainly, of course—to figure out the chess puzzle in *The Big Sleep*: "a problem laid out on the board, a six-mover. I couldn't solve it, like a lot of my problems. I reached down and moved a knight, then pulled my hat and coat off and threw them somewhere."

Marlowe leads with his knight whether the situation calls for it or not. His instinctive reliance on romantic gestures distinguishes him from the grandmaster sleuth of old faced with an endgame he unfailingly solves. Able to see six moves ahead, the Great Detective checkmates the culprit—though only after he reconstructs, from the arrangement of the pieces on the board, the game from its origins, move by move. Hammett and Chandler played by different rules. For them, the game and the puzzle were always subordinate elements in the composition. Murder illustrated the "normative" workings of a criminal milieu and not the ingenuity of a lone culprit. Action, not cogitation, was needed in response. And so the armchair genius was replaced by the highly fallible shamus in the nondescript city office, while rare, untraceable poisons gave way to guns brandished by freelance desperadoes or by thugs in the employ of a racketeer. "Hammett took murder out of the Venetian vase and dropped it into the alley," Chandler wrote in a famous passage. "Hammett gave murder back to the kind of people that commit it for reasons, not just to provide a corpse."[14]

Yet romance, rather than bare-knuckles realism, defines the genre of Hammett and Chandler.

Chandler proclaimed himself a "realist in murder," but it wasn't realism that distinguished the hard-boiled novel from the tradition it broke with. Privately he acknowledged that the "realism" he professed to value was achieved through stylistic sleight-of-hand. The mystery story, he wrote in a notebook entry, "must consist of the plausible actions of plausible people in plausible circum-stances, it being remembered that plausibility is largely a matter of style."[15] That puts the matter in the right light: What Chandler's novels did was to convey the *illusion* of realism, the illusion or con-viction of a real time and place. Once *that* was accomplished, the most baroque complications could be integrated into plots no one could quite follow, and no one would complain that this was an artificial world.

Read Hammett's *The Dain Curse* (1929), for instance, and you come across the familiar staples of gothic melodrama: a family curse, a homicidal ghost, enough dope to knock out a tribe, and a sinister religious cult whose leader seems to favor human sacrifice. True, the hero of the book is presented to us as a deliberately anti-romantic figure: he is the middle-aged "nervous little fat man" Hammett calls the Continental Op. But what he endures in *The Dain Curse*—in which he is attacked by gun and by ghost, by dag-ger and by poison gas, on his way to solving eight assorted mur-ders—stretches credibility at least as much as do the complex plot contrivances of a Christie or a Sayers. *The Dain Curse* is Hammett at his weakest, but the superiority of his other books isn't a conse-quence of greater realism. Sam Spade in *The Maltese Falcon* is certainly a convincing character, but you would hardly call him a monument to realism. The very occupation of a Sam Spade makes the chronicle of his exploits fail a strict realism test—such as that proposed by Ed McBain in *Long Time No See:* "The last time Carella had met a private detective investigating a homicide was never."

Chandler's paradigmatic example of the hard-boiled sleuth is an utterly romanticized figure, a man with a mission. "He is the hero, he is everything," wrote Chandler in "The Simple Art of Murder." "He must be a complete man and a common man and yet an un-usual man. He must be, to use a rather weathered phrase, a man of honor, by instinct, by inevitability, without thought of it, and certainly without saying it. He must be the best man in his world and a good enough man for any world."[16] That's hardly what you'd call the voice of unflinching realism—and Chandler was well aware of it. In a letter he declared that the fictional private eye "is the personification of an attitude, the exaggeration of a possibility." Marlowe in particular was "a sentimentalist," whose "toughness has always been more or less a surface bluff."[17]

What was new in the hard-boiled novel wasn't an increase in

realism but an insistence that plausibility—the reader's willingness to suspend disbelief—was "largely a matter of style." The effect of all those made-for-the-movies touches—the bitter sarcasm, the menacing shadows, the unfiltered cigarettes—is a calculated dose of "brutal" reality, but it is realism only if one is convinced that an urban criminal milieu is inherently more "real" than any other locale. The hard-boiled novel, done right, just *feels* real. Analyze it and it is as mannered as the stuff Chandler loved to lampoon.

The legacy of Hammett and Chandler is, in more ways than one, stylistic. The necessary ingredients include an urban setting; a specifically American spin on the language; the determination to be spare of dialogue and laconic in description, in the Hemingway manner; the interplay of menace and dark humor, in the knowledge that the one will enhance the other. The gestures add up to a coherent way of meeting an adverse world, a way that is all the more attractive since it is clearly beyond the reader's (or the viewer's) reach. What is communicated is not a message, but an attitude: a style of being, chosen by the protagonist, that defines his essence and enables him to act on his destiny.

The hard-boiled romance has, in a specifically contemporary sense, an *attitude*—which is Manhattan shorthand for "a bad attitude," meaning an insolent and sometimes frankly hostile manner, as on the part of waitpersons in fashionable restaurants. (The posher the place, the more common the phenomenon.) Philip Marlowe's attitude implies an unwillingness to be placated, a vigilance against being duped. It coexists with a smoldering resentment of people better off than himself and a quality of moral outrage that must express itself ironically since nothing is less socially acceptable than a direct expression of moral outrage. You can hear this attitude in every snarling wisecrack of *The Big Sleep* or *The Long Goodbye*—the books are inconceivable without it.

The hard-boiled romance prizes a stylized approach toward dialogue (witty insults are favored) and description (the simile is the trope of choice). It is spiced with streetwise slang, the tang of an underworld argot. Hammett's Continental Op stories are especially good at capturing gangster "razzle-dazzle," the language of the "arch-*gonif*" and his "moll." Consider the list of nicknames in Hammett's story "The Big Knockover," which "read like *Who's Who in Crookdom*":

> There was the Dis-and-Dat Kid, who had crashed out of Leavenworth only two months before; Sheeny Holmes; Snohomish Shitey,

supposed to have died a hero in France in 1919; L.A. Slim, from
Denver, sockless and underwearless as usual, with a thousand-dollar
bill sewed in each shoulder of his coat; Spider Girrucci wearing a
steel-mesh vest under his shirt and a scar from crown to chin where
his brother had carved him years ago; Old Pete Best, once a
congressman; Nigger Vojan, who once won $175,000 in a Chicago
crap-game—*Abracadabra* tattooed on him in three places; Alphabet
Shorty McCoy; Tom Brooks, Alphabet Shorty's brother-in-law, who
invented the Richmond razzle-dazzle and bought three hotels with
the profits; Red Cudahy, who stuck up a Union Pacific train in 1924;
Denny Burke; Bull McGonickle, still pale from fifteen years in Joliet;
Toby the Lugs, Bull's running-mate, who used to brag about picking
President Wilson's pocket in a Washington vaudeville theater; and
Paddy the Mex.

Hammett was able to convey the rhythms of violence by means of
syntax alone:

> A door shut sharply downstairs.
> A body came out of nowhere, hit my back, flattened me to the
> landing.
> The feel of silk was on my cheek. A brawny hand was fumbling at
> my throat.
> I bent my wrist until my gun, upside down, lay against my cheek.
> Praying for my ear, I squeezed.
> My cheek took fire. My head was a roaring thing, about to burst.
> The silk slid away.
> Pat hauled me upright.
> We started down the stairs.
> Swish!
> A thing came past my face, stirring my bared hair.
> A thousand pieces of glass, china, plaster, exploded upward at my
> feet.
> I tilted head and gun together.
> A Negro's red-silk arms were still spread over the balustrade
> above.
> I sent him two bullets. Pat sent him two.
> The Negro teetered over the rail.
> He came down on us, arms outflung—a deadman's swan-dive.
> We scurried down the stairs from under him.[18]

The depiction of criminal violence in *Red Harvest* and the short
stories—rendered as though it were a species of urban guerrilla

warfare—has never been bettered. But the height of Hammett's achievement as a prose stylist is the third-person narration in *The Maltese Falcon*, which switches almost imperceptibly between omniscience and Sam Spade's point of view. The prose is reticent, noncommittal, studiously detached—a style suited to a morally ambiguous universe in which the hero's alignment with the forces of law and order can never be taken for granted. For his hero's dialogue lines, Hammett favored a form of insult humor that depended on a deadpan delivery. The Fat Man wonders what happened to Wilmer's guns. Spade, who disarmed the gunsel, replies: "A crippled newsie took them away from him, but I made him give them back."

Chandler went further in developing a set of rhetorical gestures into a distinctive literary style. The voice of his first-person narratives belongs to a speaker who specializes in the wisecrack. His is a style of wit that is also a style of rhetoric: a first-person-singular way of encountering events by warding them off. A favorite rhetorical device is the muted hyperbole. Consider these back-to-back examples in *The High Window* (1942): "On the chair beside her was a white-straw garden hat with a brim the size of a spare tire and a white satin chin-strap. On the brim of the hat lay a pair of green sunglasses with lenses the size of doughnuts." Chandler compiled lists of such pleasantly outlandish similes, and used them cunningly. In *The Long Goodbye* we come across an ugly man with "short red hair and a face like a collapsed lung" and a cop with a stare that could "have frozen a fresh-baked potato." In *Farewell, My Lovely* Marlowe goes through hell ("I felt like an amputated leg") for his client, the ex-con Moose Malloy, "a big man but not more than six feet five inches tall and not wider than a beer truck," who "looked about as inconspicuous as a tarantula on a slice of angel food." The effect in each case is due to calculated exaggeration and the speaker's dash. Chandler is also quite willing to let words metamorphose as they will. "Abyssinia," says a character in the story "Pearls Are a Nuisance," ending a phone conversation. In all the old familiar places. If your ear is fine-tuned to the American vernacular, *I'll be seeing you* does become *Abyssinia* and the Joycean pun is the reader's bonus.

Chandler's wisecracks are classic figures of speech with the prettiness removed. His similes describe two things: the thing they're supposed to describe and Marlowe's reaction to it. A girl in *Farewell, My Lovely* gives Marlowe "one of those looks which are supposed to make your spine feel like a run in a stocking." He walks into an elevator in *The Lady in the Lake* and detects "an elderly perfume, like three widows drinking tea." On the other hand, he can be quite insistently literal, as when in *Farewell, My Lovely,* he comes face to face with a piece of modern sculpture. The sculpture's owner "negligently" identifies it as "Asta Dial's *Spirit of Dawn.*" "I thought it was Klopstein's *Two Warts on a Fanny,*" Marlowe replies.

Perhaps the funniest bit of writing in all of Chandler is the parody of Hemingway that he serves up in *Farewell, My Lovely,* which like all really inspired parodies argues a high degree of respect and admiration for the parodied master. Two cops are giving Marlowe a hard time. One of the two, in a pathetic display of "policeman's humor," adopts the tactic of repeating Marlowe's responses to his questions. Marlowe has finally had enough: "Listen, Hemingway, don't repeat everything I say." To which one of the cops says: "I think the guy is nuts. He just called me Hemingway. Do you think he is nuts?" "I think possibly he is a little unbalanced," says the second cop. "I can't think of any reason why he should call me Hemingway," the first cop adds. "My name ain't Hemingway." A few pages later, "Hemingway" confesses that Marlowe has got his goat. "Who is this Hemingway person at all?" he asks. "A guy," Marlowe answers, "that keeps saying the same thing over and over until you begin to believe it must be good."

13

---◆---

Hammett and Chandler

*T*here is pathos, too, in the idea that a man who can write like
a fallen angel should be a mere private eye.

—Ross Macdonald, "The Writer as Detective Hero"

The chief difference between Dashiell Hammett and Raymond
Chandler is equal to the difference between their sleuths. It may
not be evident on the screen, where Humphrey Bogart personified
both Hammett's Spade and Chandler's Marlowe with the same zest.
But it's there in the top paragraphs of the books. Indeed, from the
page-one descriptions of Spade and Marlowe in *The Maltese Falcon* and *The Big Sleep,* one can deduce the entire range of moral
possibilities open to the hero of the hard-boiled romance.

"There is pathos," wrote Ross Macdonald, "in the idea that a
man who can write like a fallen angel should be a mere private
eye." Macdonald was writing about Chandler—and about the relation between Chandler the aging author and Philip Marlowe, his
persona and voice, the perennially thirty-eight-year-old private eye
and narrative "I." Macdonald's line applies to Sam Spade in a
different sense. Spade gives off a strong Luciferean odor in *The
Maltese Falcon*—he is the angel who fell out of grace with the sky.
On the first page of *The Maltese Falcon* Spade is described as looking "rather pleasantly like a blond Satan." The "pleasantly" and

the "blond" convey the moral ambiguity of the statement. Everything about Spade turns out to be ambiguous, not to say contradictory. The Fat Man is right to call him "unpredictable." There's no telling what he'll do next; he keeps his options in reserve and is therefore able to respond flexibly and spontaneously to events. He is an enigma to those who know him, because his behavior (what he does) and his manner (what he says) seem often to point in opposite directions. His relations with people are especially puzzling. There's his hostility to the police, which goes well beyond the stylized rivalries in older detective tales. And then there's his affair with Brigid O'Shaughnessy, that femme fatale disguised as a damsel in distress. He sees through her, knows she's a liar, suspects she's a murderess. Yet he takes her case. His dialogue with her—repeated almost verbatim in the movie—nearly always seems at odds with what is going on between them, a tendency that culminates when he declares, in the end, that he won't "play the sap" for her "because all of me wants to."[1]

With Spade, it is never clear, can never be clear, whether he would have acted differently if the avian statuette had turned out to be the real thing—and the temptation of money were added to the temptation of sex. Spade decides to turn over Brigid to the police only after the financial part of the equation has been unsatisfactorily resolved. "Would you have done this to me if the falcon had been real and you had been paid your money?" Brigid asks. "Don't be too sure I'm as crooked as I'm supposed to be," he answers, but she is right to have her doubts. Spade is a man who has trained himself to make his moral calculations coldly and on the basis of shrewd self-interest. "Well," he adds after a momentary delay, "a lot of money would have been at least one more item on the other side of the scales." There's something diabolically sardonic about the way Bogart delivers his lines at the end of the movie, and it's perfectly in keeping with the character as written. A blond Satan, like Marlene Dietrich's blond Venus, means trouble. There's a reason that The Maltese Falcon—the book, though not the movie—ends with Spade's secretary, Effie Perine, recoiling from his touch. Effie is frightened by his pragmatism—or cold-heartedness. "Your Sam's a detective," Spade tells her, reasonably. "She did kill Miles, angel." "I know—I know you're right. You're right," she says. "But don't touch me now—not now."

Philip Marlowe is a very different kettle of fish. He describes himself on the first page of The Big Sleep as "neat, clean, shaved and sober"—"everything the well-dressed private detective ought to be" if he is "calling on four million dollars"—but the more interesting self-revelation occurs, as it often does when Marlowe is talking, when he describes what he sees. In this case, Marlowe anticipates his own predicament in the process of describing the entrance doors of the Sternwood estate. The wisecracks are there to keep you from noticing too clearly the brand of chivalry Marlowe is proposing:

> Over the entrance doors, which would have let in a troop of Indian elephants, there was a broad stained-glass panel showing a knight in dark armor rescuing a lady who was tied to a tree and didn't have any clothes on but some very long and convenient hair. The knight had pushed the vizor of his helmet back to be sociable, and he was fiddling with the knots on the ropes that tied the lady to the tree and not getting anywhere. I stood there and thought that if I lived in the house, I would sooner or later have to climb up there and help him. He didn't seem to be really trying.

This "stained-glass romance" clearly foreshadows what happens to Marlowe in *The Big Sleep*—and in Chandler's other novels as well. He is the "knight in dark armor," all right; he even calls himself, in *The High Window*, a "shop-soiled Galahad"; the trouble is, his knightly mission is doomed to fail regardless of whether he solves the mystery. For the naked lady he is supposed to rescue is herself part of the corruption.

Where Spade appears to enjoy his association with Brigid O' Shaughnessy, Marlowe can't be said to derive any pleasure from attempting to rescue Carmen Sternwood. As Mary Astor plays Brigid in the movie (it's hard to imagine her any other way), Brigid is so obviously and splendidly histrionic that she's hard to resist:

Spade: "What makes it [the falcon] so important?"
Brigid: "I don't know."
Spade: "What's it made of?"
Brigid: "Porcelain."
Spade: "You *are* a liar."
Brigid: "I *am*. I have always been a liar."

Spade happily goes to bed with her. Perhaps his sexual appreciation of her is enhanced by the constant threat of treachery she embodies; the text doesn't say. Carmen Sternwood, on the other hand, can arouse only disgust in Marlowe. She is a drug addict, a nymphomaniac, a creature of sybaritic self-indulgence wholly lacking in restraint and feminine modesty, virtues Marlowe looks for in a lady. But the moralist's anachronistic code of honor has put him in a double bind. He cannot simply turn Carmen over to the police—that wouldn't be playing by the rules of the "stained-glass romance." In short, and this is the pathos of his situation, he cannot serve both justice and the demands of his romantic ideal.

The conscience of the "blond Satan" is clear at the end of *The Maltese Falcon*. Spade is not going to give himself a hard time about Brigid O'Shaughnessy's fate. "If they hang you I'll always remember you," he tells her equably, between embraces, before the police arrive. Marlowe, on the other hand, feels ultimately compromised by the chivalrous gesture he makes at the end of *The Big Sleep* when, rather than identify Carmen as the killer, he lets her sister "take her away." "Me, I was part of the nastiness now," Marlowe says melodramatically on the last page of the book. Maybe Marlowe's part in covering up Carmen's crimes is Chandler's version of the cover-up lie at the end of Conrad's *Heart of Darkness*— in which, as it happens, the narrator is named Marlow.

Think back to page one, and Carmen Sternwood's symbolic significance in Marlowe's spiritual predicament becomes clear. The one time we see him in an absolute rage is when he discovers her in his bed; she has slipped into his room and is waiting for him, naked. After spurning her, he makes her dress and throws her out. Then, he says, he "tore the bed to pieces savagely." With that strong phrase the chapter ends. A few pages earlier Marlowe had picked up the theme of the knight that he left on page one. Here he combines it with the motif of the chess puzzle, a prop used to remind us that the dilemmas facing the hero differ radically from the neat, soluble, aesthetically pleasing mannerist artifice we find in the classic whodunit. But Carmen in her nakedness, "hissing" like a serpent in the shabby Eden of his bedroom, puts the chess puzzle on his coffee table in an entirely new light. "I looked down at the chessboard," says Marlowe, using the laconic syntax and key-word repetition that Chandler liked in Hemingway. "The move with the knight was wrong. I put it back where I had moved it from. Knights had no meaning in this game. It wasn't a game for knights."

Marlowe knows he is doomed to play the part of the chivalrous hero—though he is without the illusion that the rest of the script can accommodate the fantasy. If he weren't so determined to meet every contingency with tough talk and wisecrack ("'I'm not tough,' I said. 'Just virile'"), he would be in danger of looking as priggish as a Victorian gentleman with muttonchop sideburns in President Nixon's White House. But his superior sense of humor, which he directs at himself as frequently as not, saves the day. This example of his self-lacerating irony appears in *The High Window*:

> Twelve hours to tie up a situation which I didn't even begin to understand. Either that or turn up a client and let the cops go to work on her and her whole family. Hire Marlowe and get your house full of law. Why worry? Why be doubtful and confused? Why be gnawed by suspicion? Consult cock-eyed, careless, clubfooted, dissipated investigator, Philip Marlowe, Glenview 7537. See me and you meet the best cops in town. Why despair? Why be lonely? Call Marlowe and watch the wagon come.

Chandler intended Marlowe's first-person voice to blend the qualities of idealism and contempt. The reality he goes out to encounter would be utterly impalatable if not for his ability to transform what he sees with what he says or how he says it. It is Marlowe's voice that unites him with his readers. We see things with his eyes and flatter ourselves into thinking that his biting similes have issued from our lips. This is what we'd like to sound like if we lived in the world of a *film noir*.

——————◆——————

Both Hammett and Chandler took a stab at formulating the parable at the heart of the hard-boiled detective novel. Chandler's candidate, "the Cassidy case," is in *The High Window*. Marlowe is doing the talking:

> Cassidy was a very rich man, a multi-millionaire. He had a grown-up son. One night the cops were called to his home and young Cassidy was on his back on the floor with blood all over his face and a bullet-hole in the side of his head. His secretary was lying on *his* back in an adjoining bathroom, with his head against the second bathroom door, leading to a hall, and a cigarette burned out between the fingers of his left hand, just a short burned-out stub that had scorched the skin between his fingers. A gun was lying by his right hand. He was shot in the head, not a contact wound. A lot of drinking had been done. Four hours had elapsed since the deaths

and the family doctor had been there for three of them. Now, what did you do with the Cassidy case?

Detective-Lieutentant Jesse Breeze, the cop Marlowe is talking to, wasn't involved in investigating the Cassidy case. It boiled down to "murder and suicide during a drinking spree," he guesses. "The secretary went haywire and shot young Cassidy. I read it in the papers or something." That's what the newspapers reported, Marlowe agrees. But it's not what happened. What happened was a cover-up. The secretary "was made out to be a drunken paranoiac because his boss's father had a hundred million dollars."

> There was no inquest. But every crime reporter in town and every cop on every homicide detail knew it was Cassidy that did the shooting, that it was Cassidy that was crazy drunk, that it was the secretary who tried to handle him and couldn't and at last tried to get away from him, but wasn't quick enough. Cassidy's was a contact wound and the secretary's was not. The secretary was left-handed and he had a cigarette in his left hand when he was shot. Even if you are right-handed, you don't change a cigarette over to your other hand and shoot a man while casually holding the cigarette.

The Cassidy case displays Marlowe's ability—as both a narrator and a sleuth—to spot a telling clue (the cigarette in the left hand, the contact wound) and extrapolate a scenario from it. But the synopsis is also a parable about the way detective stories work. As in the example, detective stories frequently involve the substitution of one solution for another; the true solution is reached by way of a critique of a false but plausible solution. The detective, in reconstructing the story of a crime, is also, invariably, debunking an expedient cover-up, an official version of the events, the version announced by the police and publicized by the newspapers.

For Chandler, what lifts the Cassidy case to the level of a parable is its didactic thrust (the detective's mission is "to seek the truth out and find it and let the chips fall where they may") and its dire political implications. As Marlowe tells it, the moral of the tale is that justice is a commodity that can be bought and sold like any other—and that the inequality of citizens before the law mocks the ideals of a democratic society. "Until you guys own your own souls you don't own mine," Marlowe tells Breeze. "Until you guys can be trusted every time and always, in all times and conditions, to seek the truth out and find it and let the chips fall where they may—until that time comes, I have a right to listen to my conscience, and protect my client the best way I can. Until I'm sure you won't do him more harm than you'll do the truth good. Or until I'm hauled before somebody that can make me talk.'' This is Marlowe's testament, full of pride, defiance, and romantic idealism: the testament of a man with an unrequited passion for justice. But even Marlowe must recognize that the moral he draws from the Cassidy case clashes with his sense of things as they are. ''Say, I'd like to read up on that Cassidy case,'' says Spangler, another cop on the scene. Up goes Marlowe's guard; out comes the reflexive irony that he uses to mask his native romanticism. ''It was a long time ago,'' Marlowe says. ''And it never happened. I was just kidding.''

The Cassidy case is a parable about truth and justice and how hard it is to attain either. The man who would undertake to solve the case must circumvent official channels; he must himself be uncompromised; he is the last, lone just man, fired by a furious sense of moral indignation. In short, he could not possibly exist except on the printed page. The final, tongue-biting irony is that Chandler endows his hero with enough self-consciousness to see that he has come too late to make a difference; it all happened ''a long time ago.'' He can ascertain the truth, if belatedly, but he can't really publicize his findings, let alone undo the damage that has already been done. Still, Chandler insists that we ascribe a positive allegorical meaning to the Cassidy case—and, by extension, to the genre of fiction he practices. On the last page of *The High Window,* Lieutenant Breeze tells Marlowe that there really was a Cassidy case ''under another name'' and that, because of it, ''I sometimes give a guy a break he could perhaps not really deserve. A little something paid back out of the dirty millions to a working stiff—like me—or like you.''

The Flitcraft parable in *The Maltese Falcon* lacks such trumped-up optimism. Also absent is the furious idealism that makes Marlowe feel so self-conscious and defensive. Flitcraft's story, as Sam Spade tells it to Brigid O'Shaughnessy, is about neither truth nor justice but about chance and providence—and about what is a ''reasonable'' way to behave in a universe not known for its reasonableness. Arguably, it reveals a more fundamental truth about the hard-boiled genre than does Chandler's Cassidy case; unquestionably, the Flitcraft episode is more enigmatic and more resonant.

A successful real-estate man named Flitcraft, who lived in a Tacoma suburb with his wife and two sons, disappeared one day ('' 'like that,' Spade said, 'like a fist when you open your hand' '') for no apparent reason. Five years go by. Spade, then an operative with a Seattle detective agency, tracks down Flitcraft in Spokane. The man now goes by the name of Charles Pierce; he operates a successful car business, has a wife and a baby son, lives in a Spokane suburb. "Flitcraft had no feeling of guilt. He had left his first family well provided for, and what he had done seemed to him perfectly reasonable. The only thing that bothered him was a doubt that he could make that reasonableness clear to Spade. He had never told anybody his story before, and thus had not had to attempt to make its reasonableness explicit."

What happened to Flitcraft on the day of his disappearance is that he walked past a construction site on his lunch hour and narrowly missed being hit by a falling beam. "It brushed pretty close to him, but didn't touch him, though a piece of the sidewalk was chipped off and flew up and hit his cheek. It only took a piece of skin off, but he still had the scar when I saw him. He rubbed it with his finger—well, affectionately—when he told me about it. He was scared stiff of course, he said, but he was more shocked than really frightened. He felt like somebody had taken the lid off life and let him look at the works."

To Flitcraft, the falling beam—and his luck in avoiding it—becomes an admonition or a reprimand, which he translates into an injunction to change his life. "The life he knew was a clean orderly sane responsible affair. Now a falling beam had shown him that life was fundamentally none of these things. He, the good citizen-husband-father, could be wiped out between office and restaurant by the accident of a falling beam. He knew then that men died at haphazard like that, and lived only while blind chance spared them."

Flitcraft is determined to adjust to his new understanding of life. "Life could be ended for him at random by a falling beam: he would change his life at random by simply going away." He had led his life in an orderly way; henceforth he would throw caution to the winds. The wonderfully ironic twist is that Flitcraft abandons his identity and his family—he frees himself of all connections and responsibilities—only to replicate with a stunning fidelity the circumstances of his former existence: Spokane rather than Tacoma, the automobile business rather than real estate, a wife like the echo of his first. "It seemed reasonable enough to him," Spade concludes. "I don't think he even knew he had settled back naturally into the same groove he had jumped out of in Tacoma. But that's the part of it I always liked. He adjusted himself to beams falling, and then no more of them fell, and he adjusted himself to them not falling."

The signal importance of the Flitcraft parable has been recognized by many commentators and doubted by only one, Julian Symons. "With Hammett the most straightforward, least high-flown view of the Flitcraft story is likely to be the one he had in mind," Symons writes. "It is possible that he was not contemplating a grand application of the story to all human existence but merely a personal reference to his own career to date. . . . Up to the time of his departure from San Francisco, Hammett had done his best to order his life sensibly, without much success. For several years afterward, however, he made no attempt to order it at all." The comment lacks imagination. It also sells Hammett short. If Symons is right about the Flitcraft episode, it is merely a gratuitous bit of storytelling, a judgment that is hard to square with Symons's own high regard for Hammett's artistry.[2]

Equally unacceptable is the interpretation proffered by Robert I. Edenbaum, who draws a contrast between Spade's life "in which beams are expected to fall, and do fall, and that of the suburban businessman, in which they do not—or, at least, do not until they do." After extricating himself from this syntactical thicket, Edenbaum concludes that Spade, via the Flitcraft parable, is telling Brigid "that her appeals to Spade's sense of honor, his nobility, his integrity, and finally, his love, will not and cannot work." What Edenbaum overlooks is that Spade cannot know—at the time he is telling Brigid the Flitcraft story—how his own affair with her will turn out: He's not prescient, after all. But Edenbaum has a stake in seeing things this way; he cites the Flitcraft story to support his reading of Spade as the victimizer and Brigid the victim—a reading that conflicts with just about anybody's experience of either the novel or the film.[3]

John G. Cawelti gets closer to the heart of the Flitcraft mystery when he situates it in the context of an "existentialist" discussion. "The existentialist believes that recognizing the irrationality and absurdity of the universe can be the prelude to a new spiritual depth," Cawelti writes. "The Flitcraft parable seems to come out at the other end. Only a rejection of all emotional and moral ties can help man survive in a treacherous world." According to this reading, the narrative function of the Flitcraft story is that it's Spade's way of warning Brigid that he is unreliable, unpredictable, a man who, in Cawelti's words, "has adjusted himself to a world that is likely to betray him at any time.''[4] Maybe. But Cawelti's interpretation, like Edenbaum's, concentrates on Flitcraft's escape from Tacoma—and neglects the part about how he settled down in Spokane to a life almost identical to the one he'd left behind.

Like Cawelti, Steven Marcus dwells on the theme of "irrationality"; the Flitcraft parable is about, he says, "the ethical irrationality of existence, the ethical unintelligibility of the world." What makes Marcus the best commentator on this passage is his attentiveness to the twist with which the Flitcraft story ends, the way that Flitcraft reproduces the very set of circumstances from which he had escaped. Marcus reminds us that this is the part of the story that Spade says "he 'always liked,'" which means the part that he liked best. For here we come upon the unfathomable and most mysteriously irrational part of it all—how despite everything we have learned and everything we know, men will persist in behaving and trying to behave sanely, rationally, sensibly, and responsibly." Later in the narrative, the lesson is repeated in the accents of the taxi driver who doesn't envy Sam Spade his profession. "Well, hack-drivers don't live forever," Spade says. "Maybe that's right," the cabbie retorts, "but, just the same, it'll always be a surprise to me if I don't."

If the falling beam underscores the randomness of experience and the decisiveness of chance, the new life Flitcraft chooses for himself shows that he remains—despite his intentions—the prisoner of a pattern. Life may be, as Marcus has it, "inscrutable, opaque, irresponsible, and arbitrary," but life is full of patterns to which we conform—without even being fully aware of them. We repeat ourselves, compulsively, and that creates an order in our lives, though at the same time we are haunted by the conviction that this order, any order, is perfectly arbitrary, governed by chance. "It is this sense of sustained contradiction that is close to the center—or one of the centers—of Hammett's work," Marcus writes. "The consciousness is not ethical alone; it is metaphysical as well. And it is not merely sustained; it is sustained with pleasure. For Hammett and Spade and the Op, the sustainment in consciousness of such contradictions is an indispensable part of their existence and of their pleasure in that existence."[5]

That there are existential overtones to the Flitcraft parable is undeniable. The hard-boiled sleuth is a version of the existential hero in part because he stands alone, unwilling to compromise his freedom and his capacity for "unpredictable" behavior. But in larger part, it's because he recognizes the absurdity of his situation, recognizes that events are the products of chance, yet commits himself nevertheless to a search for truths and certainties. He knows that the relativism of the law renders it useless as a moral guide; he has seen police corruption and police brutality close up. But if the law is no guarantee of peace and goodwill, the absence of the law would be even worse; the hard-boiled sleuth assumes (or would, if he gave the matter any thought) that life in a state of nature is Hobbesian, every man for himself, at war with every other man—that man is neither perfectible nor is he the tragically chained descendant of an original noble savage. The nobility of the gumshoe rests in the fact that he has freely chosen to thrust himself into danger for the sake of the action itself and not out of a practical regard for likely consequences. He is an example of a Flitcraft who left his job and wife and kids and never looked back—never stopped moving, alone and unprotected—and never settled back down, the way Flitcraft does, as though nothing had happened.

Compare the Flitcraft parable to the remarkably similar synopsis of a movie in the opening pages of Walker Percy's novel *The Moviegoer*:

> The movie was about a man who lost his memory in an accident and as a result lost everything: his family, his friends, his money. He found himself a stranger in a strange city. Here he had to make a fresh start, find a new place to live, a new job, a new girl. It was supposed to be a tragedy, his losing all this, and he seemed to suffer a great deal. On the other hand, things were not so bad after all. In no time he found a very picturesque place to live, a houseboat on the river, and a very handsome girl, the local librarian.

The amnesia-inducing accident—like the falling beam in the Flitcraft parable—snaps the man out of his "everydayness," as Percy calls it. And any man not sunk in the everydayness of his life will take up, must take up, "the search." Yet the amnesiac in the movie, like Flitcraft in Hammett's story, reverts back to type with dazzling speed:

> The movies are onto the search, but they screw it up. The search always ends in despair. They like to show a fellow coming to himself in a strange place—but what does he do? He takes up with the local

librarian, sets about proving to the local children what a nice fellow he is, and settles down with a vengeance. In two weeks time he is so sunk in everydayness that he might just as well be dead.[6]

The protagonist and narrator of Percy's novel defines himself in opposition to the forgetful fellow in the film: He will go on the search, though he mightn't be able to say in so many words what he's searching for. And similarly, the hard-boiled hero measures himself and his calling by his distance from Flitcraft's "reasonable" way of adjusting to beams falling, and then not falling, in the parable Sam Spade spins out. It's Flitcraft's orderly life that Marlowe is rejecting when, in a memorable passage in *The Long Goodbye,* he paints a picture of his life as it might have been: "small-town rich, an eight-room house, two cars in the garage . . . the wife with a cast iron permanent and me with a brain like a sack of Portland cement. You take it, friend. I'll take the big sordid dirty crooked city." The hard-boiled sleuth, wanting at all costs to avoid the strangling "everydayness" Percy describes, embarks on his life of jeopardy. He, too, like Percy's moviegoer, is on a search.

The Flitcraft episode is exemplary in one last way: It may be interpreted as a parable about our experience of detective novels. The form postulates a time before the crash, a time when life had been "a clean orderly sane responsible affair." The corpse on page one, like the falling beam in the Flitcraft story, has dashed that view irrevocably. And just as Flitcraft returns to "the same groove he had jumped out of," we return, at the end of the novel, to the state of rest at which we began.

However you read it, the Flitcraft parable does nothing to make less ambiguous the detective's moral orientation in *The Maltese Falcon.* "Be reasonable, Sam," pleads Tom Polhaus, the one cop on the force with whom Spade has decent relations, but Sam is, as Brigid maintains, the wildest, most unpredictable man. It is asking a lot of us to suppose that he goes through all the trials and errors of *The Maltese Falcon* for the sake of collecting his fee—to have us suppose, in other words, that Spade himself does not to some extent get involved in the general obsession with the bejeweled "dingus." Nor can we write off his involvement with the lovely lady; there's something thrilling about his rejection of her at the end, but only because of the sexual spark between them—the sense that he really is giving something up. If Chandler had written *The Maltese Falcon,* it would have been a tale of greed; in Hammett's hands, it's the tale of a fatal, seemingly irresistible obsession. It offers a bleak and radical skepticism that is far more interesting than Chandler's soak-the-rich brand of moralism. The complexity and ambiguity of Sam Spade's attitude in *The Maltese Falcon*—as he expresses it in the story of Flitcraft and as he lives it with Brigid and the rest—make it the one Hammett novel superior to Chandler at his best.

14

Ross Macdonald and After

"I know your type. You have a secret passion for justice.
Why don't you admit it?"
"I have a secret passion for mercy," I said. "But justice is
what keeps happening to people."

—ROSS MACDONALD, *The Goodbye Look*

Ross Macdonald, the finest crime novelist of his generation, enlarged the possibilities of the hard-boiled novel and endowed it with a degree of high-minded seriousness it had never before known. Macdonald built on Chandler's example but adapted it to the 1960s and 1970s, the era of the generation gap and the ubiquitous identity crisis, two themes in which he specialized. In bringing Chandler up to date, he altered the sociological rules of the game. Macdonald reduced the amount of physical violence and swagger in his work, increased the mental anguish, and shunned the milieu of racketeers and cheap hoods in favor of the respectable, discontented middle class. Less hooch was consumed, and more compassion openly displayed, by Lew Archer, Macdonald's private eye. The result could be parodied, as by Geoffrey Hartman: "Down these polluted freeways goes a man with undimmed vision, cutting through sentimental fog and fiery smog to speak face to face in motel or squalid rental or suburban ranch with Mr. and Mrs. and

Young America!''[1] The danger in the approach was sentimentality; the gain was a greater sense of psychological depth, the result of a shift in the detective novel's basic orientation—from justice to mercy.

Macdonald's stroke of genius was to transform the hard-boiled romance into a species of what Freud called the family romance. In Hammett and Chandler, the investigation of a crime leads to the illumination of a social condition: political and financial corruption, organized greed, urban chaos. In Macdonald, the investigation of a crime leads to the illumination of a "family constellation"—and the revelation that all unhappy families are more or less alike.

The Lew Archer novels resemble gothic psychodramas. They have one peculiarity in common with Agatha Christie's mysteries, which they otherwise do not resemble in the slightest: In many of them, just about everyone in the story is revealed in the end to be related to everyone else. In *The Goodbye Look,* a consummate example, a woman in her early forties tries to explain to Archer the nature of her relationship with a much younger man: "I call him my boyfriend," she says. "Actually we're more like brother and sister, or father and daughter—I mean mother and son." Actually, Archer discovers, they *are* brother and sister, though neither of them knows it yet. The incest taboo is flirted with constantly by such characters. When one of them has an identity crisis, it's a real identity crisis. A man's mother turns out to be his wife (in *The Chill*); in self-defense a boy shoots a tramp who is revealed many years later to have been the boy's natural father (in *The Goodbye Look*). Every murder is a consequence of an earlier murder, which it resembles, in a fearful pattern that the sleuth must try to break.

The tone of Macdonald's novels is one of weary resignation. The sleuth is powerless to undo what has already happened, and that is everything: Everything is foredestined and foredoomed. If homicide is the end product of a series of compulsions, to what extent can any individual perpetrator be held accountable? If criminality is a function of disease rather than of viciousness—if, that is, the proper response to a crime is mercy, not justice—to what extent can the perpetrator be said to have free will? And without free will, what kind of moral system are we left with? At work in Macdonald is a degree of psychological determinism that is totally at odds with the existential (or absurdist) spirit of Flitcraft and Sam Spade. If Macdonald were telling the Flitcraft story, the falling beam would illustrate the providential workings of destiny—since it didn't fall on Flitcraft—rather than the arbitrariness of fate; there is, in Hamlet's words, a special providence in the fall of a sparrow. In Macdonald's novels, everything means something. Nothing occurs in isolation; guilt connects the present and the past in a web of inevitability. If we learn early on, as in *The Goodbye Look,* that a character's mother died in a car crash back in 1945, we can bet that this seemingly inconsequential piece of background detail will prove neither innocent nor content to remain in the background. There are no car accidents. They are all homicides.

The hero in a Hammett or Chandler novel gets beaten up or knocked out, mandatorily. In Macdonald's version of the myth, only the sleuth's psyche gets bruised. In that region, however, bruises don't go away; Archer is wounded more deeply (or more obviously) than his predecessors. The insistent references to Dante tell us he is living among the damned, who may be divided into two groups: the sinners and the sinned against. "Abandon hope all ye who enter here," Archer tells a potential client on the first page of *The Zebra-Striped Hearse*; the house of destiny in *The Goodbye Look* is on a street that "rose like a slope in purgatory." These allusions would seem merely "literary" if they didn't reinforce an atmosphere so heavy with guilt that any excess in description can be justified as a baroque touch. Archer is like a man who read T. S. Eliot in college and never got over it. Macdonald doesn't say, but one imagines Archer as the graduate of a small college, a place like Antioch or Swarthmore, where he determined to do well by doing good. As a sensibility, Archer is the closest parallel in the literature to Josiah "Tink" Thompson, the practicing philosopher who gave up a tenured professorship at Haverford College in order to become a private eye on the streets of San Francisco.[2] As a narrator Archer is a clever and companionable fellow, though a mite too earnest and sensitive for his own good. A woman with whom he is having an affair accuses him of having "a secret passion for justice." "I have a secret passion for mercy," he replies. "But justice is what keeps happening to people."

Like Chandler, Macdonald favored first-person narration and invested his sleuth with a suave and persuasive speaking voice. Macdonald was nearly as brilliant a maker of similes as the master and copied him in making the simile a central element of his style. But Chandler's similes were, at their most interesting, gratuitous and digressive; he used them with almost surrealistic abandon. Consider this artfully hyperbolic example from the story "Trouble Is My Business": "She was sitting behind a black glass desk that looked like Napoleon's tomb and she was smoking a cigarette in a black holder that was not quite as long as a rolled umbrella." Macdonald's similes, in contrast, are seldom weightless; they remind us a bit naggingly of the author's thematic obsessions. In *The Chill,* one simile after another sounds the theme of the past's stranglehold over the present. "Dr. Godwin was talking in a small dead voice that sounded like the whispering ghost of the past." "The questions Mrs. Deloney had raised, or failed to answer, stuck in my mind like fishhooks which trailed their broken lines into the past." "Hoffman's damaged mouth opened and shut mechanically, like a dummy's, as if the past was ventriloquizing through him." Without Lew Archer's saving presence, *The Chill* would be a pure example of gothic melodrama, California-style.

The characters in *The Goodbye Look* and *The Chill*—Macdonald at his best—are the prisoners of a past only dimly remembered; their minds resemble jail cells. We know they are doomed even before we ascertain their part in the play. The sins of the fathers condemn them; they are the victims of somebody's guilty secret, somebody's buried past. The opening chapters of *The Goodbye Look* adumbrate a moralized landscape of guilt and chastisement, and it is the similes that paint the picture. Lew Archer announces himself to a "pink-haired receptionist," and the first thing he notices about her is this: "The heavy dark lines accenting her eyes made her look like a prisoner peering out through bars." That's on page one. On page two Archer meets his client, a lawyer whose "eyes and voice were faintly drowsy with the past." The lawyer directs him to the house on Pacific Street, which "rose like a slope in purgatory from the poor lower town to a hilltop section of fine old homes." The sleuth enters the house and finds himself in an "austere" room within the large mansion where an oedipal riddle is about to unfold: "The single small window, barred on the outside, made it resemble a prison cell. As if the prisoner had been looking for a way out, there were shelves of old law books against one wall." The theme is guilt and the desire for punishment. The guilt is contagious and spreading rapidly; it expresses itself hyperbolically (and sometimes homicidally) because it has been so long repressed.

There is one sense in which Macdonald's originality is nearly complete. In all detective novels, there is a gap in time between the story of the crime and the story of the investigation. Macdonald complicates the time scheme brilliantly by factoring the remote past into his calculations. Since the corpse in the present corresponds to a homicide long hushed up in the past, the duties of the sleuth necessarily include a species of time traveling. In a Macdonald novel, we move from the present (the detective making his inquiries and his calculations) to the immediate past (the disappearance of a character: a young man in *The Goodbye Look,* a young woman in *The Chill*) to the remote past (murder or embezzlement among civilians in California during the last days of World War II). The effect, oddly or logically enough, is that figures of memory appear to have greater solidity and substance than their here-and-now offspring. "I looked," says Lew Archer in *The Chill,* "like a ghost from the present haunting a bloody moment in the past."

Macdonald's best novels are variations—marvelous, ingenious variations—on the Oedipus theme. The plot is a Byzantine web of causality. The case begins with some trivial pretext—a missing Florentine gold box, say—but the search for a missing child or parent is the real problem Archer needs to solve. Invariably Archer's detective work brings to light a past trauma in which long-repressed fantasies of incest and parricide got played out. The puzzle in *The Zebra-Striped Hearse* hinges on the revelation that not only the blustering army colonel but his daughter—long assumed dead—is prepared to kill for the sake of an incestuous passion. *The Underground Man* begins with a man who abandons his family in order to search for his father, who abandoned *his* family fifteen years earlier—it's like an ode to the repetition compulsion Freud describes in *Beyond the Pleasure Principle.* The missing gold box in *The Goodbye Look* contains letters written twenty-five years earlier, and the letters help prove that Nick Chalmers's father isn't the man sitting in the family study but a bank embezzler named Eldon Swain, who was shot fifteen years ago with the same gun that was used to kill Jean Trask last week. No accident: Swain was Jean Trask's father, too. Was Swain the man Nick killed when he was eight, the man who called himself Nick's father, the man who abducted Nick and then made a pass at him?

In *The Chill,* no fewer than three oedipal problems emerge. Each in a sequence of three murders corresponds to an unresolved problem between a character and his or her parent of the opposite sex. The murdered Helen Haggerty, a college teacher, suffered from a "father fixation." Haggerty's student Dolly Kincaid is ambivalent about *her* father, which is understandable enough since he is serving time for allegedly slaying his wife, Dolly's mother, ten years ago. And ten years before that, in Haggerty's home town, there occurred a third murder, that of Luke Deloney, son-in-law of a senator. This, the third in the series, holds the key to the other two. The summer that Luke Deloney was killed, his sister is supposed to have died. In fact, she is very much alive; she is the older woman who was introduced to us as the college dean's mother—but who is, we learn in the end, his wife. It is a stunning revelation. It ties up the three murders neatly with one string. But if the murders are solved, the incestuous wife-as-mother masquerade leaves a more enduring mystery behind.

To solve the riddle of *The Chill,* Lew Archer must return to the scene of crimes committed ten and twenty years before. The three plots intersect like the three roads that meet where Oedipus slays Laius in *Oedipus Rex.*[3] Detection in these circumstances becomes, in part, a means of separating neurotic fantasy from homicidal actuality. Lew Archer's labors become, in this light, a metaphor for the work of the psychoanalyst.

As a detective, a catalyst of plots, Lew Archer leaves little to be desired. Mercy is his business; he has a way of getting people to open up to him, as though he were a combination of father confessor and therapist. But lest this description make the author sound too positivistic, Macdonald complicates his message quite cunningly in *The Chill.* A supporting member of the cast is a psychoanalyst, who offers the familiar sixties idea that criminals are sick rather than morally culpable—and that criminality is environmental rather than freely chosen. Given Macdonald's Freudian attachment, we might expect the shrink to be a sympathetic character, and through much of the book he seems to be. But that portrayal is crucially qualified in the end when we realize that this advocate of an enlightened social policy has been covering up a murderer's tracks. Again, in *The Goodbye Look,* a psychotherapist is one of the characters, and here there is less ambiguity about him: From the start he is pompous, officious, disagreeable; Archer has an affair with the man's wife. As in *The Chill,* the therapist in *The Goodbye Look* is revealed to have covered up for one of his patients and become a partner in a guilty secret. It is an act of personal greed that has dire consequences, since the patient in question is capable of murder. By making the psychotherapist in both cases a Judas figure, Macdonald issues a strong critique of liberal social assumptions even as he seems to advance them. He is willing to concede that crime is and should be treated as the product of mental illness or emotional deprivation rather than as a moral violation; but the Freudian therapist in his failings is proof that Freudian categories do not make all morality obsolete. In the hedging of his bets—this radical departure from the allegory he has taken some pains to establish—lies the writer's considerable savvy.

Chandler was clearly Macdonald's master, his literary father. It was a painful irony that Chandler should have criticized his protégé's reliance on exuberant figurative language—precisely the stylistic trait announcing Macdonald's indebtedness to the master. Which prompts a final word about the oedipal drama enacted in *The Chill*. The story's pivotal plot secret centers on a man married to a woman old enough to be his mother. And Chandler, as Macdonald could not help knowing, lived with his mother until she died when he was thirty-five; a month later, he wedded a woman who was eighteen years his senior, and he remained married to her until her death (when he was sixty-six, and she eighty-four). It's hard not to think of *The Chill* as a kind of gothic elaboration of Chandler's predicament—or as a literary psychodrama occasioned by what Harold Bloom calls "the anxiety of influence."

Time and again in Lew Archer's world people are caught trying to escape from the past, to run away, but the past cannot be escaped. Every homicide, no matter how remote, is assured of having a sequel, just as dreams are repeated from night to night whether the dreamer is willing or not. The family romance ends invariably in violent self-destruction, with too much justice and not enough mercy. The implications of the murder spread out like concentric circles in a stone-rippled pond; everyone is affected, except perhaps the sleuth, who looks doleful but remains true to code, a loner whose alliances are temporary. He is a far sadder man than Philip Marlowe, and his sadness tells us that it is a late time in the history of the detective novel. The environment at large is, Archer knows, contaminated. The murders he investigates are merely local instances of a fatal, irrevocable split between man in his corrupt state and nature. Ecological disasters on a spectacular scale—the oil spill in *Sleeping Beauty*, the forest fire in *The Underground Man*—roar out the wrong man has done to his world.

———◆———

Contemporary examples of the private-eye novel are haunted by a powerful sense of nostalgia for the 1940s. The books acknowledge their debt to Hammett and Chandler indirectly—by summoning up Hollywood images and sound bites. The protagonist of Arthur Lyons's *Three With a Bullet* (1985), true to form, salutes the Beverly Hills Hotel in Los Angeles as "a monument to another era, an era of glamour and gaiety, an era of Gable and Lombard and Bogie and Bacall, an era in which I'd always thought I should have lived." The knowledge that Spade and Marlowe were the originals—and that nearly everyone since is a pale imitation—translates into the self-deprecating humor that enlivens some of the best hard-boiled writing now being done. It's the note that Lyons sounds on the first page of *Hard Trade* (1981) when his detective, Jacob Asch, is visited by a new client. He describes her as "a Munchkin," and adds: "The heavy-breathing, leggy blondes all went to Spade and Marlowe; I wound up with the refugees from Barnum and Bailey."

Other writers impose on themselves the technical requirement of setting their books in the period of nostalgic desire. William Hjortsberg's *Falling Angel* (1977) is unorthodox in many ways— among them the fact that it is set in New York City in 1959, an unusual choice of year. Andrew Bergman situates *The Big Kiss-Off Of 1944* (1974) in more familiar hard-boiled turf: the New York City of Thomas E. Dewey, crime-busting district attorney and presidential aspirant, a favorite player in such scripts. (On the first page, Jack LeVine—Bergman's detective—treats his client with the breeziness of Groucho Marx. "I need what they call a shamus," she says. "Is it Yom Kippur already?" he replies, thoroughly mystifying her.) Robert Mitchum playing Marlowe in the 1975 movie version of *Farewell, My Lovely* keeps reminding us that it's supposed to be 1941. In his search for "little Velma," Marlowe pauses only long enough to keep track of Joe DiMaggio's fifty-six-game hitting streak.

Sometimes all these nostalgic elements coalesce in one composition. Thomas Maxwell's *Kiss Me Once* (1986) is a good example. It is set in New York around the time of the Japanese attack on Pearl Harbor. DiMaggio's hitting streak punctuates the text. The book's heroine is described as looking like Philip Marlowe's ideal lady—"like the symbol of beauty and chastity for whom Saint George might have slain any number of dragons. Either that or a Vassar girl at the Yale Bowl in a cigarette ad, though maybe that was only another version of the same thing. You never knew when it came to symbols." (And all this about a gangster's moll!) The plot of *Kiss Me Once* involves the ambitions of Thomas Dewey—

come to us straight from the groom's position on top of the wedding cake—and the machinations of an incarcerated Lucky Luciano. The hero imagines himself in combat with "a crippled newsie," a figure of speech that will forever be associated with Bogart playing Sam Spade in 1941. Most of the time, indeed, it's the Bogart figure that Cassidy, Maxwell's hero, tries to evoke. Two cops strong-arm him into their car. "Cassidy chuckled and shook his head like Bogart in the movies. 'Two bashful suitors. What a pair. Sure, sure, I'll come. But you gotta give me my arm back, Harry.'" Those lines really do sound if they were written for Bogart to bite them off. The problem is that a text so haunted by its predecessor is trapped into becoming at best an inspired parody or act of fealty.

One way around the problem of nostalgia is to take liberties with the depiction of the sleuth. In recent hard-boiled novels he remains, fundamentally, the same old Galahad figure he was when his name was Philip Marlowe, but that fact is buried behind some artful disguises. Unshaven and debauched he may be, a boozed-up rent-a-cop in Montana who snorts lines of cocaine in his pick-up truck, as in James Crumley's *Dancing Bear.* For that matter, he remains a compelling figure even when you strip him of his hard-boiled accoutrements, his whiskey and his wound, and replace then with Yuppie essentials—a jogging suit and live-in girlfriend with a sexy career of her own. In Richard Rosen's *Strike Three, You're Dead* (1984), you'll find him in the guise of a professional baseball player who lives a stone's throw from Harvard Yard. Harvey Blissberg, Rosen's sleuth, used to play center field for the "Providence Jewels" expansion team. He has a mother out of Philip Roth ("it's not easy telling people my son is thirty years old and plays baseball"), a girlfriend who's a TV sports announcer, and an older brother who's an English professor and a baseball statistics freak. Ever the projection of his author's irony, Blissberg is tough enough to "take a licking and keep on ticking"—and it's entirely characteristic that his experience of a beating should be rendered in the self-mocking accents of a Timex commercial.

The ultimate Yuppie sleuth is the hard-boiled heroine. She may be a Chicago-based feminist with a unisex name, like V. I. Warshawsky (her friends call her "Vic") in Sara Paretsky's novels. Or perhaps she is an endearingly frisky wisecracker, like the capriciously named Kinsey Millhone in Sue Grafton's series of alphabetical murder mysteries (such as *'C' Is for Corpse* and *'D' Is for Deadbeat*). The recent emergence of such female gumshoes may be inevitable, given the course of contemporary feminism, but it is really quite startling when you consider the genre's initial ambivalence at best and hostility at worst toward its women characters. Women in the world of Sam Spade and Philip Marlowe tended to be temptresses or villains. (The nice ones didn't have much sex appeal. "You're a damned good man, sister," Sam Spade says to his secretary, Effie Perine.) With Grafton and Paretsky, the wheel has come full circle. The women in these crime novels have other choices available to them besides the roles of victim and villain. They're more likely to be cast as role models rather than parole models or damsels in distress.

In *"C" Is for Corpse,* Grafton's sleuth meets her client in Yuppiedom's answer to the traditional girl-meets-boy scene: They're doing leg curls together at a fitness club. Aside from her cloyingly confected name, Kinsey Millhone is an admirable creation. Twice divorced at thirty-two, she's a loner with a sharp eye and tart tongue who lives in a converted garage ninety-five miles north of Los Angeles. In the Chandler tradition, Kinsey defines her character through the quality of her perceptions. Santa Teresa Hospital, she says, "looks like an enormous art deco wedding cake," is more expensive than most hotels, and offers "many personal services that didn't interest me, autopsy being one." When Kinsey tells us that Lila Sams's "breasts looked like two five-pound flour sacks from which some of the contents had spilled," we know that the sexagenarian thus described is sure to cause trouble. But while Kinsey can crack wise with the best of them, she's also capable of bursting into tears at the news of her client's murder. Nor is she above poking fun at herself in the ironic hard-boiled manner. In one scene, she approaches the resplendent Spanish Revival mansion where the suspects are disporting themselves. Dressed inappropriately in slacks, Kinsey improvises an outlandish getup featuring high heels, panty hose, and a flimsy black gauze tunic. "If I walked in front of a light, they'd see my bikini underpants, but so what?" she reasons. "If I couldn't afford to dress well, at least I could provide a distraction from the fact."

Sara Paretsky is more doctrinaire, less whimsical. Her work has a strong political dimension; it practices the fictional equivalent of affirmative action as programmatically as if it were an enforceable law. The most reliable characters in Paretsky's *Bitter Medicine* are almost exclusively women. In addition to the intrepid sleuth, other women in the cast include a resourceful black sculptor and a dedicated doctor (and Holocaust survivor) who forsakes the high-powered, high-paying job that could be hers for the asking in favor of running a clinic in a downscale Chicago neighborhood. The novel's suitably complicated plot centers on a case of hospital malpractice that allows the author to score a number of political points. A nasty anti-abortion demonstration, as Paretsky depicts it, makes "right to life" seem not only a hollow phrase but a tragically dangerous one.

Paretsky's culprits are invariably men, who run the gamut from obnoxious attorneys and corrupt city officials to vicious punks; in *Bitter Medicine* her victims, as predictably, are a pregnant Hispanic teenager and a young black surgeon. We suspect the author of resorting to feminist typecasting more than once. The sleuth's ex-husband, an unscrupulous and avaricious lawyer, is described by a sympathetic character as "a prick"; we may be quite certain that no female character will be called "a cunt," and with the author's tacit approval at that. A critique of Paretsky's novels might dwell on her didacticism—it is not necessarily the substance of her message but its redundancy that irritates. On the other hand, a political defense of Paretsky's procedures can easily be mounted. Surely, her depiction of men is no more objectionable than the depiction of women in Hammett or Chandler. What's more, if her novels reinforce the sexes in their mutual hostility, that may be justified under the heading of consciousness-raising. What Paretsky does—and does brilliantly—is turn the hard-boiled novel's original masculine-feminine hierarchy upside down. To the extent that any deconstructionist program depends on a reversal of received hierarchies, Paretsky may be said to practice a form of feminist deconstruction. In *Bitter Medicine,* for example, the love interest is a man who goes to bed with the sleuth, turns out to be implicated in the crime, and in time is condemned to the precise degree of humiliation that a Chandler or Hammett would have reserved for a deceitful mistress.

The point, however, is not the author's sexual politics but the fact of their easy coexistence with the traditional traits of the hard-boiled genre. V. I. Warshawsky's Chicago is a city of ethnic neighborhoods and violent contrasts, few illusions and considerable chaos—which may be why the sleuth prides herself on her disorderly housekeeping ("I found a pint of blueberries that could have saved the world if we'd run out of penicillin"). Her mission, to "put some order into life," is a perfectly appropriate paradox, since the hard-boiled sleuth characteristically adds to the chaos before getting to the heart of the case. Foster child of Philip Marlowe that she is, Warshawsky reminds us that the hard-boiled novel emphasizes action to the same extent that the classic murder mystery emphasizes cogitation. She herself favors the "Dick Butkus approach to detection"—butting heads at the line of scrimmage—rather than the fancy intellectual gymnastics of a Sherlock Holmes or a Nero Wolfe. Her tart, no-nonsense wit has a political edge, but the tone—that of anger and fatigue almost but not quite brought to a boil—is instantly recognizable. Days after getting slashed in the mandatory scene where the sleuth is roughed up by hired thugs, she is getting tired of explaining the scar on her face. "I cut myself shaving," she tells one importunate asker.

V. I. Warshawsky could be speaking for all her predecessors, male or female, when she says: "Not only do I not think I can save the world, I suspect most people are past redemption. I'm just the garbage collector, cleaning up little trash piles here and there." Grafton's Kinsey Millhone, for her part, announces the hard-boiled sleuth's credo on page one of *'D' Is for Deadbeat.* "I credit myself with an easygoing disposition, tempered (perhaps) by an exaggerated desire for independence," says this self-supporting survivor of two broken marriages. "I'm also plagued with the sort of doggedness that makes private investigation a viable proposition for someone with a high school education, certification from the police academy, and a constitutional inability to work for anyone else." That is a pithy pronunciamento of the hard-boiled attitude, transposed though it be to an urban environment inhabited by prosperous, upwardly mobile materialists, whose smugness would seem so inimical to the spirit of the private eye.[4]

15

A Portrait
of the Reader as Escapist

*L*et me lend you the *History of Contemporary Society*. It's in
hundreds of volumes, but most of them are sold in cheap
editions: *Death in Piccadilly, The Ambassador's Diamonds, The
Theft of the Naval Papers, Diplomacy, Seven Days' Leave, The
Four Just Men . . .*

—GRAHAM GREENE, *The Ministry of Fear*

The world's most distinguished opponent of detective novels exco-
riated them as escapist. "The reading of detective stories is simply
a kind of vice that, for silliness and minor harmfulness, ranks somewhere between smoking and crossword puzzles," Edmund Wilson
told his *New Yorker* readers in 1945.[1] Though wrongheaded, Wilson wasn't entirely wrong. There is no denying the escapist nature
of the genre's appeal, though one may turn the tables—as the critic
Robert Warshow did a few years later—and say that escapism in
the service of "a particular aesthetic effect" is no vice. Warshow
wrote a celebrated essay on gangster movies, "The Gangster as
Tragic Hero," at a time when the culture of escapism was not yet
an intellectually respectable subject for inquiry. The gangster,

Warshow asserted, expresses a disaffected part of the American psyche; he "speaks for us."[2] The detective story may be defended—if it requires defense—on similar grounds. It aims at aesthetic effects that would be interesting whatever the means or the vehicle—effects that become doubly so in the work of a master novelist or filmmaker.

It is possible to modify the charge of escapism by pointing to the many contemporary thrillers that enjoy a symbiotic relationship with headlines and other tabloid truths. The symbiosis is evident enough in spy novels and crime thrillers. The distinguishing characteristic of this class of books is that, unlike detective stories and murder mysteries, they do not begin with the corpse and work their way backward; the emphasis is on the chase, the escape, the heist, or the scheme about to take place rather than on the investigation of a murder that has already occurred. Something resembling journalistic research must go into a John Le Carré spy novel, an Eric Ambler or Ross Thomas novel of skulduggery and intrigue, an Elmore Leonard crime novel, a Donald E. Westlake comic caper. These writers set store by their accuracy of detail—the way Elmore Leonard's dialogue always rings true—and by their fidelity to the newspapers' conception of reality. An airliner has been hijacked in Greece. There is a plot to assassinate the rebel leader in the Philippines. Terrorists take hostages in Lebanon. A Florida cocaine scam goes sour. A foolproof plan to fleece a millionaire has its headquarters in a bookie joint run by spurious nuns in Queens. The sequence of events is plausibly outlandish—that is, outlandish enough to get your attention but no more improbable than what you might read in tomorrow's tabloids ("Headless Corpse in Topless Bar!") or even sobersided newspapers of record ("Bolivia Blooms With Cocaine Kingpin's Cash").

It sometimes seems as though journalists and op-ed-page pundits are recapitulating the events of a particular thriller and pondering their implications. In Ambler's *The Intercom Conspiracy* (1969), for example, two veteran NATO hands conspire to blackmail rival intelligence outfits by taking over a disreputable right-wing newsletter and using it to leak highly classified information. The novel becomes a parable of the mimetic relationship between nominally antagonistic intelligence operations. In the world of espionage, we're meant to see, each side knows the other's secrets but knows also that "the conventions must be observed and the pretences maintained, that outsiders may not look in on our foolishness and that both sides have a common enemy—the small boy who saw that the emperor was naked." The point—that the CIA and KGB are more concerned with one another than either is with the world of external events—has been made often enough, and often enough by intelligence insiders, in the years since Ambler adumbrated the theme with his customary wit and polish in *The Intercom Conspiracy.* That is one of Ambler's acknowledged strengths: His novels are like predictions couched in the past tense. Events generally prove them right.

By contrast, detective novels aren't famous for reflecting tomorrow's news today. We associate them with nostalgia—for a privileged society or a romanticized past—and with the desire to escape from the world of bulletins and fast-breaking stories. Yet a trait of recent American detective novels is that they're grounded in hard news. Richard Rosen's *Strike Three, You're Dead* is a prime example. It was published in 1984—two years before a Brown University prostitution-ring scandal made front-page news. In Rosen's novel, Detective Sergeant Linderman of the Providence police force agrees to meet Harvey Blissberg, a professional baseball player and amateur sleuth, at a bar on the Brown campus. "Nice place," Linderman spits out. "We pinched a couple hookers there last month."

The headlines anticipated in *Fadeaway,* Rosen's second novel, are "Hoop Homicides Horrify Hub" and "Did Two NBA Careers Go Up In Coke?" If headlines are the haiku of journalism, these are fine inventions. They seem to take pleasure in their own artifice, as if to mimic and exaggerate journalistic form, but at the same time they're not too good to be true. They come close to the headlines one actually *did* encounter in the spring of 1986—after the novel was written but before it was published—when college "phenom" Len Bias died of a cocaine overdose just days after the Boston Celtics made him their first-round draft pick. With Bias's death fresh in their minds, *Fadeaway's* first readers stumbled on the murdered bodies of Tyrone Terrell (forward, Boston Celtics) and Gus Sturdivant (guard, Washington Bullets) in a luggage locker and a trash barrel, respectively, at Boston's Logan Airport. Terrell is found with "a suspicious white powdery substance adhering to his mucous membrane," Rosen writes; Sturdivant's well-known prescription for basketball success was "toot 'n' shoot."

Even Rosen's choice of villain seems to fit as the prophecy of a future headline. In *Fadeaway,* that role is played by "a basketball coaching legend," who plans on becoming Rhode Island's next

governor—and who, between bites of "custid pie," extempora-
neously delivers this send-up of a "man of the people" speech:
"I'm a people person. I'm a person person. I'm a good people
people. I may dress like this, but I'm a man of the people." (Dress-
ing "like this" means wearing "a double-breasted navy chalk-
stripe suit and cap-toe cordovans" at a sleazebag diner, the effect
as cheerfully incongruous as a fashion ad "in which the model is
photographed next to 'real people' in a debased urban location.")
Sure enough, as if in response to Rosen's summons, 1987 provided
a newsworthy incident involving college athletics and the governor's mansion: In March of that year, the national media were full
of stories about the role of Texas governor Bill Clements in a re-
cruitment scandal at Southern Methodist University.[3]

Rosen places his emphasis on characters and quips, not on whodunit or how or why. In this regard, *Strike Three, You're Dead* and
Fadeaway fall squarely within the American hard-boiled tradition,
though a patina of wit lightly mocks that tradition. But not only
murder mysteries in the Hammett-Chandler mode are able to anticipate newspaper realities. Scroll down the *New York Times* back to
February 21, 1987, and you'll find this front-page headline: "Judge
Sent Poisoned Candy; Man He Sentenced Arrested." Read on and
you learn that on Valentine's Day that year, a box of poisoned chocolates was sent to the home of Chief Judge Charles L. Brieant, Jr.,
of the Federal District in Manhattan; the Valentine's Day card it
came with was signed with a question mark in lieu of a signature.
Four of the "Golden Godiva" chocolates—which had been treated
with deadly nightshade—were consumed not by the judge but by
his wife, who collapsed and was rushed (in time, luckily) to the
hospital. The affair eerily echoes the plot of Anthony Berkeley's
The Poisoned Chocolates Case (1929), a British classic from the
days when the genre's supreme value was conceived to be the craft-
ing of ingenious puzzles, no matter how implausible. Such stories
are supposed to have a rather tenuous relation to actuality. More's
the surprise, then, when you turn to Berkeley's novel and read
about the box of adulterated chocolates that has been sent to Sir
Eustace Pennefather at his club in London. Not having a sweet
tooth, Sir Eustace gives the chocolates to his fellow club member
Graham Bendix, who gives them to his wife, who eats them and
dies.

The candy caper culprit of 1987 was apparently careless enough
to leave one of his fingerprints on the box of chocolates. Since the
fingerprint matches up with that of the anthropology professor

Judge Brieant sent to prison six years earlier, the police feel they have an open-and-shut case on their hands. This is, of course, where the classic puzzler has it all over the stuff of the headlines. In Berkeley's *Poisoned Chocolates Case,* we get not one putative solution but six of them in turn, as each member of London's "Crimes Circle Club" takes a stab at the case. On successive nights, different solutions are proposed and discussed. Sir Charles, the barrister, argues that Sir Eustace Pennefather's *wife* sent the poisoned sweets, meaning to kill her philandering husband; the death of Mrs. Bendix was an unfortunate accident. Fielder-Flemming, the dramatist, points an accusing finger at *Sir Charles,* whose daughter was being wooed by Sir Eustace. Bradley, the detective writer, "proves" that it must have been *he* who did it. Roger Sheringham, founder and president of the Crimes Circle Club, maintains that the deceased really was the intended victim all along—and that *her husband* did it. Miss Dammers, the novelist, proposes a yet-more-sophisticated reading: She agrees that Mrs. Bendix was the intended victim but argues that the culprit was *Sir Eustace.* His motive? Mrs. Bendix, his discarded mistress, was threatening to make their affair public. On the last night, Miss Dammers is herself trumped by the unheralded Mr. Chitterwick, who explains that *Miss Dammers* herself set out to kill both Sir Eustace and Mrs. Bendix, her rival for Sir Eustace's affections. Each solution erases the last; the whole stands as a kind of epistemological parable, proving that a well-made problem admits of more than one plausible explanation, that different detective methods produce different results, and that the detective may be implicated by and in his own findings. But the ingenuity of the solutions gives a pleasure beyond this clever multiplicity. The crime in *The Poisoned Chocolates Case* is, says one of the armchair sleuths, "so exactly right—ingenious, utterly simple, and as near as possible infallible." The speaker is all admiration. "A perfect murder makes me feel lyrical," he explains. "If I was this particular criminal I should have been writing odes to myself for the last fortnight."

——◆——

Grant the truth in Edmund Wilson's charge, and we're left with a couple of questions. What does it mean to be a literary escapist, if that's what each of us is? Is *escapist* necessarily a pejorative term, or can we accept it as descriptively appropriate and evaluatively neutral? Bearing in mind that the detective novel as a phenomenon peaked between the two world wars, we might look to the fiction of this period for three possible portraits of the reader as escapist—fictional stand-ins for us, the detective story's ideal readers. My candidates are Joseph K. in Franz Kafka's *The Trial* (1925), Arthur Rowe in Graham Greene's *The Ministry of Fear* (1943), and Charles Latimer in Eric Ambler's *A Coffin for Dimitrios* (1939). The first two share the common attribute of exaggerated guilt; the second is likened to a detective novelist and the third is in fact a detective novelist. First, however, something further does need to be said about escapism, why we are guilty of it, and what it means.

A rhetorical defense of escapism was furnished by T. S. Eliot, though that wasn't exactly his intention when he asserted that poetry was "an escape from emotion" and "an escape from personality." He added a flourish: "But, of course, only those who have personality and emotions know what it means to want to escape from these things."[4]

There is, equally of course, an obvious distance between Eliot's sense of poetic escapism and Eliot's own love of detective stories. Eliot had no trouble seeing high art and pop culture as distinct and irreconcilable categories, though he himself promoted an easy commerce between the two by raiding music hall lyrics for "The Waste Land." The argument in defense of escapism begins with the recognition of such acts of easy commerce. There is no need to judge the works of Raymond Chandler in the context of Marcel Proust. One need only remark, first, that the detective story has clearly had an influence on the course of modern fiction, and second, that the influence has been a salutary one. The first of these points is easy to prove. Elements of detective stories are appropriated with a startling frequency by novelists not considered genre writers. In the past several seasons, one thinks of new books by such authors as Mario Vargas Llosa, Peter Ackroyd, Joyce Carol Oates, John Hawkes, John Fowles, and Robert Coover, each of which was or could be described as having the plot (or structure) of a detective story.[5] The second point—that the detective novel's influence has been salutary—may be advanced by testimonial (Auden's praise of Chandler), by citation of signal achievements (Chandler's vision of a mercenary inferno), and by analogy (compare Chandler's prose style with that of our leading minimalists, and the advantage goes to the former). We need to remind ourselves not to hold a work's popularity against it even as we recall that few detective writers profit from being treated as literary artists.

There is a narrow sense in which the detective novel aspires to perform an aesthetic function precisely *because* it is escapist and not in spite of that condition. Art, wrote W. H. Auden in "Caliban to the Audience," possibly the greatest of his poems on the subject, classically presents "the perfectly tidiable case of disorder, the beautiful and serious problem exquisitely set without a single superfluous datum and insoluble with less." The description applies more obviously to the old-fashioned art of the murder mystery than to most forms of modern art. Infallible sleuths on the order of Sherlock Holmes and Hercule Poirot operate on the confident assumption that problems are neatly soluble and all disorder "perfectly tidiable." This has become a purely escapist notion; it obtains in less and less fiction that is, or purports to be, advanced in technique and serious in aim. The art of our century has characteristically emphasized disorder, feeling anything but confident about its—or our—ability to tidy it up.

Detective stories are the nostalgic alternative. One reason we are drawn to them is our conviction that neither life nor high art is really *like* that. We live, or read, in a state of constant uncertainty, among unreliable narrators, amid equivocal clues, faced with mysteries that turn out to be unsolvable muddles. How pleasant, then, to escape into a universe founded on logic and order, where violations are temporary, transgressions are punished, and justice is expected to prevail! At this point in the argument, it is customary for the defender of detective stories to cite the example of Dickens, who was popular and wrote for the ages: "And besides, where does escapism leave off and transcendence begin?"

A well-made thriller is an insomniac's dream—or a recurrent nightmare, albeit one that ends well; when we wake up, we're ready to start dreaming again. And that's not to denigrate the impulse. On the contrary, it gets us closer to the art of the matter. It was a wise man who observed that art is a criticism of life primarily in the sense that a jailbreak is a criticism of the penitentiary. The ex-convicts on the loose, free at last, find something to nourish them in the imagination—something that will hold them in good stead in their next stint behind bars.

❖

In affirming its old-fashioned values—a strong plot, a clear resolution, a sense of closure—the detective novel paradoxically provides the means by which it can be subverted into an alien form of art. It would be fruitful to consider *The Trial* in this light. "Everyday life is the greatest detective story ever written," Franz Kafka once told a friend. "Every second, without noticing, we pass by thousands of corpses and crimes. That's the routine of our lives. But if, in spite of habit, something does succeed in surprising us, we have a marvellous sedative in the detective story, which presents every mystery of life as a legally punishable exception."[6] In an important sense, Kafka echoes the circumstances of a detective novel in *The Trial*—only he situates it in metaphysical space, a place where the genre's governing assumptions do not apply. The sole "sedative" Kafka is willing to dispense is guaranteed to send readers to a nightmare of bureaucratic terror, which also happens to be a parable about justice and damnation.

Auden described the hero of *The Trial* as "a portrait of the kind of person who reads detective stories for escape."[7] Though Joseph K. is never shown to us with a detective novel in hand, we can tell he's the sort of fellow who—if he lived on our street— would have a stack of detective novels beside his bed. He needs to escape. His sense of guilt is overwhelming; what's more, he feels imprisoned by circumstance, trapped in the labyrinthine corridors of his nightmare—he cannot wake up to find it was all a dream. There can be no better example of an escapist mentality than that of the condemned man, who faces prison or the death sentence, if he doesn't somehow escape. And in Joseph K.'s case, there is the added pathos of the born victim who knows that he cannot escape.

Detective novels depend on the premise that the truth can be known and acted upon. But *The Trial* subverts this principle—Joseph K.'s nightmare has the logic of lies. His adventures begin with this remarkable opening sentence, which can be taken as either literal fact or childish paranoia: "Someone must have been telling lies about Joseph K., for without having done anything wrong he was arrested one fine morning." The truth—in a place where lies are credited—becomes irrelevant. The first fact of K.'s cosmos is that he is guilty without knowing why. The last fact is that he assists his own executioners and dies, as he says, "like a dog." The guilt is real, though we remain convinced that K. never did do anything wrong. The cosmos is neither rational nor just but it doesn't need to be. As the priest explains in the great cathedral episode, "It is not necessary to accept everything as true, one must only accept it as necessary." "A melancholy conclusion," K. replies. "It turns lying into a universal principle." Melancholy, indeed: If lying is a universal principle, how can we ever know anything for certain?

A citizen in the land of *The Trial* would perhaps inevitably favor detective novels if the law of compensatory imagination holds—if readers look to books for what's lacking in their lives. Joseph K. can never even find out what he's being charged with, and no one resembling a detective—amateur or professional, hard-boiled or refined—steps forward to help him find out. Yet guilt as a psychological (or symbolic) fact can exist without empirical causes, and K. is convinced beyond the shadow of a doubt that he is the guilty party. His guilt is irrevocable, his punishment inevitable, though no evidence speaks against him and nothing like a corpse turns up. That could never happen in a narrative game played according to Doyle. No doubt that is why Joseph K. is (or would be) so responsive a reader of detective stories. In detective stories he finds what's missing in his life; there the puzzle, in the end, makes sense. In the world *he* inhabits—where guilt is certain and universal but never rationally explained—it is easy to see the charms of a literary form that holds out the promise or at least the possibility of closure and disclosure, the restoration of order, the achievement of justice, and the vindication of the innocent many by the banishment of the guilty one.

A second fictional portrait of the reader as an escapist is Arthur Rowe, the hero of Graham Greene's *The Ministry of Fear* (1943), whose own favored form of escapism is amnesia. The setting here is wartime London, ravaged by enemy bombs. As the result of an explosion, Rowe loses his memory. He is told that his name is Digby and that he saved a girl's life by falling on the bomb. What he doesn't know is who he is or what he had done, for good or ill, in the days and years before the bomb went off. Desperate to sleuth out the facts about his past, Rowe becomes an amateur Oedipus, asking questions, pleading for answers. Eager to learn about the world at large, he is an avid reader of newspapers when he can get his hands on them and sets his mind on puzzling out the mysterious episode of a government leak that the papers have reported. The episode fascinates him. Was he perhaps a detective before the explosion wiped out his past? "You weren't a detective," exclaims a good-natured orderly in the asylum where Rowe is attempting to recover his memory. "You were a detective writer." A sheen of irony coats this high-spirited exchange. By the end of *The Ministry of Fear,* the orderly is dead; the asylum turns out to be a false

Bower of Bliss, and the amnesiac is a man who gave his wife a glass of poisoned milk, and killed her.

Arthur Rowe's amnesia and his newspaper addiction are the twin sides of the reader's experience of detective stories. What Rowe reads in the newspaper contains cryptic clues to his own predicament—and hints at the global consequences of private lives. What Rowe forgets is his terrible guilt. Before the explosion wiped out his memory, he always felt like a murderer. He was obsessed with his guilt and would have been suicidal except that a still, small voice inside warned him off. True, there were extenuating circumstances: His wife was terminally ill. The jury acquitted him, preferring to view her death as a mercy killing. But Rowe's court of conscience could not be so easily appeased: "He believed against all the experience of life that somewhere there was justice, and justice condemned him." Graham Greene's portrait of the reader as an escapist is, then, a person with a past who fears damnation. The narrative is his purgatory.

Rowe's predicament is a variant of Joseph K.'s. Both regard their guilt as self-evident, the one real thing and probably the key ingredient in the escapist personality. But unlike the hero of *The Trial,* Rowe has a past that makes his current situation credible. There is an end to Rowe's amnesia in *The Ministry of Fear.* There is no end to Joseph K.'s terminal uncertainty. Joseph K. has no past; history doesn't exist in *The Trial.* The place is Anywhere, the time is Always, the leading character has a cipher instead of a name and must, since causality cannot be ascertained, endure consequences without knowing their causes. His plight is a pitiless parable about justice, the remoteness of humanity from any kind of deity except a cruel and implacable one. By contrast, Graham Greene's "entertainment" is a parable of conscience and mercy set in a London that remains in significant ways unchanged from the urban Edwardian fairyland that Chesterton invoked and praised in *The Club of Queer Trades* and the Father Brown stories. *The Ministry of Fear* designates a purely metaphorical zone, a sinister funhouse of mirrors and illusions, where a charity bazaar may be the front for a spy ring and a cake ("baked with real eggs") their chosen vehicle for smuggling state secrets—a most unconventional "MacGuffin."[8]

To an extent, Greene intends a critique of—and a lament for—the literature of escapism. Before he undergoes the adventures that transform and redeem him, the hero of *The Ministry of Fear* yearns for the books of his childhood. These are conjured up in a memorable passage:

> In childhood we live under the brightness of immortality—heaven is as near and actual as the seaside. Behind the complicated details of the world stand the simplicities: God is good, the grown-up man or woman knows the answer to every question, there is such a thing as truth, and justice is as measured and faultless as a clock. Our heroes are simple: they are brave, they tell the truth, they are good swordsmen, and they are never in the long run really defeated. That is why no later books satisfy us like those which were read to us in childhood, for those promised a world of great simplicity of which we knew the rules, but the later books are complicated and contradictory with experience: they are formed out of our own disappointing memories—of the V. C. in the police-court dock, of the faked income-tax return, the sins in corners, and the hollow voice of the man we despise talking to us of courage and duty.

Our detective novels are like those books of childhood. We may yearn for them, their certainties and simplicities, but there is no returning to that naive state of being. We have outgrown the romances and the detective stories in whose bourne "justice is as measured and faultless as a clock."

Greene goes out of his way to depict the professional detective in *The Ministry of Fear* as a pathetically weak, ineffectual, ignoble figure. It's as though, by contrast with the hero-worshiping books of childhood, *this* book were a critically revised detective novel, as though Greene's method in his entertainments were simply to take certain thriller elements and divest them of their air of unreality. One often-quoted passage from *The Ministry of Fear* speaks of a multivolume *History of Contemporary Society*: "It's in hundreds of volumes, but most of them are sold in cheap editions: *Death in Piccadilly, The Ambassador's Diamonds, The Theft of the Naval Papers, Diplomacy, Seven Days' Leave, The Four Just Men . . .*" It should be noted, however, that Rowe, the speaker, is delirious when he says this—and that he has just described himself as the librarian of a madhouse.

Like Greene, Eric Ambler retained key elements of received thriller formulas but cut deeply against their grain. In his great prewar thrillers—*Journey into Fear, A Coffin for Dimitrios, Cause for Alarm*, and *Epitaph for a Spy*—Ambler intended a critique of the escapist mind, identifying it with the isolationist Briton who needed to be persuaded that neutrality in the age of Hitler was folly. It made literary sense to parody, though lightly, detective novel routines in *A Coffin for Dimitrios* (1939)—it distracted readers from noticing just how much energy Ambler was generating out of the very conventions he was sending up. As a portrait of the reader as an escapist, the hero of *A Coffin for Dimitrios* is triumphant in a key sense: He survives. Ambler waited until *The Intercom Conspiracy* in 1969 to kill him off on the grounds that the detective as a hero and the detective story as a form were through.

It could be said that Ambler did for the spy thriller what Hammett did for the detective novel. Before Ambler revolutionized the genre, espionage in fiction was largely a matter of drawing-room intrigue, madcap escapades in Monte Carlo casinos, and tuxedo-clad secret agents on whose glamorous shoulders the fate of Western civilization depended. Ambler gave espionage back to the people who conspire for a cause, not just to provide the pretext for an international incident. The assassins in Ambler's prewar thrillers were deliberately prosaic thugs as opposed to the larger-than-life or uglier-than-sin villains who had previously populated the genre. Of the hired killer reeking of scent in *Journey into Fear*, for example, we're told that "his very insignificance was horrible. It leant a false air of normality to the situation." The menace in Ambler's novels was ever in inverse proportion to the apparent "normality" of the circumstances; the threat of violence, the logic of its inevitability, loomed greater than the actual violence depicted. Ambler always made sure his readers knew who was paying for the bullets. Espionage was business by other means: Behind the eponymous international criminal of *A Coffin for Dimitrios* stand the resources and prestige of the "Eurasian Credit Trust."

Unlike the spiffy, well-bred agents in E. Phillips Oppenheim's early espionage novels, Ambler favored rank amateurs, examples of "the wrong man." Unlike John Le Carré's professionals, Ambler's prewar protagonists are versions of his ideal reader, ordinary chaps thrust willy-nilly into extraordinary circumstances. The complacent ballistics engineer in *Journey into Fear* (1940) and the nervous production engineer in *Cause for Alarm* (1939) are alike in being middle-class innocents abroad who get disabused of their illusions despite wishing hard to cling to them. The education of these politically neutral English naïfs begins once they cross the channel and learn "that civilization was a word and that you still lived in the jungle." Then danger descends, the threat of imminent death, "waiting"—we're told in *Journey into Fear*—"to make nonsense of all your comfortable ideas about your relations with time and chance."

Ambler's reader is *you*. The aim of the exercise was, in part, to shatter "your" complacency. Paradoxically, Ambler used the escapist form of the thriller to dramatize the idea that danger was everywhere in the European thirties and that escape from its consequences was impossible. The European jungle lived by the application of Nietzschean principles. "What a man does depends on what he needs," says a character in *Journey into Fear*. "A man is an ape in velvet." Strip off the velvet and you get a man like Dimitrios, whose existence is proof that good and evil "were no more than baroque abstractions. Good Business and Bad Business were the elements of the new theology. Dimitrios was not evil. He was logical and consistent; as logical and consistent in the European jungle as the poison gas called Lewisite."

The heroes of *Journey into Fear* and *Cause for Alarm* acquit themselves well in the end; they are resourceful enough to survive. But there is one Ambler character who seems as emblematic of the reader as escapist as Kafka's condemned man and Greene's amnesiac. Charles Latimer, the hero of *A Coffin for Dimitrios,* is a professional detective writer—which makes him a confirmed amateur at "real murder." The plot of the book is supposed to further Latimer's education in reality. In Istanbul the mild-mannered mystery writer meets Colonel Haki, the genial chief of police, an avid reader of detective novels. But Colonel Haki—unlike the policemen in detective novels—is not a figure of fun. The corpse of a notorious desperado has turned up on shore, requiring the colonel's attention. "I wonder if you are interested in real murderers," he says and proceeds to tell Latimer about the drowned Dimitrios Makropoulos. Fascinated, the novelist decides to trace Dimitrios's footprints as an "experiment in detection." It is expected that the experience will act as a corrective to the exaggerated puzzles and the archaic notions of the detective stories Latimer writes.

The structure of *A Coffin for Dimitrios* approximates the backward structure of detective novels: It begins with a corpse and works its way backward. As in a detective story, the story of Dimitrios's past—episodic crimes in exotic places—is enveloped inside the story of Latimer's present. Latimer goes, for example, to Geneva to find out about an espionage gambit involving Dimitrios in

Belgrade in 1926. The story of the crimes and the story of the investigation proceed on their separate tracks until they suddenly intersect at the moment of revelation: in Paris, where the ostensibly dead Dimitrios returns to life. Latimer is even given a sidekick and traveling companion, the ambiguous Mr. Peters (Sydney Greenstreet to Peter Lorre's Latimer in the movie version), in a conscious nod at detective story form.[9]

Yet when Latimer talks to the sometimes ruthless characters who are in charge of educating him, they constantly use *detective story* as a synonym for *bosh* and *rubbish*. Colonel Haki: "In a *roman policier* there is a corpse, a number of suspects, a detective and a gallows. That is artistic. The real murderer is not artistic." Peters, less politely: "Mr. Latimer, this is not a detective story. There is no *need* to be so stupid."

Latimer's "experiment in detection" is, then, a critique of detective novel naïvetés. Dimitrios is an assassin, a mercenary spy, the organizer of a drug-smuggling ring; he kills when that is the profitable or expedient thing to do. "Here [Latimer tells himself] was *real* murder: not neat, tidy book-murder with corpse and clues and suspects and hangman, but murder over which a chief of police shrugged his shoulders, wiped his hands and consigned the stinking victim to the coffin." As he reconstructs Dimitrios's life of crime, Latimer begins to see him as a biographer would his subject: "not as a corpse in a mortuary but as a man, not as an isolate, a phenomenon, but as a unit in a disintegrating social system." Dimitrios prefigures the death of the detective novel, for he has moved beyond the detective novel's moral system. He has gone beyond good and evil. Not through an appeal to moral values but to superior force is he to be subdued.

The detective story as a form is rejected as too unsophisticated to accommodate either the criminal mind or the political realities of Europe on the verge of the Second World War. Yet after Dimitrios's story ends, Latimer's continues—and the final twist is that he ends where he began, dreaming up the plot of an escapist detective novel. Latimer is returning home, riding on the Orient Express. He reads a letter from a friend in Sofia, who fills in some missing details about Dimitrios and concludes with heartiness and a grand illusion: "My latest information is that war will not break out until the spring; so there will be time for some ski-ing." (The "now" of the book is either 1938–39, the time of writing, or 1939–40, when its first readers came to it.) Latimer puts away the letter with a sigh.

Then he thinks of "more important matters," such as "a motive, a neat method of committing a murder and an entertaining crew of suspects" for his next book. It apparently doesn't occur to him to appropiate the story of Dimitrios to this end. "The scene? Well, there was always plenty of fun to be got out of an English country village, wasn't there? The time? Summer; with cricket matches on the village green, garden parties at the vicarage, the clink of tea-cups and the sweet smell of grass on a July evening. That was the sort of thing people liked to hear about. It was the sort of thing that he himself would like to hear about." And this, too, describes us, this confirmed addiction to the very genre whose premises have just been exploded. We know that escape is impossible and yet the wish for escape is too strong and too urgent to resist.

The last sentence of *A Coffin for Dimitrios*—"The train ran into a tunnel"—has a plainly ominous charge (whereas the same image, at the end of Hitchcock's *North by Northwest,* signifies conjugal merriment). We are in the darkness, entering a tunnel, proceeding blindfolded into a future of fear and danger, distracting ourselves by thinking of a detective story plot. There is pathos in the know-ledge that Latimer, the escapist hero, goes back to writing his sort of novel—goes back to the old illusions, willingly and with a sigh of contentment. He remains in that condition for thirty years—until Ambler revived the character, only to eliminate him, in *The Intercom Conspiracy.* Latimer's death in *The Intercom Conspiracy* is deeply disturbing. It's as if a true innocent such as he can no longer be expected to survive the mischief he may stumble into—as though, as of 1969, any true "experiment in detection" is likely to end not with knowledge but in death.

16

---◆---

At the Heart of the Maze

‘‘*E*veryone thought that the encounter of the two chess players was accidental.’’ This phrase allows one to understand that the solution is erroneous. The unquiet reader rereads the pertinent chapter and discovers *another* solution, the true one. The reader of this singular book is thus forcibly more discerning than the detective.

—JORGE LUIS BORGES, ‘‘An Examination of the Work of Herbert Quain’’

In the case of any escapist literature, it is reasonable to ask where the escapists are going and where they are fleeing from. The question is easy enough to answer with respect to classic detective novels and thrillers. There the escape is from guilt into fear. The story interrupts one kind of anxiety with another. A problem of murder—so long as it is somebody else’s murder and somebody else’s guilt—is easier to bear than one’s own immediate concerns, mundane though these may be. Many readers have remarked on the disparity between the terminal violence in even the cosiest murder mystery and the mild-mannered disposition of the commuter reading the book on a train, who escapes thereby from the anxiety of not knowing what awaits him when he reaches his destination.[1]

But if the reader of mysteries is necessarily an escapist, he’s a

special one—a participant. Either he collaborates in his own mystification or he participates in the plot by trying to puzzle out the
solution ahead of the sleuth. (To anticipate the correct solution
without an expenditure of effort is taken as an indication of the
writer's inadequacy and not the reader's skill.) There's a metaphorical sense in which the armchair reader equals the armchair sleuth,
who metaphorically wills himself into the locked room—Room 101,
place of torture, world of no exit and no escape—in order to affirm
his mental or spiritual superiority to stone walls and iron bars. The
avid reader of mysteries wills himself into the very maze from
which, during the course of the reading, he will try to escape. The
author is in the same position but with the added burden of having
to construct the artifice in the first place. The author is the Daeda-
lus of the plot, who creates both the maze and the means by which
it can be escaped.

Then there is the case of that putative escapist, the unquiet
reader of an unorthodox study in detection. Into what are they
escaping, the readers of a book that is self-conscious and uneasy
about its relation to detective story tradition—a book that may explode the genre's conventions? Such readers need to be sophisticated ironists: able to recognize and act on their desire for escape
despite the resigned awareness that such attempts must in the order of things be sabotaged. The aim of the exercise is to enjoy
the vicarious or palpable pleasures associated with the thriller—the
suspense, the surprise, the suspicion, the danger, the sense of taking a journey into the unknown—without needing to credit any of
the genre's premises.

The detective story has become a sort of refuge for writers and
readers who are reluctant to give up their love of illusion—even
while priding themselves on having "no illusions" about art and
fantasy. This double impulse is at the heart of the postmodernist
maze: The love of artifice and the intolerance of it are simultaneous, and the writer tries to duplicate that simultaneity by giving
you an experience and its negation at once. You are led to the heart
of the maze, where you *do* confront a Minotaur—though when you
look at it up close, you can tell it's just a clumsy piece of stage
machinery. The postmodernist detective novel equals its form emp-
tied of content, or otherwise adapted, subverted, parodied, revised.
Thus the form of the detective novel is guaranteed a posthumous,
metaphysical existence independent of the life of the genre.

The ludic postmodernist impulse was put into play by the great Argentine writer Jorge Luis Borges, who yielded to no one in his devotion to detective stories. He wrote admiringly of Poe, Doyle, and Chesterton. Under his editorial direction, a series of detective novels—collectively titled The Seventh Circle—introduced Argentine readers to (in his words) "the idea that a detective story could also be literary." Approximately 150 novels, including works by Wilkie Collins, Dickens (*The Mystery of Edwin Drood*), Nicholas Blake, and Michael Innes, were published in the series, which enjoyed a handsome success. "Those books did a lot of good," Borges remarked, "because they reminded writers that plots were important. If you read detective novels, and if you take up novels afterwards, the first thing that strikes you—it's unjust, of course, but it happens—is to think of the other books as shapeless."[2] For Borges, the importance of the plot went beyond its structural value, the insistence that a story have a definite shape with a clearly defined beginning, middle, and end. The plot was understood to be the structural element that reflects cunning, craft, and design. A coherent plot was an assertion of order—though often, alas, a malevolent order—like a maze.

Borges favored the synopsis as a literary form; he liked its artistic economy. "The composition of vast books is a laborious and impoverishing extravagance," he wrote in a prologue to his 1941 collection, *The Garden of Forking Paths*. "To go on for five hundred pages developing an idea whose perfect oral exposition is possible in a few minutes! A better course of procedure is to pretend that these books already exist, and then to offer a résumé, a commentary."[3] In several of his stories, Borges offers in few pages the concentrated essence of a detective novel. (An enterprising writer, mindful of the relative commercial value of novels and short stories, might consider elaborating certain of these stories into full-length books or films.) The recurrent elements in Borges's detective plots (or plot summaries) are fallible sleuths, sham appearances, death-dealing doubles, multiple outcomes and, above all, tortuous mazes. Some examples:

—*The God of the Labyrinth* by "Herbert Quain" is a purely conceptual detective novel summarized in "An Examination of the Work of Herbert Quain," a story in the form of a eulogy to (or obituary for) an imaginary author. All we're told of *The God of the*

Labyrinth is that it is self-subversive in the subtlest possible way. From a sentence near the end of *The God of the Labyrinth*, a clever reader can see that the solution proffered in the text is erroneous: "The unquiet reader rereads the pertinent chapters and discovers *another* solution, the true one. The reader of this singular book is thus forcibly more discerning than the detective."

—Herbert Quain's putative novel *April March* is said to be thirteen chapters long. Chapter 1 presents an inconsequential episode at a train station. Chapter 2 describes what happened the night before. The third chapter is another possible version of that night. The fourth chapter, a third version of the same night. Each of these three evenings is similarly subdivided into three parts with the result that the book comprises nine novels containing three chapters apiece. "The temper of one of these novels is symbolic; that of another, psychological; of another, communist; of still another, anticommunist; and so on." The imaginary novel enacts both the symbolic pattern of a maze and the backward narrative motion of a classic detective story.

—"The Garden of Forking Paths" is a Borges story that might have been conceived by "Herbert Quain." The action in the story occurs in curious and tantalizing counterpoint to a conversation between two men about a labyrinthine novel. Everything the story's narrator does is acted out for the benefit of one particular newspaper reader: an intelligence officer in Germany during World War I. Combing the English newspapers, this reader will decipher the story of an apparently motiveless murder. He will recognize that the narrator's "problem was to indicate (through the uproar of the war) the city called Albert, and that [he] had found no other means to do so than to kill a man of that name." This we learn in the story's penultimate sentence; until then we had no idea why the narrator, a Chinese agent in the employ of the Germans, tracks down and kills the eminent Sinologist Stephen Albert. The homicidal blow is struck only after a learned and cordial conversation between Albert and his assassin. During the course of their conversation, we learn that an ancestor of the narrator constructed "an invisible labyrinth of time" in the form of a novel. "In all fiction, when a man is faced with alternatives he chooses one at the expense of the others. In the almost unfathomable Ts'ui Pên, he chooses—simultaneously—all of them. He thus *creates* various futures, various times which start others that will in their turn branch out and bifurcate in other times."

—"Theme of the Traitor and Hero" is a parable about clandestine activities and official appearances: The execution of a traitor is stage-managed to look like the assassination of a statesman. The parable—about crowd control and propaganda but also about the problematic relationship between reality and "official" appearances—is fundamental to the espionage novel, or to any thriller with a political dimension, in which nation-states become in effect plural characters in the plot.

It is possible to consider several of Borges's parables as metaphoric extensions of an imagined conflict between the world of the text (or the library) and the world beyond its reach and its power. The library, an image of mind and order, is opposed to the chaos and flux of experience. The deadliest image of chaos is the knife, which stands in Borges not simply for violence but for all that is gratuitous and unexplainable, primitive and urgent. Between the word and the world there are correspondences and points of mutual intersection, enough to quicken the hope that artistic design governs lawless actuality after all. It even sometimes happens that events on earth, be they tragic or comic, seem to illustrate ancient verses, benedictions, or imprecations—as when, in the magnificent "Death and the Compass," a sequence of murders seems to draw a homicidal or even diabolical link between the four letters of the sacred Hebrew name of God and the four points of the compass. The melancholy in Borges is the resigned awareness that such symmetries are human creations, fearful and often fatal.

That the maze is very nearly as emblematic of the detective story as the locked room is enough to explain the form's great appeal to Borges. The symbol for the intricate puzzle and the quest to solve it is the labyrinth; a fundamental irony in Borges is his simultaneous celebration of human ingenuity (which is capable of constructing such extravagant artifices) and denigration of it (for the products of our ingenuity defeat and sometimes destroy us). Of the many mazes in Borges's stories, none is more disturbing than the conceptual labyrinth postulated by the criminal and entered by the sleuth in "Death and the Compass." The detective in the story penetrates to the heart of the maze, where his own destruction awaits him at the hands of his double.

"Death and the Compass" is a parable of the end of detection—*end* in the sense of *aim, goal,* and *completion* as well as of *demise.*

The hero likens himself to Poe's Dupin and is indeed nothing if not subtle in anticipating the criminal's next move. "It is true that Erik Lönnrot did not succeed in preventing the last crime, but it is indisputable that he foresaw it," the opening paragraph dryly informs us. Good detective that he is, Lönnrot collects the evidence and submits it to scrutiny. He continues his investigation past the point where Treviranus, the police commissioner, gives it up as hopelessly muddled. There have been three murders, at points north, east, and west; each occurs on the night of the third of the month, and each victim is Jewish. The plodding Treviranus is only as smart as a cop. Weary of the case, he is inclined to credit the anonymously sent letter declaring that the murder series is over. But the more imaginative Lönnrot, having done his homework and his mental arithmetic, recognizes that the geometrical design of the plot is a rhomb rather than an equilateral triangle. He knows there will be a fourth murder. The compass tells him where it will take place; the calendar tells him when. On the appointed night, he travels to Triste-le-Roy—only to learn that he himself is the intended victim, scheduled to die that night. The clues were concocted to lure him to the spot. The series of murders was arranged with Lönnrot in mind.

Not because he is inadequate is Lönnrot destroyed; on the contrary, the plot against him would not have succeeded if Lönnrot had been any less brilliant. In the best detective tradition, he has used the past to predict the future; his method could be called retrospective prophecy. Yet the knowledge costs him his life. A victim of his own ingenuity, he has collaborated in his own demise. And with his death the genre quite explodes. If the end of true detection is knowledge, and knowledge means death, the very premises of the detective story are overturned. "To Treviranus I sent the equilateral triangle," Red Scharlach tells Lönnrot before shooting him. "I sensed that you would supply the missing point. The point which would form a perfect rhomb, the point which fixes where death, exactly, awaits you." The police chief may be a dullard, but at least he survives. The pattern has caught the sleuth in its web. This murder is his.

Borges is the most radical of detective story writers, not only because *his* form of escapism takes the reader from certitude to its opposite but because he was the first to proclaim the death of the detective—an event comparable in local significance to Nietzsche's pronouncement that God was dead. Borges adopts the genre's conventions lovingly—and explodes them decisively. In his hands the detective story is an exercise in nostalgia but also a parable about the chimerical pursuit of knowledge. What could be called the subversive tradition begins with a handful of Borges's stories in which, invariably, the detective is defeated in the end—defeated because the conditions that made detection possible have ended, or because the theory of detection was founded on untenable assumptions all along, or because there is no way of knowing the truth. And for the detective, defeat is indistinguishable from death.

The logic of the subversive tradition goes like this: The detective's occupational hazard is to discern a conspiracy where others see only random violence. But say he's wrong. Postulate a vision of epistemological confusion and moral anarchy; say that the violence on the city's streets really is random, unmotivated, and only as coherent as a paranoid fantasy, which may be absolutely real to the paranoiac but to everyone else is a synonym for chance. What happens then? What happens if the world refuses to behave in compliance with the expectations of a rationalist? In other words, it's as though you retained the plot and structure of the detective story but removed the article of faith on which the whole contraption stood. What happens to the detective story—and to our escapist impulses—when it outlives the optimistic assumptions that once governed the genre but now no longer hold?

One subversive possibility is explored by Mark Smith in *The Death of the Detective* (1974), a vision of Chicago as inferno. Smith's detective goes from being a catalyst to being an emissary of death; his obsessive search for the criminal triggers off more corpses and more chaos. Another subversive possibility is the elevation of the criminal as hero: the scamp heroes of Ross Thomas's *Chinaman's Chance* (1978), the confidence men Donald E. Westlake favors when writing in his own persona and the mercenary tough guy he likes when using the name of Richard Stark. In many of Patricia Highsmith's novels, such as *The Talented Mr. Ripley* (1955), the absence of a detective goes together with an absence of any moral restraint; the killer invariably gets away with murder. ("Criminals are dramatically interesting, because for a time at least they are active, free in spirit, and they do not knuckle down to anyone," Highsmith has said. "I find the public passion for justice quite boring and artificial, for neither life nor nature cares if justice is ever done or not.'')[4] A third possibility, and surely the most Borgesian, is that the detective may be hanged by his own ingenuity—as happens in Friedrich Dürrenmatt's *The Pledge* (1958).

Matthai, Dürrenmatt's ingenious detective, predicts a crime with all the assertive confidence of Lönnrot in ''Death and the Compass.'' But Matthai's antagonist, unlike Lönnrot's, simply doesn't appear. The detective has done everything right. He has figured out the culprit's identity and knows what he will do next. He sets his trap accordingly—only to be stood up. The sleuth fails though his logic has been impeccable: The reason the villain doesn't show up is that he has been killed in a car accident on the way. Everything else Matthai had factored into his thinking, but a car crash he could not have anticipated. Chance and accident have sabotaged the best-laid plans of the mind; reality refuses to conform to our mental models of it. The fate of sheer intellect is like the fate of the single throw of dice in Mallarmé's poem ''Un Coup de dés jamais n'abolira le hasard''—''A Throw of the Dice Will Never Abolish Chance.''

The detective, being the paradigm of the intellectual hero, is necessarily a casualty of any such breakdown in our confidence in reason and ratiocination. That is why *The Pledge* is subtitled *A Requiem for the Detective Story*. The detective in a cosmos where detection is necessary but impossible to achieve is doomed from the start. Dürrenmatt's Matthai, waiting for the culprit to arrive, never stops waiting, turning gradually into a grotesque figure, an absurdity—like the man in Kafka's parable waiting for years at the portals of justice until he dies there and the door, meant for him, is shut—or like Vladimir and Estragon, waiting for Godot and doomed to wait in vain.

The world according to Alexander Pope's rationalist eighteenth-century model was ''a mighty maze, but not without a plan.'' Borges echoes the notion but revises it critically in his parables. Life is a labyrinth and each of us is Theseus in search of the Minotaur in the center. But the labyrinth Borges postulates is infinite: It is, for example, the universe in the form of a labyrinthine library (''The Library of Babel''). The maze either has no center and no exit or an infinite number of them. It can be solved over and over again but never definitively. And the Minotaur may be a papier-mâché fake or it may be one's own mirror image, looming large and wielding engines of destruction.

Borges is the presiding deity of Umberto Eco's *The Name of the Rose,* an encyclopedic medieval extravaganza that uses the murder mystery's structure much as James Joyce used that of the Homeric epic in *Ulysses.* Eco's book demands to be read in the context established by Borges; *The Name of the Rose* is simply the most brilliant and accomplished of the books inspired by Borges's example. Eco acknowledges Borges in numerous ways, overt and subtle, in his book. An important character is suggestive of Borges in name ("Jorge of Burgos"), attributes (he is blind, learned, venerable), and occupation (professional librarian). The figure of the labyrinth is crucial to Eco's plot. At the heart of *The Name of the Rose* is a labyrinthine library that seems to be patterned after the one in Borges's "The Library of Babel," with its spiral staircases and mirrors and sense of infinitude. The first sentence of "The Library of Babel" announces that some people regard "the universe" and "the Library" as synonymous. Eco spins out this Borgesian conceit to an apocalyptic end in *The Name of the Rose.*

The Name of the Rose opens with a gambit that Borges made familiar: A preface explains the history of the work we have before us, which is said to have surfaced in an antiquarian book shop in ... Buenos Aires. As in "Death and the Compass," Eco's plot centers on fearful parallels between a sacred text (in this case, the Book of Revelation) and destructive events on earth (a series of violent deaths in a Benedictine monastery in northern Italy in the year 1327). Seven monks die in as many days, victims of suicide or murder; each death corresponds to a prophetic verse. Is the end of the world at hand? The gullible are ready to panic, but Brother William of Baskerville, staunch champion of the rational spirit, resists. Codes need to be cracked, clues collected, "signs" interpreted; and like the baroque elaboration of a locked-room puzzle, the riddle of the labyrinthine library must be deciphered before Eco's detective—an avatar of Sherlock Holmes—can distinguish accident from design. At last he lights on a plot to suppress a scroll containing Aristotle's long-thought-lost writings on comedy. But by then it is too late: The sleuth is powerless to prevent the novel's climactic holocaust, the fire that destroys the labyrinthine library and all its treasures. The irony is that *The Name of the Rose* has all along debunked apocalyptic fantasies in the name of reason. Yet the book's ending is nothing if not apocalyptic: The conflagration of the books seems as much a modern as a medieval myth of the imagined end of the world.

Near the end of the novel, William of Baskerville makes a Borgesian point that would be anathema to Sherlock Holmes. In his valedictory speech, he acknowledges the possibility of understanding "the truth of signs" while misinterpreting their relation, which may be accidental and unplanned. Individual clues may make sense—with his footprints a man *does* leave his signature on the snow—but may not cohere. And so, Eco's hero explains, he arrived at the identity of the right culprit for the wrong reason. He discerned "an apocalyptic pattern" in a series of crimes, not realizing that the pattern was fortuitous, the product of chance and gullible minds. He pursued "the plan of a perverse and rational mind," but there was no plan, only the illusion or intimation of one—"a sequence of causes, and concauses, and of causes contradicting one another, which proceeded on their own." Like Erik Lönnrot in Borges's "Death and the Compass," then, Eco's hero is a Great Detective, in whom the glories of human reason shine forth. And as in Borges, his story is a parable of the limits of detection and the inefficacy of human intelligence.

Given the book's many debts to Borges, and all these echoes of Borges's plot devices and themes, the question that lingers in the air long after one shuts *The Name of the Rose* is perplexing indeed. For the villain of the novel is none other than that obvious fictional stand-in for Borges, Jorge of Burgos—the monastery's old, blind librarian. We are bound to wonder why. The plot hinges upon Jorge's wish to suppress, at all costs, Aristotle's writings on comedy. He is a killjoy who considers laughter an abomination; he is also a censor. To the extent that Jorge of Burgos represents an image of Borges, we're in a desperate quandary. The real-life Borges was, of course, neither a humorless scold (quite the contrary) nor a grave guardian of secrets, determined to limit the flow of knowledge. Why, then, does Eco associate his fictionalized Borges with censorship in the abstract and with the repression of the comic impulse in particular?

Eco takes up the question briefly in his *Postscript to The Name of the Rose*:

> Everyone asks me why my Jorge, with his name, suggests Borges, and why Borges is so wicked. But I cannot say. I wanted a blind man who guarded a library (it seemed a good narrative idea to me), and

library plus blind man can only equal Borges, also because debts must be paid.... When I put Jorge in the library I did not yet know he was the murderer. He acted on his own, so to speak. And it must not be thought this this is an "idealistic" position, as if I were saying that the characters have an autonomous life and the author, in a kind of trance, makes them behave as they themselves direct him. That kind of nonsense belongs in term papers. The fact is that the characters are obliged to act according to the laws of the world in which they live. In other words, the narrator is the prisoner of his own premises.[5]

One of the most interesting things about this paragraph is that the line endorsed by the author doesn't differ tremendously from the "idealistic" position that Eco ridicules. What, after all, is the difference between "acting on one's own" and "having an autonomous life"?

Perhaps any novelist would fudge the question in print. No novelist, especially one as clever and as knowing as Eco, would wish to rob his readers of the pleasure of puzzling out such an issue for themselves. And surely no novelist can come right out and endorse Harold Bloom's theory of "influence-anxiety"—though one need scarcely adhere down the line to that theory to see its attractions in this case. How better to overcome the anxiety provoked by the literary father's influence than by killing him on paper? And besides, making Borges the culprit of a murder mystery would be a good side joke, considering Borges's love of the form, wouldn't it?

As I say, one cannot expect a novelist to examine his own motives so clinically and coldly. Still, the paragraph in *Postscript* about Borges struck me when I read it as remarkably unsatisfactory, especially given Eco's reputation as a brilliant critic. I therefore wrote to Professor Eco in Milan, hoping to cajole him into making further disclosures. I identified myself as one who greatly admired *The Name of the Rose*; I reminded him that I had reviewed it in *Newsweek* on its publication in the United States in 1983. Then I put my question:

The book would seem an act of homage to Borges, and yet it is Borges who is vilified. Perhaps, I reasoned, this was yet one more "labyrinthine" touch in the novel, a twist that was itself quite Borgesian. Perhaps. But another possibility also proposed itself: was it possible that the author wished secretly (and subversively) to proclaim that Jorge of Burgos, and not William of Baskerville, spoke for him? Was he, to twist what Blake said about Milton, of the devil's party, consciously and deliberately?

I wondered then, too, what the author would say were the matter put to him. Would he argue that he was simply emulating Hitchcock in making the villain the most interesting character in the work? Whatever else the author's reticence allowed him to say, I doubted he would call it a matter of little consequence, since it seems to me that everything in *The Name of the Rose* has its intended significance. Was it precisely the author's design that the reader not be able to solve this conundrum? That the relation of Jorge of Burgos to Jorges Luis Borges is one of echo, Eco, or ego, and ambiguous whichever way you look at it?[6]

Eco's reply to my letter essentially restated the position he'd put forth in his *Postscript*:

The answer is very simple, even though (perhaps) disappointing.

I set up a work in which I gave to my characters certain names in order to pay homage to people I liked. Moreover, since I had a library it looked to me indispensable to have a *blind* librarian and this librarian had to be a Spaniard because of the mozarabic tradition of Apocalypses. At this point I called him as I called. At that moment I didn't know that the characters had to do what they finally did. When they did it I respected their story and their name.

I love Borges, Borges is not Jorge, and the ambiguities that are generated by the text seemed to me as a sort of contribution to the Borgesian poetics of ambiguity.[7]

In the spirit of *perhaps*—a spirit recommended warmly by both Borges and Eco—I would like to propose three further possibilities:

1. That Eco began by paying homage to Borges and caricatured him inadvertently; on realizing that he had done so, he decided to make a virtue out of an inevitability; he concluded that it would give an energetic shake to the tradition of the surprise villain by casting his real-life mentor in the role.

2. That an opposition between Sherlock Holmes and Jorge Luis Borges implies a split in the human mind—and a state of perpetual enmity between the rival parties; and that, in any conflict between reason (Holmes) and the imagination (Borges), the latter will invariably be the outlaw. (This analogy, though it sounds convincing, falls

apart as soon as one is reminded that the severe, unpleasant Jorge of Burgos can scarcely be taken to personify the imagination.)

3. That it was Eco's design, whether from the outset or determined only gradually, to provide at least one mystery that would survive the closing of the book—a riddle that cannot be solved, even by the author himself. That way there is some element of mystery to undercut the security that comes with the naming of the culprits and the meting out of suitable punishments. That way, too, the author can keep the detective novel's eternal question—"Who is guilty?"[8]—in issue even after an answer has been given. It is certainly a ploy that Borges, the creator of Herbert Quain, would have admired.

———◆———

"I believe people like thrillers not because there are corpses or because there is a final celebratory triumph of order (intellectual, social, legal, and moral) over the disorder of evil," Eco has written. "The fact is that the crime novel represents a kind of conjecture, pure and simple." Eco's intellectual thriller is essentially Borgesian (or "postmodernist") in emphasizing conjecture and possibility as distinguished from facts and certainty. The book is anachronistic twice over: It overcomes the sense of its belatedness—a detective novel written after the age of the detective novel has ended—by projecting modern figures, Sherlock Holmes and Dr. Watson, into the medieval past. Nevertheless, once you disentangle the layers of historical reference and irony and learned disputation that make it so weighty and complicated a tome, you find that *The Name of the Rose* does after all fulfill the contract between the mystery writer and reader. That is, the book affirms rather than denies a double assurance: that life is an inexhaustible source of curiosity and mystery and that we can survive the mysteries we embrace, just as William and Adso survive the events in that murderous monastery in 1327.

If reality is a puzzle, enigma, or maze, then the details of a life are clues, the cast of characters a cast of suspects—and detection becomes not only a literary motif or chain of conventions but a way of life, a mode of apprehending reality, as well as a necessary process of thought, whether or not it is fated to succeed. The detective novel as a form is predicated on the notion that the puzzles of our lives can and will be solved—and that is why the form is so easily and splendidly subverted by those who hold a rather more pessimistic view of human knowledge. The first job of the detective novelist is to convince us that our lives are not as drab and humdrum as we fear, that menace lurks under every surface and conspiracy is in the air, that we've a perfect right to be paranoid. The wrong number on the telephone was not so innocent as we naively supposed; not so anonymous are the strangers in the skyscraper elevator where later a corpse will turn up. The thrill of thrillers lies here, in the perverse delight we take in sinister possibilities. At the same time, the books promise (though they may break their word) that things will turn out all right; the truth will be known in the end, or as much of it as we can bear.

1

———◆———

Further Reading

When the literature of pleasure becomes an object of study, it's a happy moment for bibliophiles who like making lists. The recommended titles in the selected bibliography that follows were chosen either for their importance in the evolution of the mystery genre or simply for the pleasure they reliably give; in many cases, both reasons apply. Titles of singular interest in the immediate context of mystery fiction are starred.

(I) DETECTIVE NOVELS AND STORIES

(A) Origins

*Edgar Allan Poe, *Tales* (1845)
*Wilkie Collins, *The Moonstone* (1868)
*Arthur Conan Doyle, *A Study in Scarlet* (1887)
*———, *The Adventures of Sherlock Holmes* (1892)
———, *The Memoirs of Sherlock Holmes* (1894)
*———, *The Hound of the Baskervilles* (1902)
R. Austin Freeman, *The Red Thumb Mark* (1907)
Gilbert Keith Chesterton, *The Club of Queer Trades* (1905)
*———, *The Man Who Was Thursday* (1908)
*———, *The Innocence of Father Brown* (1911)
———, *The Wisdom of Father Brown* (1914)

(B) The Classic Whodunit, 1912-41

*E. C. Bentley, *Trent's Last Case* (1912)
*Agatha Christie, *The Murder of Roger Ackroyd* (1926)
*——, *Murder on the Orient Express* (1934)
*——, *The ABC Murders* (1936)
——, *And Then There Were None* (1940)
*Anthony Berkeley, *The Poisoned Chocolates Case* (1929)
Dorothy Sayers, *Strong Poison* (1930)
*——, *Murder Must Advertise* (1933)
*Ellery Queen, *The Chinese Orange Mystery* (1934)
Henry Wade, *Heir Presumptive* (1935)
*John Dickson Carr, *The Three Coffins* (1935)
*——, *The Burning Court* (1937)
——, *The Crooked Hinge* (1938)
Carter Dickson, *The Judas Window* (1938)
——, *The Reader Is Warned* (1939)
*Nicholas Blake, *Thou Shell of Death* (1936)
——, *The Beast Must Die* (1938)
*——, *The Corpse in the Snowman* (1941)
Ngaio Marsh, *Overture to Death* (1936)
Michael Innes, *Hamlet, Revenge!* (1937)
Margery Allingham, *The Fashion in Shrouds* (1938)
*Raymond Postgate, *Verdict of Twelve* (1940)

(C) The Hard-boiled Romance, 1929-

*Dashiell Hammett, *Red Harvest* (1929)
*——, *The Maltese Falcon* (1930)
——, *The Glass Key* (1931)
James M. Cain, *Double Indemnity* (1936)
*Raymond Chandler, *The Big Sleep* (1939)
*——, *Farewell, My Lovely* (1940)
*——, *The High Window* (1942)
——, *The Long Goodbye* (1954)
*Jim Thompson, *The Killer Inside Me* (1952)
——, *The Getaway* (1959)
*Ross Macdonald, *The Chill* (1964)
*——, *The Goodbye Look* (1969)
——, *The Underground Man* (1971)
*Mark Smith, *The Death of the Detective* (1974)
Roger Simon, *The Big Fix* (1974)
Andrew Bergman, *The Big Kiss-Off of 1944* (1974)
William Hjortsberg, *Falling Angel* (1977)
Arthur Lyons, *Hard Trade* (1981)
Richard Rosen, *Strike Three, You're Dead* (1984)

James Crumley, *Dancing Bear* (1985)
Thomas Maxwell, *Kiss Me Once* (1986)
*Dennis Potter, *The Singing Detective* (1986)
*Sue Grafton, *'C' Is for Corpse* (1986)
*Sara Paretsky, *Bitter Medicine* (1987)

(D) The Postwar Era, 1945-

*Kenneth Fearing, *The Big Clock* (1946)
Edmund Crispin, *The Moving Toyshop* (1946)
*Rex Stout, *Too Many Women* (1947)
——, *And Be A Villain* (1948)
*——, *The Second Confession* (1949)
Nicholas Blake, *Minute for Murder* (1947)
——, *The Widow's Cruise* (1959)
Patricia Highsmith, *Strangers on a Train* (1949)
——, *The Talented Mr. Ripley* (1957)
*Josephine Tey, *The Daughter of Time* (1951)
*Julian Symons, *The 31st of February* (1951)
Ira Levin, *A Kiss Before Dying* (1953)
Stanley Ellin, *Mystery Stories* (1956)
*——, *The Eighth Circle* (1958)
Simon Nash, *Death Over Deep Water* (1963)
Ed McBain, *Ten Plus One* (1963)
*——, *Long Time No See* (1977)
*——, *Ice* (1983)
Harry Kemelman, *Friday the Rabbi Slept Late* (1964)
Edward Candy, *Words for Murder Perhaps* (1971)
Agatha Christie, *Curtain* (1975)
Ruth Rendell, *Means of Evil* (1977)
*——, *The Killing Doll* (1985)
P. D. James, *Death of an Expert Witness* (1977)
*——, *A Taste for Death* (1986)
*Umberto Eco, *The Name of the Rose* (1983)
Elmore Leonard, *Glitz* (1985)
Paul Auster, *The New York Trilogy* (1985–86)
Barbara Vine, *A Fatal Inversion* (1987)

(II) RELATED GENRES

(A) Spies and Such

Erskine Childers, *The Riddle of the Sands* (1903)
Joseph Conrad, *The Secret Agent* (1906)
John Buchan, *The Thirty-Nine Steps* (1915)

E. Phillips Oppenheim, *The Great Impersonation* (1920)
W. Somerset Maugham, *Ashenden* (1928)
*Eric Ambler, *A Coffin for Dimitrios* (1939)
——, *Journey into Fear* (1940)
——, *The Intercom Conspiracy* (1969)
Graham Greene, *The Confidential Agent* (1939)
*——, *The Ministry of Fear* (1943)
——, *The Human Factor* (1978)
John Le Carré, *The Spy Who Came in From the Cold* (1963)
——, *Tinker, Tailor, Soldier, Spy* (1974)
Ross Thomas, *Chinaman's Chance* (1978)

(B) The Gothic Tradition

Horace Walpole, *The Castle of Otranto* (1765)
Ann Radcliffe, *The Mysteries of Udolpho* (1794)
William Godwin, *Adventures of Caleb Williams* (1794)
*Mary Shelley, *Frankenstein, or the Modern Prometheus* (1818)
C. K. Maturin, *Melmoth the Wanderer* (1820)
James Hogg, *The Private Memoirs and Confessions of a Justified Sinner* (1824)
*Edgar Allan Poe, *Tales of the Grotesque and Arabesque* (1840)
*Robert Louis Stevenson, *The Strange Case of Dr. Jekyll and Mr. Hyde* (1886)
Oscar Wilde, *The Picture of Dorian Grey* (1890)
Bram Stoker, *Dracula* (1897)
Henry James, *The Turn of the Screw* (1898)

(C) Comparative Fictions

*Sophocles, *Oedipus Rex*
*Voltaire, *Zadig* (1749)
*Franz Kafka, *The Trial* (1925)
Vladimir Nabokov, *The Real Life of Sebastian Knight* (1941)
Friedrich Dürrenmatt, *The Pledge* (1955)
*Jorge Luis Borges, *Ficciones* (1962)
Tom Stoppard, *The Real Inspector Hound* (1968)
Donald E. Westlake, *Enough: A Travesty* (1977)
Joyce Carol Oates, *Mysteries of Winterthurn* (1984)
David Thomson, *Suspects* (1985)

(D) Movies

The Thin Man (1934; dir. W. S. Van Dyke)
**The Maltese Falcon* (1941; John Huston)
Shadow of a Doubt (1943; Alfred Hitchcock)
**Double Indemnity* (1944; Billy Wilder)

Spellbound (1945; Alfred Hitchcock)
The Big Sleep (1946; Howard Hawks)
Laura (1947; Otto Preminger)
 Dark Passage (1948; Delmer Daves)
 Strangers on a Train (1950; Alfred Hitchcock)
 Rashomon (1951; Akira Kurosawa)
 Diabolique (1954; Henri-Georges Clouzot)
Rear Window (1954; Alfred Hitchcock)
Vertigo (1958; Alfred Hitchcock)
 Blow-Up (1966; Michelangelo Antonioni)
The French Connection (1971; William Friedkin)
 Dirty Harry (1971; Don Siegel)
 Sleuth (1972; Joseph L. Mankiewicz)
Chinatown (1974; Roman Polanski)
 Murder on the Orient Express (1974; Sidney Lumet)
 Farewell, My Lovely (1975; Dick Richards)
 Death on the Nile (1978; John Guillermin)
 Dressed to Kill (1980; Brian De Palma)
 Body Heat (1981; Lawrence Kasdan)
The Singing Detective (1986; Jon Amiel)
 The Thin Blue Line (1988; Errol Morris)

(E) Poems

A range of poems attests to the detective novel's attractions as a source of metaphor. Consider the following titles: W. H. Auden's "Detective Story"; James Fenton's "A Staffordshire Murderer"; Dana Gioia's "In Chandler Country"; Daniel Hoffman's "Who Done It?"; Martha Hollander's "The Detective Examines the Body"; Vickie Karp's "Police Sift New Clues in Search for Beauty"; Weldon Kees's "Crime Club"; David Lehman's "Defective Story"; Laura Mullens's "The Holmes Poems"; Howard Nemerov's "A Reader of Mysteries"; Elizabeth Spires's "Clue Sestina." James Cummins's *The Whole Truth* (1986) is a sequence of twenty-four sestinas about Perry Mason and his crew. John Hollander's *Reflections on Espionage* (1976) takes the form of coded messages sent to various secret agents by "the master-spy whose code name was *Cupcake*."

(III) CRITICAL DOCUMENTS

*Thomas De Quincey, "On Murder Considered as One of the Fine Arts"
    (1827, 1839, 1854)
 T. H. Huxley, "On the Method of Zadig" (1880)
*G. K. Chesterton, "A Defense of Detective Stories" (1901)
*Gertrude Stein, "What Are Master-pieces and Why Are There So Few
    of Them" (1936)

Roger Caillois, "The Detective Novel as Game" (1941)
*Edmund Wilson, "Who Cares Who Killed Roger Ackroyd?" (1944)
*Raymond Chandler, "The Simple Art of Murder" (1944)
*W. H. Auden, "The Guilty Vicarage" (1948)
Geraldine Pederson-Krag, "Detective Stories and the Primal Scene"
(1949)
Richard Wilbur, "The House of Poe" (1959)
*Ross Macdonald, "The Writer as Detective Hero" (1973)
Umberto Eco, *Postscript to The Name of the Rose* (1984)
Josiah Thompson, *Gumshoe: Reflections in a Private Eye* (1988)

(IV) RESOURCE BOOKS

Vincent Starrett, *The Private Life of Sherlock Holmes* (1933)
Howard Haycraft, *Murder for Pleasure* (1941)
———, ed., *The Art of the Mystery Story* (1946)
Francis M. Nevins, Jr., ed., *The Mystery Writer's Art,* (1970)
Jacques Barzun and Wendell Hertig Taylor, *A Catalogue of Crime*
(1971)
Michele Slung, ed., *Crime on Her Mind* (1975)
John G. Cawelti, *Adventure, Mystery, and Romance* (1976)
Frank MacShane, *The Life of Raymond Chandler* (1976)
Larry N. Landrum, Pat Browne, and Ray B. Browne, eds., *Dimensions
of Detective Fiction* (1976)
John Ball, ed., *The Mystery Story* (1976)
Encyclopedia of Mystery and Detection, ed. Chris Steinbrunner and
Otto Penzler (1976)
Elliot L. Gilbert, *The World of Mystery Fiction: A Guide* (1978)
David I. Grossvogel, *Mystery and Its Fictions* (1979)
Robin Winks, *Modus Operandi* (1982)
Glenn W. Most and William W. Stowe, eds., *The Poetics of Murder:
Detective Fiction and Literary Theory* (1983)
Dilys Winn, ed., *Murder Inc* (1984)
Julian Symons, *Bloody Murder: From the Detective Story to the Crime
Novel* (rev. ed.; 1985)
William Patrick Day, *In the Circles of Fear and Desire: A Study of
Gothic Fantasy* (1985)
Robert Barnard, *A Talent to Deceive: An Appreciation of Agatha
Christie* (rev. ed.; 1987)
Victoria Nichols and Susan Thompson, *Silk Stalkings: When Women
Wrote of Murder* (1988)

2

———◆———

Personal Favorites

At gunpoint a few years ago, my editors at *Newsweek* asked me to list ten of my favorite crime novels of the twentieth century. I learned that top-ten lists are something of a tradition among mystery readers and that they're particularly valued by bookshop managers and their clientele. A good list is expected to balance acknowledged classics and little-known gems—to have something for both the aficionado and the novice. Here, then, are fifteen books I'm crazy about. No more than one title per author—and even so, it was hard to limit myself to just fifteen.

———◆———

The Hound of the Baskervilles by Sir Arthur Conan Doyle (1902). Probably the best of the Sherlock Holmes novels from the point of view of craft and structure. A notable feature of the case is the prolonged absence of Holmes; a second is the gothic setting—the Devonshire moors, where a spectral hound figures in manmade homicides. Holmes solves the murders, lays to rest an ancestral curse, and converts a gothic nightmare into a triumphant display of human reason.

The Innocence of Father Brown by Gilbert Keith Chesterton (1911). Chesterton's London is a modern metropolitan fairyland—rather like what you would get if you crossed the exoticism of the Arabian Nights with the air of privilege and intrigue at a patrician club. The Father Brown stories are romances, puzzles that resemble paradoxes. In "The Blue

Cross," which opens the book, Flambeau is the famous thief and Valentin is the head of the Paris police; in "The Secret Garden," which follows, Valentin commits murder; in "The Flying Stars," three stories later, Flambeau renounces crime and thereafter becomes Father Brown's occasional sidekick.

The Maltese Falcon by Dashiell Hammett (1930). The black bird is "the stuff dreams are made of," as Humphrey Bogart playing Sam Spade says in John Huston's wonderful movie. The object of universal desire is either a fiction or a fake, and it's at the center of a morally ambiguous allegory involving a shamus, his late partner, his beautiful client, and several eccentric rogues. In November 1988, the *New York Times* ran a story about a thriving one-man mail-order business dealing in replicas of the falcon. The headline: "Falcons as Fake as the Real Thing."

The Three Coffins by John Dickson Carr (1936). Carr, the master of the impossible, regularly devised homicidal plots as ingenious as poetic conceits. The first murder in the book is an exemplary instance: No one could have entered or left the hermetically sealed chamber in which the body lies. A subsequent problem is the discovery of a corpse in an empty cul-de-sac, where no footprints but the victim's are found. Includes detective Gideon Fell's "Locked-Room Lecture" in which the various ways of constructing such a puzzle are outlined.

The ABC Murders by Agatha Christie (1936). A masterpiece of the series-murder motif. Like other of Christie's plot innovations, the puzzle and the surprise solution have been borrowed by writers ever since. The corpse of Mrs. Ascher in Andover is followed by that of Betty Barnard in Bexhill-on-Sea and then of Sir Carmichael Clarke in Churston. What did the murderer's alphabetical logic reveal?

Thou Shell of Death by Nicholas Blake (1936). A high-spirited example of Blake's artistry: clever puzzles, excellent writing, careful plot construction. Blake does English accents well, which allows him to delineate a stratified social structure with admirable subtlety. The eponymous shell is that of a walnut doctored with cyanide. Inspector Blount "solves" the case in the penultimate chapter and is trumped by detective Nigel Strangeways—loosely based on the poet W. H. Auden—in the finale.

The Big Sleep by Raymond Chandler (1939). For the sheer verve of the writing, some favor *Farewell, My Lovely* (1940), but Chandler's first novel, plot confusions and all, gets my vote. Philip Marlowe, Chandler's wisecracking mouthpiece, enters "the stained-glass romance" of the Sternwood mansion and, many corpses later, ends his quest at the source of the Sternwood fortune: the oil sump where Rusty Regan sleeps the big sleep. You can't beat the extravagant similes or the tough-guy talk: "Thanks, lady. You're no English muffin yourself."

A Coffin for Dimitrios by Eric Ambler (1939). An inspired hybrid of the spy and detective genres. Our hero is Charles Latimer, a mild-mannered detective novelist who sets out to reconstruct the life of a notorious desperado whose corpse has washed up on the shore of Istanbul. To Smyrna, Belgrade, Sofia, Geneva, and Paris goes Latimer, whose "experiment in detection" turns into a crime story—or, perhaps, a crime allegory—totally unlike the ones in his books. A fine surprise awaits him in Paris.

The Big Clock by Kenneth Fearing (1946). As a poet who loves detective novels and has written for a newsmagazine, I feel a particular kinship with Fearing, a much underrated poet who worked for *Time*. *The Big Clock*, his best mystery, is set in a newsweekly's New York City headquarters. Splendid use of both the "purloined letter" and "wrong man" motifs. Made into a memorable Charles Laughton–Ray Milland movie, it was also the source of the recent Kevin Costner vehicle, *No Way Out*.

Too Many Women by Rex Stout (1947). From Stout's finest period, the late 1940s. The division of detective labor between the irascible, orchid-loving Nero Wolfe and debonair man-about-town Archie Goodwin is very nearly as charming as the greatest partnership of all, that of Holmes and Watson. The suspects here are all deadlier than the male; eligible Archie has his arms full.

The Eighth Circle by Stanley Ellin (1958). A narrative tour de force, notable for the interest and variety of the female characters. The corpse is introduced early but in so indirect a way that no reader will notice; only with the detective's hindsight does a case of alleged police graft turn into a murder mystery. The issue in the book—the character of a cop under investigation—is an enigma shrouded in a riddle, since we never meet the man. One character was inspired by Dylan Thomas; the name of a magazine that figures in the plot is *Peephole*.

The Chill by Ross Macdonald (1964). Three violent deaths, separated by twenty years, are investigated by Lew Archer in this baroque oedipal murder mystery set in southern California. We meet daughters who are hung up on their dads and a son who may have married his mother. The psychological drama is rich, and the plotting is superb: The three murders intersect like the three roads that meet at the place where Oedipus slays Laius.

Long Time No See by Ed McBain (1978). It's pretty much a toss-up between this one and *Ice* (1983); both are terrific. The murder victims in *Long Time No See* are all blind. Crucial to the case is the posthumous interpretation of a dream. A deceased veteran's nightmare—as recorded by a military psychotherapist—holds the key to the macabre murders and brings to light a long-suppressed incident in Vietnam.

The Name of the Rose by Umberto Eco (1983). Surely the most intellectually ambitious—and demanding—of detective novels. It pays homage both to Sherlock Holmes and (enigmatically) to Jorge Luis Borges, and is in all likelihood the only international bestseller to contain long quotations untranslated from Latin. A magical medieval mystery tour.

The Singing Detective by Dennis Potter (1986). With the possible exception of the 1986 playoffs and World Series, this six-part series based
on Potter's teleplay was the best thing on TV this decade. A detective
novelist with the unlikely but very British name of Philip Marlow (without
the terminal *e*) is hospitalized with a terrible case of psoriasis. There are
four narrative levels: actuality (the circumstances of the hospital ward),
fantasy (a decrepit man on his deathbed can burst without warning into
Dick Haymes's voice singing "It Might As Well Be Spring"), memory
(traumatic incidents from Marlow's childhood), and fiction (the plot of
Marlow's detective novel, *The Singing Detective*). The result is an ingenious blend of *film noir* and musical comedy, a sense of tremendous psychological mystery and unexpected clarity at journey's end.

Notes

———◆———

INTRODUCTION

1. W. H. Auden, *The Dyer's Hand* (New York: Vintage, 1968), p. 147.
2. Jacques Barzun and Wendell Hertig Taylor, *A Catalogue of Crime* (New York: Harper & Row, 1971), p. 14.

Chapter 1
THE CORPSE ON PAGE ONE

1. Umberto Eco, *Postscript to The Name of the Rose*, trans. William Weaver (San Diego and New York: Harcourt Brace Jovanovich, 1984), pp. 78, 81.
2. George Grella, "Murder and Manners: The Formal Detective Novel," in *Dimensions of Detective Fiction*, ed. Larry N. Landrum, Pat Browne, and Ray B. Browne (Bowling Green, Ohio: Popular Press, 1976), pp. 41–42, 49.
3. W. H. Auden, "The Guilty Vicarage," in *The Dyer's Hand* (New York: Vintage, 1968), p. 151.
4. Walter Benjamin, "One-Way Street," in *Reflections*, ed. Peter Demetz, trans. Edmund Jephcott (New York: Harcourt Brace Jovanovich, 1978), pp. 64–65.
5. See François Truffaut, *Hitchcock*, rev. ed. (New York: Simon and Schuster, 1984), p. 191.
6. Interview with James filed by *Newsweek*'s Tony Clifton in London, September 18, 1986.
7. See, for example, "The Gallup Survey: American Readers Love a Mystery," *Publishers Weekly*, November 21, 1986, p. 17.
8. *Newsweek*, October 20, 1986, p. 83.
9. See Charles Nicol, "The Hard-Boiled Go to Brunch," *Harpers*, October 1987, pp. 61–65.

Chapter 2
THE BIRTH OF A NEW HERO

1. Gertrude Stein, "What Are Master-Pieces and Why Are There So Few of Them" (1936), in *Writings and Lectures 1909–1945*, ed. Patricia Meyerowitz (New York: Penguin, 1971), p. 151.

2. Richard Wilbur, "The Poe Mystery Case," *New York Review of Books,* July 13, 1967, p. 26.

3. Henry Levin observes that *grotesque,* meaning purely imaginary, "was paired against its classic antithesis, *sublime,* in the influential formula of Victor Hugo." *Arabesque,* meanwhile, denotes "the free play of fancy, a positive assertion of what is negatively implied by *grotesque.*" Levin's remarks, from his book *The Power of Blackness* (1958), are reprinted in *Twentieth Century Interpretations of Poe's Tales,* ed. William Howarth (Englewood Cliffs, N.J.: Prentice-Hall, 1971), pp. 24–25.

4. Thomas H. Huxley, "On the Method of Zadig" (1880) in *Science and Hebrew Tradition: Essays* (1896; reprint, Greenwood Press, 1968), p. 7.

5. *The Name of the Rose,* trans. William Weaver (New York: Harcourt Brace Jovanovich, 1983), pp. 23–25.

6. Marshall McLuhan, *The Gutenberg Galaxy* (New York: New American Library, 1969), p. 328.

Chapter 3
MYSTERIES AND MYTHS

1. Gilbert K. Chesterton, "A Defence of Detective Stories" (1901) in *The Art of the Mystery Story,* ed. Howard Haycraft (New York: Grosset & Dunlap, 1946), p. 4.

2. *Elijah's Violin and other Jewish Fairy Tales,* selected and retold by Howard Schwartz (New York: Harper & Row, 1983), pp. 19–24.

3. John G. Cawelti, *Adventure, Mystery, and Romance* (University of Chicago Press, 1976), p. 95.

4. Quoted in *The Guardian,* 23 October 1971.

5. Quoted in *Newsweek,* March 22, 1971, p. 108.

6. Geraldine Pederson-Krag, "Detective Stories and the Primal Scene," in *The Poetics of Murder,* eds. Glenn W. Most and William W. Stowe (San Diego and New York: Harcourt Brace Jovanovich, 1983), p. 16.

7. Robert Lowell, *Collected Prose* (New York: Farrar, Straus & Giroux, 1987), pp. 132–33.

8. Dennis Porter, "Backward Construction and the Art of Suspense," *The Poetics of Murder,* p. 333.

9. W. H. Auden, "The Guilty Vicarage," in *The Dyer's Hand,* (New York: Vintage, 1968), p. 152.

10. Edmund Wilson, "Why Do People Read Detective Stories?" in *Classics and Commercials* (New York: Vintage, 1962), pp. 236–37.

11. Nicholas Blake, "The Detective Story—Why?" in *The Art of the Mys-*

tery Story, ed. Howard Haycraft (New York: Grosset and Dunlap, 1946), p. 400.

12. Elliot L. Gilbert, *The World of Mystery Fiction: A Guide* (San Diego: University Extension, University of California, 1978), p. 76.

13. Auden, "The Guilty Vicarage," p. 151.

14. The idea that movie characters have a life before and after the film in which we know them is explored to the full in David Thomson's ingenious book *Suspects* (1985). Casper Gutman—The Fat Man—and Brigid O'Shaughnessy are two characters from *The Maltese Falcon* whose pre-movie and post-movie lives are described. In self-contained chapters meant ultimately to cohere, we learn of the fate of Kay Corleone after *The Godfather* and what Rick Blaine did before *Casablanca;* characters from *Double Indemnity, Chinatown, The Big Sleep, Body Heat, The Third Man,* and *Laura* are also included. The emphasis on *film noir* is deliberate; the effect, beyond its novelty, is meant to be disturbing.

15. Steven Marcus, "Introduction," Dashiell Hammett, *The Continental Op* (New York: Vintage, 1975), pp. xxiv–xxv.

16. Ross Macdonald, "The Writer as Detective Hero," *The Capra Chapbook Anthology* (Santa Barbara, Cal.: Capra Press, 1979), pp. 81–82.

Chapter 4
MURDER CONSIDERED AS A FINE ART

1. The little-known Edward Candy is the pseudonym for a female British physician whose literary manner has been likened to that of Ivy Compton-Burnett.

2. Cf. George Grella, "Murder and Manners: The Formal Detective Novel," in *Dimensions of Detective Fiction,* ed. Larry N. Landrum, Pat Browne, and Ray B. Browne (Bowling Green, Ohio: Popular Press, 1976), pp. 44, 45–46.

Chapter 5
DE QUINCEY'S IRONY

1. The essay was published in two parts in *Blackwood's Magazine* in 1827 and 1839, with a postscript added for the 1854 publication of *Selections Grave and Gay from the Writings Published and Unpublished of Thomas De Quincey,* volume 4.

2. *The Art of the Mystery Story,* ed. Howard Haycraft (New York: Grosset & Dunlap, 1946), pp. 189–93, 194–96, 198.

3. In *Evolutionary Ethics* (London: Macmillan; New York: St. Martin's

Press, 1967), A. G. N. Flew discusses the problem of "natural law": "The crux can be illustrated, light-heartedly but very aptly, by referring to a crisp exchange recorded in Mr. Raymond Chandler's *Farewell, My Lovely*. Philip Marlowe is conversing with Anne Riordan: 'You take awful chances, Miss Riordan.' 'I think I said the same about you. I had a gun. I wasn't afraid. There's no law against going down there.' 'Uh-huh. Only the law of self-preservation.' With his accustomed acuteness Marlowe, returning the gun, corrects himself: 'Here. It's not my night to be clever.' Certainly, interpreted as other than a wisecrack, his remark would be foolish. For, precisely in so far as there were a psychological law of self-preservation under which all our actual actions could be subsumed, there would be no point in appealing to this law as a reason for acting not in one way but another; while if after all no such law holds, then it cannot provide any reasonable ground for anything.... The point of the passage just quoted from *Farewell, My Lovely* lies in its wisecracking exploitation of this ambiguity. But, as is shown by other examples which we have given and shall give, the fact that one can draw an illustration from such a source must be interpreted not as evidence of the universal obviousness of the crucial distinction [between the descriptive and prescriptive senses of 'law of nature'] but as one more indication of the quality of Chandler" (pp. 33–34).

4. This is true of early Holmes, the Holmes of *A Study in Scarlet* and the *Adventures*. In the later works, Conan Doyle substituted a more conventional sense of morality.

5. Vincent Starrett, *The Private Life of Sherlock Holmes* (New York: Pinnacle Books, 1960, 1975), p. 11.

6. By decadence, it should be made clear, something besides moral disapprobation is implied, something at odds with it. The word can be seen to refer to an inescapable cultural condition—or to an aesthetic posture designed to make a virtue out of necessity. See Suzanne Nalbantian, *Seeds of Decadence in the Late Nineteenth-Century Novel* (New York: St. Martin's Press, 1983), pp. 1–7.

Chapter 6
NO POLICE LIKE HOLMES

1. Howard Haycraft, *Murder for Pleasure: The Life and Times of the Detective Story* (New York: Carroll & Graf, 1941, 1984), p. 5. This is a reprint of the 1941 edition.

2. Aaron Marc Stein, "The Mystery Story in Cultural Perspective," in *The Mystery Story*, ed. John Ball (New York: Penguin, 1978), pp. 36–41.

3. Quoted in slightly different form (*police* instead of *p'lice*) by Howard Haycraft, *Murder for Pleasure,* p. 55.

4. Gilbert K. Chesterton, "A Defence of Detective Stories," in *The Art of the Mystery Story,* ed. Howard Haycraft (New York: Grosset & Dunlap, 1946), p. 6.

5. Quoted in *The Craft of Crime: Conversations with Crime Writers* by John C. Carr (Boston: Houghton Mifflin, 1983), p. 21.

6. See Robert Polito's excellent piece on Thompson, "Savage Nights," *Boston Phoenix,* December 10, 1985.

7. Dorothy L. Sayers, "The Omnibus of Crime," in *The Art of the Mystery Story,* ed. Howard Haycraft, p. 77.

8. *Ibid.,* p. 94.

Chapter 7
THE LEGACY OF EDGAR ALLAN POE

1. Quoted in Edmund Wilson, "Poe at Home and Abroad," *A Literary Chronicle: 1920-1950* (Garden City, N.Y.: Doubleday Anchor, 1956), p. 68.

2. Harold Bloom, "Introduction," *Edgar Allan Poe: Modern Critical Views* (New York: Chelsea House, 1985), pp. 5-7.

3. See *The Prelude,* Book XI, lines 258-397 (1805 edition). "Such moments worthy of all gratitude, / Are scatter'd everywhere," wrote Wordsworth.

4. Richard Wilbur, "The House of Poe" in *Poe: A Collection of Critical Essays,* ed. Robert Regan (Englewood Cliffs, N.J.: Prentice-Hall, 1967), pp. 103-104, 110.

5. Ibid., pp. 110-11.

6. Ibid., p. 108.

7. Wilbur, "The Poe Mystery Case," in *New York Review of Books,* July 13, 1967, p. 27.

8. See Donald A. Yates, "Locked Rooms and Puzzles," in *The Mystery Story,* ed. John Ball (New York: Penguin, 1978), pp. 189-203, and Elliot L. Gilbert, *The World of Mystery Fiction: A Guide* (University Extension, University of California, San Diego, 1978), pp. 73-82, for an excellent discussion of locked-room mysteries.

Chapter 8
NO MASK LIKE OPEN TRUTH

1. See François Truffaut, *Hitchcock,* rev. ed. (New York: Simon and Schuster, 1984), p. 138, for Hitchcock's description of the "gimmick." "The 'MacGuffin' is the term we use to cover all that sort of thing: to steal plans or documents, or discover a secret, it doesn't matter what it is.

And the logicians are wrong in trying to figure out the truth of a Mac-Guffin, since it's beside the point. The only thing that really matters is that in the picture the plans, documents, or secrets must seem to be of vital importance to the characters. To me, the narrator, they're of no importance whatever.

"You may be wondering where the term originated. It might be a Scottish name, taken from a story about two men in a train. One man says, 'What's that package up there in the baggage rack?'

"And the other answers, 'Oh, that's a MacGuffin.'

"The first one asks, 'What's a MacGuffin?'

"'Well,' the other man says, 'it's an apparatus for trapping lions in the Scottish Highlands.'

"The first may says, 'But there are no lions in the Scottish Highlands,' and the other one answers, 'Well then, that's no MacGuffin!' So you see that a MacGuffin is actually nothing at all."

Chapter 9
THE DOUBLE

1. Richard Wilbur, "The Poe Mystery Case," in *New York Review of Books,* July 13, 1967, pp. 16, 25–28.
2. *Ibid.,* p. 27.
3. Daniel Hoffman, *Poe Poe Poe Poe Poe Poe Poe* (Garden City, N.Y.: Doubleday, 1972), p. 217.
4. William Patrick Day, *In the Circles of Fear and Desire* (Chicago: University of Chicago Press, 1985), p. 50–51, 54.

Chapter 10
FUNERALS IN EDEN

1. W. H. Auden, *The Dyer's Hand* (New York: Vintage, 1968), p. 151.
2. Ross Macdonald, "The Writer as Detective Hero," in *The Capra Chapbook Anthology,* ed. Noel Young (Santa Barbara, California: Capra Press, 1979), p. 80.
3. Roger Caillois, "The Detective Novel as Game," trans. William W. Stowe, in *The Poetics of Murder,* eds. Glen W. Most and William W. Stowe (San Diego and New York: Harcourt Brace Jovanovich, 1983), p. 3.
4. A murder is simulated; the passengers examine the clues and grill the suspects; prizes are given for the correct solution.
5. Raymond Chandler, "The Simple Art of Murder," in *The Art of the Mystery Story,* ed. Howard Haycraft (New York: Grosset & Dunlap, 1946), pp. 230–31.
6. Macdonald, "The Writer as Detective Hero," p. 80.

7. David I. Grossvogel, *Mystery and its Fictions* (Baltimore, Md.: Johns Hopkins University Press, 1979), p. 42.

8. *Ibid.,* p. 52.

9. For a penetrating analysis of "Death and the Compass," see Elliot L. Gilbert, *The World of Mystery Fiction: A Guide* (University Extension, University of California, San Diego, 1978), pp. 129–32, to which I am indebted.

10. From, respectively, "The Assistant Producer," p. 69, and "Time and Ebb," p. 132, in *Nabokov's Dozen* (New York: Penguin, 1960, 1971).

11. Vladimir Nabokov, *The Real Life of Sebastian Knight,* Chapter 10 (Middlesex, England: Penguin, 1964, 1971), p. 78.

Chapter 11
FROM PARADISE TO POISONVILLE

1. Howard Haycraft, *Murder for Pleasure: The Life and Times of the Detective Story* (New York: Carroll & Graf, 1984) p. 56.

2. Rex Stout, *Too Many Women* (1947) (New York: Bantam, 1981), p. 6.

3. Gilbert K. Chesterton, "A Defence of Detective Stories," in *The Art of the Mystery Story,* ed. Howard Haycraft (New York: Grosset & Dunlap, 1946), p. 4.

4. *Ibid.,* pp. 5–6.

5. Jorge Luis Borges, "On Chesterton," in *Other Inquisitions 1937–1952,* trans. Ruth L. C. Simms (New York: Washington Square Press, 1966), pp. 88–89.

6. Ross Macdonald, "The Writer as Detective Hero," in *The Capra Chapbook Anthology,* ed. Noel Young (Santa Barbara, Cal.: Capra Press, 1979), p. 85.

7. John C. Carr, *The Craft of Crime: Conversations With Crime Writers* (Boston: Houghton Mifflin, 1983), p. 8.

Chapter 12
THE HARD-BOILED ROMANCE

1. See Frank MacShane, *The Life of Raymond Chandler,* (New York: Dutton, 1976), pp. 44–51, for an excellent account of *Black Mask* and its importance for both Hammett and Chandler.

2. Raymond Chandler, "Introduction," *Pearls Are a Nuisance* (Middlesex, England: Penguin, 1964, 1969), p. 7.

3. Ross Macdonald, "The Writer as Detective Hero," in *The Capra Chapbook Anthology,* ed. Noel Young (Santa Barbara, Cal.: Capra Press, 1979), pp. 84–85.

4. MacShane, *The Life of Raymond Chandler,* p. 62.

5. *Ibid.,* p. 202.

6. As it happens, Spade's sleuth work with the newspaper in Joel Cairo's wastebasket is a nod in the direction of *The Hound of the Baskervilles,* in which Sherlock Holmes attempts to find out the culprit's identity by having one of his Baker Street irregulars track down the rubbish in London hotels. They are looking for the leader page that supplied the words on a warning message sent to Holmes. A telephone's automatic "memory," which when activated rings up the last phone number dialed on the machine, is a useful clue in Arthur Lyons's *Three With a Bullet* (1985).

7. Raymond Chandler, *Farewell, My Lovely* (1940), Chapter 18.

8. Chandler, "The Simple Art of Murder," in *Pearls Are a Nuisance,* p. 197.

9. MacShane, *The Life of Raymond Chandler,* p. 70.

10. Murray Kempton, "Son of Pinkerton," *New York Review of Books,* May 20, 1971, p. 24.

11. Quoted in Bruce Kawin, *Faulkner and Film* (New York: Ungar, 1977), p. 114.

12. Chandler, "The Simple Art of Murder," p. 189.

13. Jessica Mann, *Deadlier than the Male: An Investigation into Feminine Crime Writing* (London: David and Charles, 1981).

14. Chandler, "The Simple Art of Murder," pp. 194–95.

15. *The Notebooks of Raymond Chandler,* ed. Frank MacShane (New York: Ecco, 1976), p. 35.

16. Chandler, "The Simple Art of Murder," p. 198.

17. MacShane, *The Life of Raymond Chandler,* pp. 70, 206.

18. Dashiell Hammett, "The Scorched Face," in *The Big Knockover and Other Stories* (Middlesex, England: Penguin, 1969), p. 109.

Chapter 13
HAMMETT AND CHANDLER

1. See Barbara Deming's discussion of the "tough boy" character in her book *Running Away from Myself* (New York: Grossman Publishers, 1969), pp. 140–71.

2. Julian Symons, *Dashiell Hammett* (New York: Harcourt Brace Jovanovich, 1985), p. 71.

3. Robert I. Edenbaum, "The Poetics of the Private Eye: The Novels of Dashiell Hammett," in *The Mystery Writer's Art,* ed. Francis M. Nevins, Jr. (Bowling Green, Ohio: Popular Press, 1970), p. 102.

4. John G. Cawelti, *Adventure, Mystery, and Romance* (University of Chicago Press, 1976), pp. 167–68.

5. Steven Marcus, "Introduction" to Dashiell Hammett, *The Continental Op* (New York: Vintage, 1975), pp. xiv–xviii.

6. Walker Percy, *The Moviegoer* (New York: Noonday Press, 1967), pp. 4–5, 13.

Chapter 14
ROSS MACDONALD AND AFTER

1. Geoffrey Hartman, "Literature High and Low: The Case of the Mystery Story," in *The Poetics of Murder,* eds. Glenn W. Most and William W. Stowe (San Diego and New York: Harcourt Brace Jovanovich, 1983), p. 222.

2. In *Gumshoe: Reflections in a Private Eye* (Boston: Little, Brown, 1988), Thompson cites his experiences in "detectivery" as Zen-like illustrations of philosophical concepts learned less graphically in the works of Kierkegaard, Sartre, Heidegger, and Merleau-Ponty.

3. Macdonald, who held a Ph.D. in English literature, published a novel titled *The Three Roads*—"which got its title from *Oedipus Tyrannus,*" he noted—in 1946, a decade before undergoing the successful course of psychotherapy that prompted him to make his detective novels more consciously Freudian in their assumptions and their mythic secrets.

4. See Charles Nicol, "The Hard-Boiled Go to Brunch" in *Harper's,* October 1987, pp. 61–65.

Chapter 15
A PORTRAIT OF THE READER AS ESCAPIST

1. Edmund Wilson, *Classics and Commercials* (New York: Vintage, 1962), p. 263.

2. Robert Warshow, "The Gangster as Tragic Hero," in *The Immediate Experience* (New York: Doubleday, 1962), p. 130.

3. Governor Clements, the former chairman of the SMU board of governors, admitted that he had approved improper payments to student athletes. See *Newsweek,* March 16, 1987.

4. "Tradition and the Individual Talent," in *Selected Prose of T. S. Eliot,* ed. Frank Kermode (New York: Harcourt Brace Jovanovich and Farrar, Straus and Giroux, 1975), p. 43.

5. This tendency remains strong even after one allows for the fact that "like a detective novel" is as basic to the blurbs of the 1980s as "Kafkaesque" was a decade ago.

6. Gustav Janouch, *Conversations with Kafka,* trans. Goronwy Rees, rev. ed. (New York: New Directions, 1971), p. 133.

7. W. H. Auden, "The Guilty Vicarage," in *The Dyer's Hand* (New York: Vintage, 1968), p. 158.

8. See chapter eight, note one. The idea that a cake could play a part in a clandestine international escapade was demonstrated during the secret arms-for-hostages negotiations between Iran and the United States.

9. Both the movie and the British edition of the novel are titled *The Mask of Dimitrios.*

Chapter 16
AT THE HEART OF THE MAZE

1. Walter Benjamin was struck by the phenomenon of the train-riding thriller reader, who suppresses one fear with another. See Ernest Mandel, *Delightful Murder: A Social History of the Crime Story* (Minneapolis: University of Minnesota Press, 1984), p. 9.

2. Richard Burgin, *Conversations with Borges* (New York: Avon/Discus, 1970), p. 51.

3. Jorge Luis Borges, *Ficciones,* ed. Anthony Kerrigan (New York: Grove, 1962), p. 15.

4. Quoted in Julian Symons, *Bloody Murder* (New York: Viking, 1985), p. 167.

5. Umberto Eco, *Postscript to The Name of the Rose,* trans. William Weaver (New York: Harcourt Brace Jovanovich, 1984), pp. 27–28.

6. David Lehman, Ithaca, N.Y., letter to Umberto Eco, 12 February 1986.

7. Umberto Eco, Milan, Italy, letter to David Lehman, 26 February 1986.

8. Eco, *Postscript,* p. 54.

Index of Concepts

———◆———

Absolution, 4, 31, 32, 34, 124, 141
Aesthetics, xvii, 37–49, 53
Allegory, 35, 75–76, 124
Ambiguity, 128, 129, 156, 167
Armchair detective, the, 52, 78–79, 122, 148, 198
Artist, the, 42–44, 48, 49, 96, 102, 186

Bourgeois interior, 9

Cassidy case, the, 159–161
Chance, 108, 161, 164, 165, 193, 204, 206
Chess, 64, 148, 158
City (metropolis), the, 24, 72, 117–120, 121–123, 126–130, 131–134, 136–137, 147, 179–180
Classic whodunit, xvii, 12, 57, 58, 71, 75, 76, 79, 101–116, 117, 122, 129, 133, 137, 141, 147–148, 158, 180, 197
Closed murder, the, 102, 106, 107, 109, 117, 130

Clues, 3, 29, 30, 76, 83–84, 95, 101, 115, 116, 160, 187, 190, 206
Corpse in the drawing room, the, 9, 11
Corpse on page one, the, xvi, 1–12, 13–15, 22, 26, 30–31, 73, 141, 166
Country house, the (remote), 24, 102–103, 115–116, 118
Critic, the, xii, 38, 42–43, 44, 58, 96, 102, 120
Cruise (as setting), 103–104
Culprit, the, xii, xiii, 7, 14, 26–27, 28, 37–44, 46–49, 94, 95, 110

Damsel in distress, the, 24, 34, 138, 156
Dandy, the, 43, 61
Dead nature, 14, 18, 22
Decadence, 51, 65, 96, 129
Deconstruction, 179
Deduction, 15, 20
"Deep crime," 72, 118, 131

Detection, xii, xiv, xviii, 2–3, 13, 19–22, 26, 27, 55, 71, 83, 87, 110, 118, 120, 139, 174, 194, 195, 198, 201–203, 206, 209

Detective, the, xii–xiii, xvii, xviii, 4–5, 18, 19, 21, 22, 28, 38, 42–43, 55–65, 77, 94, 99, 110, 114, 120, 128, 191, 192, 202–204

Doppelgänger, 26, 99

Double, the, xvii, 16, 26–27, 43, 72, 94–100, 102, 113–114, 201

Dream, the, 6, 24, 25, 29, 73, 75, 76, 80, 114, 131, 187

Eccentricity, 52–53, 57, 65, 66–69, 139

Ego, the, xvii, 17, 26, 98

Ennui, 49–50, 69

Escapism, xviii, 181–187, 189–190, 202

Escapist hero, 188, 191–195

Eternal triangle, 6, 27

Existential hero, 30, 129, 163, 164, 170

Fairy tales (folktales), 24–26, 111, 122–124

Faith, 125, 131

"Family romance," the, 27, 30, 170, 175

Feminism, 177–179

Femme fatale, 24, 138, 156

Film noir, 34, 136, 147, 159

Films policiers, 97

First-person killer, 62, 63

Flitcraft parable, the, 161–166, 170–171

Flowers of evil, 50–52

Fratricide, 27

French symbolism, 73

Golden age, the, xiv, 8, 117

Gothic tradition, the, 15–17, 94–95, 98–99, 123

Grail, the, 33, 35, 36

Great Detective, The, xiv, 18, 21, 31, 42, 44, 49, 68, 78, 90, 100, 148, 206

Grotesque (and arabesque), 17, 94

Guilt, xiii, xvi, 1, 3, 4, 5, 6, 27–28, 29, 30–32, 34, 36, 124, 172, 188–189, 190, 197

Hard-boiled detective, the, 61, 117, 138–141, 142, 149, 164–166

Hard-boiled heroine, the, 177

Hard-boiled novel, the, xiv, xvii–xviii, 12, 34, 47, 58, 99, 102, 106, 126, 127–131, 135–153, 155–167, 169–180

Hero, the, xvii, 13–22, 99, 118, 138–142, 155–159, 193

Hitchcock's law, 10, 46, 208

Holmes figure, the, 67–68

Human nature, 14, 16, 18, 19, 22, 45, 48, 101

Humor, 124, 128, 152–153, 159, 176

Id, the, xvii, 17, 26

Imagination, 14, 15, 27, 39, 58, 93, 208–209

Imp of the perverse, the, 17, 52, 98

Impossible, the, 40, 76, 79–81

Innocence, xiii, 15, 34, 86

Irony, 46–53, 142, 159, 161, 201, 205, 209

Isolated setting, 103, 105, 109, 117

Justice, 96, 128, 133, 160–161, 170, 171, 175, 190, 191

Knight-errantry, 34, 59, 128, 158

Labyrinths (mazes), 37, 133, 114, 198–201, 204, 209

Law of compensatory imagination, the, 189

Law of progressive homicide, the, 1, 31–32

Least likely suspect, the, xvii, 2, 24, 85, 111–112

Library, 201, 204, 205
Locked room, the, xii, xvii, 24, 71, 76–
    81, 103, 198, 201
Logic, 6, 14, 18, 20, 77, 80, 96, 116,
    148, 187, 188

MacGuffin, the, 88, 190
Male-female paradigm, 11–12, 34,
    178–179
Malice domestic, 9, 11
Mercy, 169–172, 175, 190
Metaphor, 4, 20, 42, 48, 73–75, 104,
    114, 118, 174
Metonymy, 73–74
Mimetic relationship, 94, 182
Mirror, the, 1, 97, 98, 99, 114, 190
Modern fiction, 186
Modernity, 13, 23, 26
Morality, 42–43, 48, 194
Most obvious hiding place, the, xvii, 3,
    86–91
Motive, 109, 129, 195
Motiveless murder, the, 38, 132, 200
Murder, 3–4, 11, 15, 31, 32, 38, 46, 197
Murder addicts, 3, 37, 41, 43, 51
Myth, 24–36, 72

Narrator, 5, 62, 63, 69, 119, 187
Newspapers, 64, 160, 182–184, 189,
    190, 200
Nihilism, 63–64
Noble savage, xvii, 14, 15, 165
Nostalgia, 121, 175–177, 183, 187, 203

Oedipus Rex, 24, 28
Oedipus theme, 27–30, 99, 173–175
Open murder, the, 102, 107
Original sin, 30–31

Parable, 27, 85, 86, 88, 159–167, 182,
    190, 200–201, 203, 206
Paradise, xvii, 102
Paradox, 3, 41, 42, 47, 59, 65, 83, 101,
    102, 112, 124, 179

Paranoia, 1, 85, 114, 188
Parody, 2, 103, 115, 153, 169, 177, 192
Partnership, 67–69, 141–142
Pastoral, 33, 111, 116
Patricide, 27
Perfect murder, the, xix, 2, 8, 37–42
Perfect murderer, the, 38, 49
Perfect victim, the, 7–8
Poisonville, xvii, 58, 127
Police, the, 55–64, 95–96, 106, 131–
    134, 193, 202
Police procedurals, xv, 59–60, 102,
    131–134
Postmodernism, 24, 198, 209
Prohibition, 135, 142–143
Psychoanalysis, 26–30, 174
Psychological thriller, 10, 11, 62
Purloined letter, the, 84, 86–91
Puzzle, the, xiv, xv, xvii, xix, 8, 11, 22,
    39–42, 77, 80, 101, 111, 113,
    114, 141, 142, 148, 184, 189, 193,
    201, 209

Quest romance, 25, 33, 34, 36, 99, 129,
    139

Ratiocination, xii, 16, 17, 29, 43, 72,
    73, 94, 204
Readers, gender of, 11–12
Realism, xvii, 60, 109, 130, 148–150
Red herring, the, 112, 115
Religious rituals, 32, 33
Retrospective prophecy, 6, 19–22, 202
Romance, 148–150, 157
Romanticism, 14–15
Rules of the game, 1, 46–47

Science, 18, 19, 20, 21, 93
Serial murders, 112–114, 131, 201–
    203
Setting, 11, 101–116, 117–134
Simile, xviii, 29, 114, 123, 129, 136,
    150, 152–153, 171–172

Sleuth, the, xiii, xiv, 3, 4, 5, 20, 21, 26–
    27, 28, 56, 58–59, 77, 79, 96
Sphinx's riddle, 16, 27, 28
"Spots of time," 15, 19
Spurious corpse, 33, 34
Spy novels, xiii, xvi, 182, 192
State of nature, 15, 19, 21
Style, 149–153
Superego, xvii, 17, 26
Suspicion, 1–2, 47

Terror, 4, 17, 93
Thriller, the, xiii, 182, 191–193, 197,
    198, 201

Thriller of manners, the, 8–9
Truth, 15, 29, 42, 76, 84, 102, 118, 133,
    141, 160–161, 188, 210

Victim, the, 4, 6–11, 9, 10, 18

Watson figure, the, xiii, xiv, 24, 66–69
Williams's maxim, 46
Wrong man, the, xvii, 85, 91, 192

Yuppie, the, 12
Yuppie sleuth, the, 177–180

Index of Names and Titles

———◆———

ABC Murders, The (Christie), 4, 32, 112, 218

Adventure, Mystery, and Romance (Cawelti), 29

"Adventure of the Norwood Builder, The" (Doyle), 100

Adventures of Caleb Williams, The (Godwin), 73

Against the Grain (Huysmans), 51

Allen, Nancy, 18

Allingham, Margery, 11

Ambler, Eric, 16, 33, 182–183, 186, 191–193, 195

Ambrose, Ianthe, 7

And Then There Were None (Christie), 111

April March ("Quain" [Borges]), 200

Archer, Lew, 29–30, 140, 141, 169–175

Archer, Miles, 47, 141

"Art and Evil" (Lowell), 31

Asch, Jacob, 138, 176

Auden, W. H., xiii, 9, 31, 33, 102, 186, 187, 188

Bacall, Lauren, 145

"Backward Construction and the Art of Suspense" (Porter), 31

Barlach, Hans, 59

Barzun, Jacques, xvi

Baudelaire, Charles, 50, 51, 72, 119

Beast Must Die, The (Blake), 8, 58

Beaumont, Ned, 128

Bell, Joseph, 56

Benjamin, Walter, 9

Bentley, E. C., 8, 43, 106

Bergman, Andrew, 176

Berkeley, Anthony, 102, 184–185

Berowne, Sir Paul, 10–11

Beyond the Pleasure Principle (Freud), 173

Big Clock, The (Fearing), 90–91, 109, 219

Big Kiss Off of 1944, The (Bergman), 176

"Big Knockover, The" (Hammett), 150

Big Sleep, The (Chandler), 129, 138,

140, 144–147, 148, 150, 155, 156–157, 158

Big Sleep, The (film), 144–147, 218

Bitter Medicine (Paretsky), 178–179

"Black Cat, The" (Poe), 17, 93, 98

Blake, Nicholas, xii, xiv, 7, 8, 32, 33, 44, 58, 109

Blissberg, Harvey, 177

Block, Lawrence, 2, 66

Bloom, Harold, 72, 175, 207

Blow-Up (film, De Palma), 36, 113

"Blue Cross, The" (Chesterton), 42, 79, 124

Body in the Library, The (Christie), 111

Bogart, Humphrey, 35, 145, 155, 156, 177

Borges, Jorge Luis, 113–114, 125, 199–203, 204–209

Bow Street Runners, 56

Breathless (film, Godard), 116

Brown, Father, 5, 26, 39, 56, 66, 78, 89, 123, 124–125, 190

Buñuel, Luis, 77

Burden, Mike, 61

Burning Court, The (Carr), 81

"C" Is for Corpse (Grafton), 178

Caillois, Roger, 103

Cain, James M., 63

"Caliban to the Audience" (Auden), 187

Candy, Edward, 40

Carr, John Dickson, xiv, 1, 39, 40, 43, 67, 79–80, 81, 83

"Cask of Amontillado, The" (Poe), 17, 94

Catalogue of Crime (Barzun and Taylor), xvi

Cause for Alarm (Ambler), 191, 192, 193

Cawelti, John G., 29, 163, 164

Chandler, Raymond, xiv, xviii, 12, 34, 48, 58, 105, 127, 128–130, 136–

138, 142, 143, 144–150, 152, 155, 158, 159–161, 166–167, 169, 170, 171, 175, 186

Chesterton, Gilbert K., 23, 24, 26, 38–39, 41, 42, 56, 59, 78, 79, 89, 102, 118, 122–125, 190

Chill, The (Macdonald), 29, 170, 172, 173–174, 175, 219

Chinaman's Chance (Thomas), 203

Chinese Orange Mystery, The (Queen), 19, 41

Christie, Agatha, xiv, 3, 4, 5, 11, 12, 32, 37–38, 42, 47, 103, 106–108, 111–112, 115, 170

Club of Queer Trades, The (Chesterton), 24, 124, 190

Coffin for Dimitrios, A (Ambler), 33, 186, 191–193, 195, 218

Coleridge, Samuel, 14

Collins, Wilkie, 3, 56–57, 86, 91

Confessions of a Justified Sinner (Hogg), 98

Congreve, Richard, 90

Continental Op, 144, 149, 150

Corpse in the Snowman, The (Blake), 44

"Coup de dés jamais n'abolira le hassard, Un" (Throw of the Dice Will Never Abolish Chance, A [Mallarmé]), 204

Crime and Punishment (Dostoyevski), 65

Crispin, Edmund, 40

Crofts, Freeman Wills, 59

Crooked Hinge, The (Carr), 1, 40, 43, 79

Crumley, James, 138, 177

Cuff, Sergeant, 57, 66

"Curse of the Golden Cross, The" (Chesterton), 39

Curtain (Christie), 37–38, 42, 43, 108

"Curtain, The" (Chandler), 145

"D" Is for Deadbeat (Grafton), 180

Dagger of the Mind (Fearing), 84, 109

"Dagger with Wings, The" (Chesterton), 89

Dahl, Roald, 89

Dain Curse, The (Hammett), 149

Dalgliesh, Adam, 10, 60–61

Dancing Bear (Crumley), 138, 177

Darwin, Charles, 16

Day, William Patrick, 99

De Palma, Brian, 18, 113

De Quincey, Thomas, xvii, 4, 14, 38, 45–49, 51, 53, 95, 98

Death Comes as the End (Christie), 3

"Death and the Compass" (Borges), 113, 201, 206

Death of the Detective, The (Smith), 203

Death of an Expert Witness (James), 11

Death of the King's Canary, The (Thomas), xii

Death on the Nile (Christie), 106

Death Over Deep Water (Nash), 104, 105

"Defence of Detective Stories, A" (Chesterton), 59, 122

Des Esseintes, Duc Jean, 51–53, 64

"Detective Story Decalogue, A" (Knox), 47

Dickens, Charles, 187

Dickinson, Angie, 18

Dickson, Carter, 67, 79, 80

Dirty Harry, 60

Dostoyevski, Fyodor, 64

Double Dealer, The (Congreve), 90

Double Indemnity (Cain), 63

Doyle, Arthur Conan, 18, 51, 56, 68, 100, 118, 121

Doyle, Popeye, 97

Dressed to Kill (film, De Palma), 18

Dupin, C. Auguste, xii–xiii, 14–15, 16, 17, 18, 27, 52, 64–66, 69, 76, 78, 84, 86–89, 94–97, 99, 120, 122

Dürrenmatt, Friedrich, 59, 204

Eco, Umberto, xiv, 2, 83, 205–209

Edenbaum, Robert I., 163, 164

"Elijah's Violin" (fairy tale), 24–25

Eliot, T. S., 3, 44, 186

End of Chapter (Blake), 109

Endgame (Beckett), 67

Epitaph for a Spy (Ambler), 191

"Eureka" (Poe), 93

Evolutionary Ethics (Flew), 226

Exterminating Angel (film, Buñuel), 77

Fadeaway (Rosen), 183

"Fall of the House of Usher, The" (Poe), 65–66, 75, 93

Falling Angel (Hjortsberg), 99, 176

Farewell, My Lovely (Chandler), 34, 48, 152, 153, 176

"Fascinating Problem of Uncle Meleager's Will, The" (Sayers), 90

Fatal Inversion, A (Vine), 61

Fearing, Kenneth, 84, 90–91, 109

Fell, Dr. Gideon, 79, 80

Fenton, James, 7

"Final Problem, The" (Doyle), 100

Fitzgerald, Scott, 93, 126

Flambeau, 39, 56, 79, 124–125

Flew, A. G. N., 48

"Flying Stars, The" (Chesterton), 39

Ford, Lou, 62–63, 126–127

Francis, Dick, xv

French, Inspector, 59

French Connection, The (film, Friedkin), 97

Freud, Sigmund, 26, 27–28, 30, 57, 99, 170, 173

Friedkin, William, 97

Funeral in Eden, A (McGuire), 105

Futrelle, Jacques, 77

"Gangster as Tragic Hero, The" (Warshow), 181

Garden of Forking Paths, The (Borges), 199

"Garden of Forking Paths, The"
    (Borges), 200
Gaudy Night (Sayers), 4
Gilbert, Elliot, 32
Glass Key, The (Hammett), 128
God of the Labyrinth, The ("Quain"
    [Borges]), 199
Godard, Jean-Luc, 116
Godwin, William, 73
"Gold Bug, The" (Poe), 83
Goodbye Look, The (Macdonald), 29,
    140, 170, 171, 172, 173, 174
Goodwin, Archie, 67, 69, 122
Grafton, Sue, 12, 177, 178, 180
Gray, Dorian, 16, 26
Great Gatsby, The (Fitzgerald), 126
"Greek Interpreter, The" (Doyle), 78
Greene, Graham, 186, 189–191
Grella, George, 8
Grossvogel, David, 107, 111
Gumshoe: Reflections in a Private Eye
    (Thompson), 231

Haig, Leo, 66
Hamlet, Revenge! (Innes), 39
Hammett, Dashiell, xiv, 34, 35, 36, 58,
    127, 128, 129, 136, 143, 144,
    148, 149, 150, 151, 152, 155, 159,
    163, 164, 166–167, 170, 171
Hard Trade (Lyons), 138, 176
Hartman, Geoffrey, 169
Hastings, Captain, 4, 5, 32
Hawks, Howard, 145–146
Haycraft, Howard, 55, 121
Heart of Darkness (Conrad), 158
Hemingway, Ernest, 137, 153, 158
High Window, The (Chandler), 129,
    152, 157, 159, 161
Highsmith, Patricia, xv, 203
Hitchcock, Alfred, 38, 85, 88, 195, 208
Hjortsberg, William, 99, 176
Hoffman, Daniel, 73, 98
Hogg, James, 98
Hollow, The (Christie), 111

Holmes, Mycroft, 52, 78
Holmes, Sherlock, xiv, 3, 5, 18, 19, 20,
    21, 27, 49–53, 56, 57, 66, 78, 85,
    87, 99, 100
"Honour of Israel Gow, The" (Ches-
    terton), 41, 123
Hornung, E. W., 57
Hound of the Baskervilles, The
    (Doyle), 15–16, 52, 217
"House of Poe, The" (Wilbur), 74
Huston, John, 35, 136
Huxley, T. H., 19, 21
Huysmans, J-K., 51

Iago, 38
Ice (McBain), 133, 134
"Imp of the Perverse, The" (Poe), 98
In the Circles of Fear and Desire
    (Day), 99
"In the Penal Colony" (Kafka), 6
Innes, Michael, 39
Innocence of Father Brown, The
    (Chesterton), 125, 217
Intercom Conspiracy, The (Ambler),
    182–183, 192, 195
Interpretation of Dreams, The
    (Freud), 28
"Invisible Man, The" (Chesterton), 89

James, P. D., xiv, 10–11, 60
Jekyll/Hyde, 16
Jorge of Burgos, 205, 206
Journey into Fear (Ambler), 16, 191,
    192, 193
Judas Window, The (Dickson), 79
Judge and the Hangman, The (Dür-
    renmatt), 59

K., Joseph, 186, 188–189, 190
Kafka, Franz, 6, 186, 188, 204
Kant, Immanuel, 48
Keats, John, 15
Kempton, Murray, 144

Killer Inside Me, The (Thompson), 62, 126–127
"Killer in the Rain" (Chandler), 145
Killing Doll, The (Vine), 61
Kiss Me Once (Maxwell), 176
Knox, Ronald, 47
Krutch, Joseph Wood, 17, 72

Lady in the Lake, The (Chandler), 34, 153
"Lamb to the Slaughter" (Dahl), 89
Latimer, Charles, 186, 193–195
Le Carré, John, 182, 192
Leonard, Elmore, xv, xvi, 182
Lewis, C. Day, xii, 32, 33
"Library of Babel, The" (Borges), 204, 205
Lightning (McBain), 132
London Detective Club, 47
Long Goodbye, The (Chandler), 130–131, 140, 143, 150, 152, 166
Long Time No See (McBain), 112, 132–133, 149, 219
Lönnrot, Erik, 113–114, 202, 206
Lowell, Robert, 31
Lyons, Arthur, 138, 176

McBain, Ed, xv, 3, 60, 112, 131–134, 149
Macdonald, Ross, xiv, 29–30, 36, 102, 106, 119, 129, 137, 140, 141, 155, 169–175
McGuire, Pat, 105
McLuhan, Marshall, 22
Maigret, Chief Inspector Jules, xvi, 5, 10, 59, 79
Mallarmé, Stéphane, 73, 74, 204
Maltese Falcon, The (Hammett), 34, 47, 128, 129, 138, 141, 149, 152, 155, 156, 158, 161, 166, 167, 218
Maltese Falcon, The (film, Huston), 35, 136
"Man of the Crowd, The" (Poe), 119

Man Who Was Thursday, The (Chesterton), 24, 59
Manderson, Sigsbee, 8, 9
Marcus, Steven, 35, 164
Marlowe, Philip, xiv, 5, 79, 129, 130, 138, 140, 144, 146–147, 148, 150, 155, 156–157, 158, 159–161, 175, 176
Marple, Miss, 111
Marsh, Ngaio, xvii, 11
Mason, Perry, 57
Matthai, 204
Maxwell, Thomas, 176–177
Means of Evil (Rendell), 61
Merrivale, Sir Henry, 67, 79
Millhone, Kinsey, 177, 178, 180
Ministry of Fear, The (Greene), 186, 189–191
Minute for Murder (Blake), 109
Moonstone, The (Collins), 3, 57, 86
Moriarty, Professor, 100
Mousetrap, The (Christie), 103
Moviegoer, The (Percy), 165
Moving Toyshop, The (Crispin), 40
Murder Must Advertise (Sayers), 8, 78, 109
Murder on the Orient Express (Christie), 107, 111, 147
Murder of Roger Ackroyd, The (Christie), 5, 8, 47
"Murders in the Rue Morgue, The" (Poe), xii–xiii, xvii, 14, 15, 16, 17, 65, 73, 75, 84, 86, 94, 119, 120
"Musgrave Ritual, The" (Doyle), 50
Mysterious Affair at Styles, The (Christie), 107, 108
"Mystery of Marie Roget, The" (Poe), xiii, 17, 64, 65, 66, 69, 78, 84

Nabokov, Vladimir, 114–116
Name of the Rose, The (Eco), xiv, 21, 83, 205–207, 209, 219
Nash, Ogden, 66
Nash, Simon, 104, 105

No Exit (Sartre), 77
North by Northwest (film, Hitchcock), 85, 195

O'Brien, Fergus, 7
"Ode on a Grecian Urn" (Keats), 15
Oedipus, 24, 27–28
Oedipus at Colonus (Sophocles), 28
Oedipus Rex (Sophocles), 24, 28
Old Man in the Corner, 78
"On the Knocking at the Gate in *Macbeth*" (De Quincey), 4, 45
"On the Method of Zadig" (Huxley), 21
"On Murder Considered as One of the Fine Arts" (De Quincey), 46
Oppenheim, E. Phillips, 192
"Oracle of the Dog, The" (Chesterton), 78, 102
Orczy, Baroness, 78
O'Shaughnessy, Brigid, 34–36, 47, 128, 156, 157, 163
Othello (Shakespeare), 38
Overture to Death (Marsh), xvii

Panza, Sancho, 68
Paretsky, Sara, 11–12, 177, 178–179
Pederson-Krag, Geraldine, 30
Peel, Sir Robert, 56
Percy, Walker, 165–166
"Philosophy of Composition" (Poe), 73
Picture of Dorian Gray, The (Wilde), 51
"Pit and the Pendulum, The" (Poe), 17, 75
Pledge, The (Dürrenmatt), 204
Poe, Edgar Allan, xi, xii, xvii, 14, 15, 16, 17, 33, 51, 52, 56, 64–65, 68, 71–77, 83, 88, 93–96, 98, 118–119, 121, 131
Poirot, Hercule, 4, 5, 38, 66, 107, 108, 112

Poisoned Chocolates Case, The (Berkeley), 102, 184–185
Pope, Alexander, 204
Porter, Denis, 31
Postgate, Raymond, 5
Postscript to the Name of the Rose (Eco), 2, 206, 207
Prismatic Bezel, The (Nabokov), 115–116
"Problem of Cell 13" (Futrelle), 77
Prometheus Unbound (Shelley), 99
"Prufrock" (Eliot), 44
"Purloined Letter, The" (Poe), 17, 58, 84, 86–89, 95–96, 99

Queen, Ellery, 19, 41, 66
"Queer Feet, The" (Chesterton), 124
Quixote, Don, 68

Raskolnikov, 64–65
Reader Is Warned, The (Dickson), 80–81
Real Inspector Hound, The (play, Stoppard), 103
Real Life of Sebastian Knight, The (Nabokov), 115
Red Harvest (Hammett), 127, 144, 151
"Red-Headed League, The" (Doyle), 49
Rendell, Ruth, xiv, 9, 11, 61–62
Rimbaud, Arthur, 74
Robin Hood, 55, 64
Roosevelt, Elliott, xii
Rope (film, Hitchcock), 38
Rosen, Richard, 177, 183–184
Rousseau, Jean Jacques, 15
Rowe, Arthur, 186, 189–190

Saboteur (film, Hitchcock), 85
Sartre, Jean Paul, 77
Sayers, Dorothy L., 4, 8, 9, 11, 67, 68, 90, 108, 137, 147
"Scandal in Bohemia, A" (Doyle), 85, 89

Scarlet Letter, The (Hawthorne), 95

Scharlach, Red, 113

Scotland Yard, 56, 60, 61

Shakespeare, William, 38

Shelley, Percy Bysshe, 99

Sign of Four, The (Doyle), 51

Simenon, George, xvi, 59

"Simple Art of Murder, The" (Chandler), 137, 147, 149

Sins of Prince Saradine, The (Chesterton), 26, 89, 123

Sleeping Beauty (Macdonald), 175

Smith, Mark, 203

Spade, Sam, 5, 12, 34-36, 46, 128, 129, 138, 141, 149, 155-156, 157, 158, 161, 163, 164, 166-167, 170, 178

Spellbound (film, Hitchcock), 85

Spillane, Mickey, 11

"Staffordshire Murder, A" (Fenton), 7

Stark, Richard, 203

Stein, Aaron Marc, 55

Stein, Gertrude, 13, 17, 19, 22, 23

Sternwood, Carmen, 157, 158

Stevens, Wallace, 97

Stoppard, Tom, 103

Stout, Rex, 2, 67, 78, 118, 122

Strangers on a Train (film, Hitchcock), 38

Strangeways, Nigel, 32, 58

Strike Three, You're Dead (Rosen), 177, 183, 184

Strong Poison (Sayers), 34

Stroud, George, 90-91

Study in Scarlet, A (Doyle), 21, 51, 52

Suspects (Thomson), 225

Symons, Arthur, 51

Symons, Julian, 163

"Tale of the Ragged Mountains, A" (Poe), 94

Talented Mr. Ripley, The (Highsmith), 203

Talking to Strange Men (Rendell), 62

Taste for Death, A (James), 10, 61

Taylor, Wendell Hertig, xvi

"Tell-Tale Heart, The" (Poe), 17

Ten Plus One (McBain), 132, 134

"Theme of the Traitor and Hero" (Borges), 200

Thin Man, The (Hammett), 127

Thomas, Dylan, xii

Thomas, Ross, xvi, 182, 203

Thompson, Jim, 11, 62, 126

Thompson, Josiah "Tink," 171

"Thou Art the Man" (Poe), 33, 73

Thou Shell of Death (Blake), 7, 33, 109, 218

Three Coffins, The (Carr), 40, 79-80, 83, 218

Three Roads, The (Macdonald), 231

Three With a Bullet (Lyons), 176, 230

Too Many Women (Stout), 69, 219

Topless Tulip, The (Blake), 2

Trent, Philip, 43, 66

Trent's Last Case (Bentley), 8, 9, 43, 106

Trial, The (Kafka), 186, 188-189, 190

Truman, Margaret, xii

"Twenty Rules for Writing Detective Stories" (Van Dine), 47

Underground Man, The (Macdonald), 29, 173, 175

Unkindness of Ravens, An (Rendell), 9

Unpleasantness at the Bellona Club, The (Sayers), 9

Usher, Roderick, 65, 75

Van Dine, S. S., 47

Vance, Philo, 66

Verdict of Twelve (Postgate), 5

Verlaine, Paul, 74

Vertigo (film, Hitchcock), 85

Vidocq, François Eugène, 56

Vine, Barbara, 62

Voltaire, 20, 56

Warshawsky, V. I., 177, 179–180

Warshow, Robert, 181–182

Watson, Dr., 5, 21, 49–50, 69

Westlake, Donald E., xvi, 182, 203

Wexford, Chief Inspector Reginald, 61

What Mrs. McGillicuddy Saw (Christie), 108

Whicher, Inspector, 57

Widow's Cruise, The (Blake), 7

Wilbur, Richard, 14, 73, 74, 76, 94–95

Wilde, Oscar, 16, 42, 51, 69

William of Baskerville, 21, 83, 205, 206

"William Wilson" (Poe), 94, 98

Williams, John, 46–47, 49

Wilson, Edmund, xii, 31–32, 181

Wilson, William, 16

Wimsey, Lord Peter, xiv, 8, 38, 66, 78, 90

Wolfe, Nero, xiv, 2, 66, 67, 69, 78, 122

Words for Murder Perhaps (Candy), 40

Wordsworth, William, 15, 17, 74

Zadig, 56

Zadig (Voltaire), 20–21

Zebra-Striped Hearse, The (Macdonald), 141, 171, 173